PENGUIN BOOKS

THE CREATIVE ECONOMY

John Howkins has advised Time Warner, IBM, Sky TV and many other companies on strategy and business development. He has worked for more than thirty governments, including those of the UK, the USA, Japan, China, Canada, Australia and Singapore, helping to formulate policy for their creative industries. He is a board director of Handmade Films plc and Hotbed Media, Deputy Chairman of the British Screen Advisory Council and a Governor of the London Film School. He founded and directed the Adelphi Charter on Creativity, Innovation and Intellectual Property (www.adelphicharter.com). The John Howkins Research Centre on the Creative Economy was opened in Shanghai in 2006. For more information contact www.creativeeconomy.com.

John Howkins

THE CREATIVE ECONOMY

HOW PEOPLE MAKE MONEY FROM IDEAS

PENGUIN BOOKS

PENGUIN BOOKS

Published by the Penguin Group
Published by the Penguin Group
Penguin Books Ltd, 80 Strand, London WC2R 0RL, England
Penguin Group (USA) Inc., 375 Hudson Street, New York, New York 10014, USA
Penguin Group (Canada), 90 Eglinton Avenue East, Suite 700, Toronto, Ontario, Canada M4P 2Y3
(a division of Pearson Penguin Canada Inc.)
Penguin Ireland, 25 St Stephen's Green, Dublin 2, Ireland
(a division of Penguin Books Ltd)
Penguin Group (Australia), 250 Camberwell Road,
Camberwell, Victoria 3124, Australia (a division of Pearson Australia Group Pty Ltd)
Penguin Books India Pvt Ltd, 11 Community Centre,
Panchsheel Park, New Delhi – 110 017, India
Penguin Group (NZ), 67 Apollo Drive, Rosedale, North Shore 0632, New Zealand
(a division of Pearson New Zealand Ltd)
Penguin Books (South Africa) (Pty) Ltd, 24 Sturdee Avenue,
Rosebank, Johannesburg 2196, South Africa

Penguin Books Ltd, Registered Offices: 80 Strand, London WC2R 0RL, England

www.penguin.com

First published by Allen Lane The Penguin Press 2001
Published by Penguin Press 2002
Reprinted with updated material 2007
013

Typeset by Rowland Phototypesetting Ltd,
Bury St Edmunds, Suffolk
Printed in England by Clays Ltd, St Ives plc

978-0-140-28794-3

www.greenpenguin.co.uk

Penguin Books is committed to a sustainable future for our business, our readers and our planet. This book is made from Forest Stewardship Council™ certified paper.

ALWAYS LEARNING PEARSON

CONTENTS

INTRODUCTION: THE ART OF THE PATENT vii

1 THE FIRST TALENT 1

2 THE BOOM IN INTELLECTUAL PROPERTY 19

3 THE CORE CREATIVE INDUSTRIES 82

4 MANAGING CREATIVITY 125

5 THE ENTERTAINMENT GENE 166

6 CLICK-AND-GO 181

7 CAPITAL OF MY MIND 204

ACKNOWLEDGEMENTS 221

NOTES 222

SELECT BIBLIOGRAPHY 246

INDEX 253

INTRODUCTION: THE ART OF THE PATENT

NEWS FROM THE FRONT

Towards the end of the twentieth century, the nature of work changed. In 1997 America produced $414 billion worth of books, films, music, TV and other copyright products. Copyright became its number one export, outselling clothes, chemicals, cars, computers and planes. *Fortune* magazine said basketball player Michael Jordan's personal economic value, gained through copyrights and merchandising, exceeded the Kingdom of Jordan's gross national product.

In 1998 theatres in the West End and Broadway spent over three times as much on intellectual property as on the bricks-and-mortar kind. In the West End, theatre owners spent £26 million a year on copyright royalties and only £8 million a year on their buildings. Britain's music industry employed more people and made more money than did its car, steel or textile industries.

In 1999, Telecom, the world's biggest communications fair, held in Geneva every four years, attracted so many people that the Swiss Tourist board was obliged to open the city's nuclear shelters for emergency accommodation. The charge was Sw Fr 25 per night including taxes and service (the service, I was told, was minimal). Over 190,000 people wanted to see the latest developments in media, communications and the Internet.

Also in 1999, the US Patent and Trademark Office issued a record number of 169,000 patents. As well as patenting the usual mechanical inventions and gadgets, it gave patents for business methods (which raised some eyebrows). It gave Dell Computers a patent not for the computers it sold but for the *way* it sold them. It gave Amazon.com a patent for the way people ordered its books and CDs. The Amazon patent contains this phrase: 'Modifications within the spirit of the invention will be apparent to those skilled in the art.' The appeal to a person 'skilled in the art' is a standard tactic in patenting worldwide. I call this the 'art of the patent'.

During the same year, the British Patent Office awarded a patent for the technique of cloning Dolly, a sheep. The patent covers the 'possible use of the technology in cloning human cells'. In Norfolk, a housewife was reprimanded and given a legal notice when she propagated a plant bought at her local garden centre and tried to sell the cuttings. She and her parents have been propagating plants for generations, but new rules made her gardening habits a civil offence.

What is going on?

A NEW ECONOMY

These diverse activities have one thing in common. They are the results of individuals exercising their imagination and exploiting (or preventing others from exploiting) its economic value.

This book is about the relationship between creativity and economics. Creativity is not new and neither is economics, but what is new is the nature and extent of the relationship between them, and how they combine to create extraordinary value and wealth.

There has been a rapid spread of patents, copyright and trademarks. Intellectual property used to be an arcane and boring subject, something for specialists only, but within the past few years it has become a powerful influence on the way everyone has ideas and owns them, as well as on global economic output. Accountants Arthur Andersen say 'electronics, software, health-care, consumer goods, telecommunications, media and entertainment are substantially dependent upon intellectual property'; I would add biology, agriculture and education. When I look at some countries' patenting policies, I am inclined to add everything else.

When he was arguing the case for America's first federal copyright law, President George Washington said it would increase the stock of knowledge, and 'knowledge in every country is the surest basis of public happiness'. Nowadays, a US president would be more likely to say it is the surest basis of business competition.

People with ideas – people who *own* ideas – have become more powerful than people who work machines and, in many cases, more powerful than the people who *own* machines. Yet the relationship between creativity and economics remains almost invisible. I decided to see if I could bring together all these elements – creativity, intellectual property, management, capital, wealth – into a single comprehensive framework. This book is the result.

First, some definitions. *Creativity* is the ability to generate something new. It means the production by one or more people of ideas and inventions that are personal, original and meaningful. It is a talent, an aptitude. It occurs whenever a person says, does or makes something that is new, either in the sense of 'something from nothing' or in the sense of giving a new character to something. Creativity occurs whether or not this process leads anywhere; it is present both in the thought and in the action. It is present when we dream of paradise; when we design our garden; and when we start planting. We are being creative when we write something, whether it is published or not; or invent something, whether it is used or not. I use the word *creator* to describe any person who creates or invents something new.

We are all creative in our own way; in how we perceive and present ourselves to the world; in how we make sense of the world. Our sparks of creativity inform our personality. A few people go further and make their creative imaginings the core of their working life; not only in terms of their personality but commercially, in how they make a living and a profit.

An *economy* is conventionally defined as a system for the production, exchange and consumption of goods and services. Economics generally deals with the problem of how individuals and societies satisfy their wants, which are infinite, with resources which are finite; it is thus primarily about the allocation of scarce resources. Although I use both terms in these senses, I show that ideas are not limited in the same way as tangible goods, and the nature of their economy is different.

Creativity is not necessarily an economic activity but may become so when it produces an idea with economic implications or a tradeable product. This transition from the abstract to the practical, from the idea to the product, is hard to define. There is no overarching definition of the moment of change that covers all eventualities. The laws on intellectual property provide one set of criteria and the marketplace provides another. In general, the change occurs whenever an idea is identified, named and made practicable and may, as a result, be owned and traded.

The result is a *creative product* which I define as an economic good or service that results from creativity and has economic value. This book starts with creativity (Chapter 1) and then moves to creative products (Chapters 2 and 3). A creative product may be a good or a service. Traditionally a good has meant something with a physical mass (like a book) and a service has meant something that has no mass (like a broadcast), but lawmakers have not been very successful at fixing these definitions in precise terms and usually resort to the comment, 'If I drop it on my foot and it hurts, then it's a good'. The distinction becomes uncomfortably blurred when a product's economic value is largely dependent upon such intangible concepts as ideas and computer software, and has intangible property rights such as patents, trademarks and designs. The growth of e-commerce adds yet more confusion. For example, a creative product (say, a piece of music) may change category from good to service and back to good again. Throughout, however, the important characteristics of a creative product are twofold: it results from a creative activity and has recognizable economic value.

The output of creative products has tended to happen most publicly and obviously in the arts, which has caused the arts to be seen as the core creative activity and for creativity and the arts to be treated as synonyms (or, at least, creativity and good art). But artists have no monopoly on creativity, nor are they the only workers in the creative economy. The difference between creativity in the arts and elsewhere is not that artists are more creative, or more successfully creative, but that because they deal in a specific range of ideas and aesthetics, they create specific kinds of works and work according to identifiable business models with their own patterns of supply, demand, values and pricing.

Creativity flourishes equally in the sciences, especially in research and development (R & D). There is little difference between the creativity of the scientist and of the artist. Colin Ronan, author of *The Cambridge History of the World's Science*, says 'To engage in science requires a vivid creative imagination, tempered by firm discipline based on a hard core of observational experience.' Biologist Edward O. Wilson, one of the most distinguished scientists of the twentieth century, and the inventor of 'consilience', which he describes as the 'interlocking of causal explanations across different intellectual disciplines', says creativity is 'the ability of the brain to generate novel scenarios and settle on the most effective'. Both arts and sciences are attempting to imagine (to visualize) and describe (to represent) the nature and meaning of reality. Both use the same thinking and creating processes. The difference comes in why they choose to do so, how they present their imagining to the world, and how they protect its economic value. Put simply, the creativity is the same; the creative products are different.

Creativity is present at all levels of business from the management of a company to the development, branding and shape of each product. Few businesses today are the same as they were ten or even five years ago; fewer still will be the same in the next five years. Increasing competition, volatile technology and the arrival of the Internet require all companies to be imaginative in the way they do business and vigilant in protecting their products by means of intellectual property rights.

Creativity is possible in every organization where novelty and invention are possible. It flourishes most when and where they are rewarded.

Many creative products, although not all, qualify as *intellectual property*. Intellectual property has the same defining characteristic as physical property: it belongs to someone. But unlike physical property, which we can see and touch, intellectual property is intangible. It is an artificial construct which did not exist until governments invented it. Governments and the courts still define what it is, and prescribe an owner's *rights*. Intellectual property is therefore not the same as any idea or bit of knowledge that we may happen to have; it is solely what a law says we know or have.

There are several forms of intellectual property, of which the four most common are copyright, patents, trademarks and designs. Some legal systems also protect trade secrets and confidential information; others, personal secrets and privacy. *Copyright* law covers an individual's creative expression when fixed in specific works. Originally, it was limited to writings in the literary sense but more categories have been added (for example, films and sound recordings), and each category extended to include more activities (for example, the category of literary works now includes computer programs because they are, after all, a skilful and imaginative piece of writing). Copyright accrues automatically to any qualifying work and does not need to be registered. It normally lasts for the author's lifetime plus seventy years.

The second major area, *patent* law, originated in the need to protect inventions of new industrial products and processes. It gives the inventor a monopoly in the making of the new product, typically for twenty years. Patents and copyright are fundamentally different. Whereas copyright accrues automatically, a patent has to pass stringent tests before being approved. It must be novel, non-obvious and useful. None of these tests apply to copyright. Once registered, a patent gives stronger protection than does copyright.

A *trademark* does not require any artistic or creative expression (as does copyright) or any expert skill (as does a patent) but is merely a mark or symbol that represents an organization or trade. I generally restrict the word to cover trademarks that are registered, which means they have to be actively traded and to pass tests of type and uniqueness. A *design* is a shape or symbol that, like a trademark, has the character of being distinctive and unusual. In legal terms, it is something of a hybrid. It often qualifies for copyright; it may also qualify for a special design right (as in Britain); and it is usually registered like a trademark.

These systems can overlap. An artist's working sketch for a trademark qualifies as an artistic work and merits copyright protection quite separately from the trademark itself being registered as a trademark or a design. Computer programs which automatically qualify for copyright may in some countries also be awarded a patent.

The *copyright industries* consist of all industries that create copyright or related works as their primary product: advertising, computer software, design, photography, film, video, performing arts, music (publishing, recording and performing), publishing, radio and TV, and video games. Art and architecture also qualify as copyright works, but in most cases their rights are marginal to their economic value. Art is mostly valued and sold as a physical object, and new buildings are sold as physical structures, according to the rules of physical property. I follow normal practice by not including them as copyright industries (though I do include them, centrally, as creative industries). The International Intellectual Property Alliance (IIPA) makes a distinction between the 'core' copyright industries listed above, and what it calls the 'total' copyright industries, which also include the manufacturing of products which depend upon copyright goods (for example, computers and TV receivers). I do not include these related industries as copyright industries. The *patent industries* consist of all industries that produce or deal in patents. The dominant ones are pharmaceuticals, electronics, information technology, industrial design, materials, chemicals, engineering, space and vehicles. The dominant activity is scientific research and development which is carried out by commercial companies, technical laboratories and universities. The *trademark* and *design* industries are even more widespread, and their sheer size and diversity make them less distinctive. It is possible to identify the creativity involved in the creation of a trademark, but it is less easy to calculate its economic value or to identify the economic gains attributable to the trademark in the total product mix.

Together, these four industries constitute the *creative industries* and the *creative economy*. This definition is contentious. While all the definitions so far concur with international practice, there is no consensus on this one. Most countries would agree that creativity and its industries embrace the creative imagination in all its forms. But a few, including Britain and Australia, restrict the term 'creative industries' to the arts and cultural industries and exclude science and the patent industries. This is a regrettable extension of the historical tendency to keep the arts and sciences too far apart. Britain confirmed this narrow view when in 1997 the Labour Government set up a Creative Industries Task Force which, although originally including all intellectual property industries, then decided to exclude science. The Task Force was a bold initiative but had the unfortunate side effect of implying science was not creative. The same government's National Endowment for Science, Technology and the Arts (NESTA) takes a wider and more humanistic view in assuming 'creativity' is present in science, technology and engineering and, indeed, in all 'new and innovative products and services'. In general, though, Britain still uses the word 'creative' to mean something 'artistic' and 'cultural'.

The *intangible industries* is another description of the creative industries in the wider sense. I use this description seldom, because although these industries do deal in intangible values, they also produce a substantial proportion of manufactured products which are highly tangible. The people who print books and build theatre sets are as much a part of the creative economy as those who write and perform on stage.

The *creative economy* consists of the transactions in these creative products. Each transaction may have two complementary values: the value of the intangible, intellectual property and the value of the physical carrier or platform (if any). In some industries, such as digital software, the intellectual property value is higher. In others, such as art, the unit cost of the physical object is higher.

We are creative animals, *homo creator*, but our creativity does not always lead to a creative product. The *creative equation* deals only in creative products, not creativity, and differentiates between a creative product and a transaction. It states that the creative economy (CE) is equivalent to the value of creative products (CP) multiplied by the number of transactions (T); that is, CE = CP x T. Creativity itself cannot be quantified. We can say someone is more creative, even very creative, but we cannot say he is two-and-a-half times as creative. The number of creative products can be quantified, but the multiplicity of products and the confidentiality of many deals may inhibit us from making a completely accurate count.

UP THE LADDER OF DESIRES

There are powerful reasons why the creative economy will be the dominant economic form in the twenty-first century. The first and most compelling is the way we evolve as physical and social beings. The great American psychologist Abraham Maslow suggested our needs ascend up a hierarchy from the physical to the emotional and spiritual (a path described by scientist Jacob Bronowski as 'the ascent of man'). Our first needs are air, water and food; then, when these are satisfied and if the environment is hostile, for shelter and safety. Next come our social needs for belonging, our 'ego' needs for love and attention, and finally our need for personal growth and intellectual exploration. As each need is satisfied, so people become more conscious and desirous of the next one up. As they satisfy their physical needs, so some seek emotional pleasure and a few seek intellectual satisfaction. Andrew Curry of the Henley Centre in London says consumer needs in OECD (i.e., industrialized) countries have changed noticeably in recent decades from functional and practical matters to having a sense of well-being and personal fulfilment. In 1998 over 50 per cent of consumer expenditure went on 'lifestyle' and 'fun'. Paul Saffo of the Institute of the Future, California, says there is a hierarchy of consumer desires with entertainment at the top. We should not be surprised if people, whose material needs are largely satisfied and who have a high level of disposal income, remix their ambitions and put a premium on matters of the mind.

We should also not be surprised if a market evolves to meet these needs. Several different processes are under way. On the supply side, automation in the manufacturing industries and, to a smaller extent, in the service industries has cut the demand for manual labour, so young people are looking elsewhere for work. Many turn to the creative industries, which may offer an attractive lifestyle and above-average economic rewards. New industries have arisen around the new communication technologies, each with its urgent needs for skills and ideas. The cultural industries are becoming more commercial and more competitive (not always to their liking). Market economies are skilful at meeting consumer needs, especially in the field of entertainment, where consumer needs are so passionate and evanescent. Suppliers have become adept at charging for pleasure.

On the demand side, economic output continues to grow, leading to a growth in spending power; an increase in leisure budgets; and an increasing focus on leisure activities. The British, Americans and Japanese spend more on entertaining themselves than on clothing or health-care (and most clothes are chosen as much for pleasure as for utility). The British and Americans spend respectively about 17 per cent and 20 per cent of total consumer expenditure on pleasure, more than on housing or food.

As a result, the creative economy is growing faster and faster. Its annual growth in the OECD countries through the 1990s was twice that of the service industries overall and four times that of manufacturing overall. Between 1987 and 2005 the American copyright industries increased their output at the rate of 5.8 per cent a year compared to 2.8 per cent a year for other industries, and increased the number of jobs at 4.0 per cent a year compared to 1.6 per cent in the ordinary economy. The number of American patents for inventions almost doubled from 89,000 in 1977 to 169,000 in 1999. The number of European patents rose more slowly but the trend was still upward.

These products can now be distributed worldwide to ever larger audiences. The most marked growth is not actually in the creation of new products (although their number is growing remarkably) but in their exploitation, distribution and trade. The creative economy has been midwived by the technologies of information and communications. The new digital technologies have created new opportunities for content; a universe of cyberspace, of synthetic 3-D imaging and discourse, hungry for text, images and stories. The low costs of digital technology allow people to make, distribute and exchange their own material alongside, and increasingly penetrating throughout, the larger corporate markets.

Content creators have always dealt with middlemen. Now a new kind of operator has emerged who not only becomes involved in the production and distribution of each product (its volume, its price) but also creates new kinds of content and new kinds of audiences. On the Internet, these gatekeepers are redefining the concept of 'channel' and 'audience'.

These evident, desirable skills of individual creativity are being copied and borrowed by people and companies throughout society. Perhaps the greatest impact of the creative economy is not only within the traditional creative industries but in the way their skills and business models are being used to create value in other areas of life. The use of the imagination, the management of intellectual capital, the best way to incentivize and reward creative people, the short timescales, the response to success and failure; these skills, which have only recently got on the agenda of mainstream business, are the stock in trade of the creative person.

Two trends are interwoven. Creative people and organizations are becoming more businesslike; and business is becoming more dependent upon creativity. Both produce more copyrights and register more patents, and often push for privatization of what was public.

This crossover between the creative industries and the conventional economy may explain the conundrum of the above-average growth of the American economy (part of what Peter Schwartz, President of the Global Business Network, calls the 'long boom'). Many expert observers in the late 1990s were perplexed by its apparent contrary nature. Economic theory suggests that a combination of higher demand and higher growth drives up the prices of raw materials and of labour; hence inflation. But the rapid growth in America between 1996 and 2000 did not cause inflation. As output continued to grow above the long-term trend, new jobs continued to be created and inflation remained low.

One possible reason is that the growth in current output depends less on old-style raw materials that are subject to diminishing returns and whose price, if demand increases, also goes up; and increasingly on intangible resources that are, if not infinite, at least indefinitely large. According to this view, the rise in stock-market values, which increased at an even faster rate than underlying output, was caused by individuals' intuitive perception of this change, in advance of theories being developed to explain it.

LEARNING AND DOING

This book is about such basic matters as what we want and what we are good at. Someone who is or has the potential to be creative (and the latter category includes everyone) faces a basic choice which is measured at one end by creativity and at the other by repetition. It is not a division between being artistic and being businesslike, which merely rewrites the kind of duality which scientist and writer C. P. Snow expressed as dividing the 'two cultures' of science and literature. It is between life and death, between thinking and not-thinking, learning and not-learning, which is applicable to art, science, literature, business – everything.

The next seven chapters describe and analyse this new economy. Chapter 1 explores the nature of creativity. Chapter 2 starts the discussion on creative products with a look at intellectual property; at the 'property contract' between creators and governments which decides what is public and what is private. After these general chapters, Chapter 3 switches tack and gives a statistical analysis of the fifteen core creative industries: from art to video games via the R & D lab. The next two chapters delve further into business and management; and Chapter 6 into digital technologies. Finally, Chapter 7 brings us back full circle, and lays out the arguments for everyone to treat creativity as his or her chief capital asset. Each chapter starts with an interview with someone I met in the course of writing the book who exemplifies the creative spirit. There is no summary chapter beyond this Introduction which you (may) have just read and a few short paragraphs at the end.

1

THE FIRST TALENT

LAW 1: CREATE OR DIE

'That which is creative must create itself.'
John Keats

'If I had to define life in a word, it would be: Life is creation.'
Claude Bernard, nineteenth-century physiologist

THE GRAPHIC ARTIST

Harry Kroto asks to borrow my pen so he can draw something on a paper napkin. As a Nobel laureate in chemistry, he might be about to draw the shape of the C_{60} molecule he and others discovered. The Nobel Foundation, not noted for extravagant praise, described it as 'uniquely beautiful and satisfying'. As his other passion is graphic design, he might be about to draw another logo. It's another logo.

I point out that most of his logos are based on word-play and letter-play rather than abstract shapes. Kroto returns to the napkin to map out the periodic table, in which each chemical element has a letter, and circles three letters, then four; goes back to the logo for his new initiative, the Vega Science Trust; and then draws his new logo for a friend's company called Breakthrough.

C_{60} is a carbon molecule with the unusually large number of sixty atoms; it is much larger than any previously known carbon molecule. Kroto named it buckminsterfullerene, after the designer and inventor Buckminster Fuller, who used a similar structure in his geodesic domes. The essence of C_{60}, apart from its great size, is the symmetrical combination of pentagons and hexagons which give the molecule outstanding strength and stability.

The story of the discovery of C_{60} illustrates the quirks of the creative spirit. It is a story in every sense of the word: a search, a number of characters, several journeys, a fortuitous discovery ('fortune favours the brave'), celebrations, periods of intervening calm, a climax, a resolution. It started when Kroto, who says he is 'interested in puzzles', in 'following my nose', had a rather far-out idea he wanted to test about molecules in space. He wasn't looking for C_{60} at all.

He suggested an experiment, but it wasn't a priority, and eighteen months passed before the team who eventually shared the Nobel Prize came together: Harry Kroto at Sussex University, and Richard Smalley and Robert Curl at Rice University, Houston. Robert Curl, an expert in spectroscopy, picked up on Kroto's original idea and talked to his colleague, Richard Smalley, who had built the original apparatus. Each worked with their fellow researchers and students. I have a vivid sense of an open community of people who stepped in to help at each stage. Kroto mentions David Walton, who 'started me off in my love affair with carbon', someone else who 'carried out a very important experiment', someone who worked down the corridor and could answer a question. When the experiment finally took place, it supported his theory about the formation of molecules in space but it also showed something else. This, he says, was a complete surprise. Serendipitously, they had discovered evidence of a new large molecule.

There followed a hectic period of about ten days in September 1985 when their speculation on the shape of the molecule turned to conviction. Kroto says C_{60} was born on Wednesday 4 September. They published their claim in *Nature* on 14 November. The responses varied from disbelief to enthusiastic acceptance.

The *Nature* article was an assertion of possibility; a brave and confident claim that the thing existed. Five further years passed before they received spectroscopic verification. Kroto says that the colour of the magenta solution produced by C_{60} in that experiment was 'one of the most beautiful colours I have ever seen'.

The first experiments in 1985 had suggested something large was present but gave no evidence of its shape. Kroto looked at what he could see in order to visualize what he couldn't see. He found himself gazing at a pattern of bathroom tiles, a cardboard model of the night sky; anything which used pentagons and hexagons. What was the right shape? They fixed on twenty hexagonal (six-angled shapes) and twelve pentagonal (five-angled shapes), with an atom at each angle, which when put side by side can be rounded and closed into a ball. The geodesic dome modelled by Buckminster Fuller has this structure, as does a European football (the black bits are the pentagons and the white bits are the hexagons).

It's obvious, when you see it. Astronomer Fred Hoyle says that when Albert Einstein stated his theory of relativity, 'He put an issue of style ahead of all the confusion of detail ... Of course, physicists never admit to style because the word brings a picture of Beau Brummell. But style it is.'

The discovery of the fullerene was a long story, beginning in the early 1980s, published in 1985, confirmed in 1990 and meriting the Nobel Prize in 1996. The Nobel citation says 'No practically useful applications have yet been produced but this is not to be expected as early as six years after the first macroscopic quantities of fullerene became available.' But the citation says 'an entirely new brand of chemistry has developed' and there are high expectations of commercial exploitation in superconductivity, astrophysics and materials.

How does one attribute the credit? This is a story full of determination and vision but also full of adventure and accident. This is true *research*, in which failure is more common than success. Kroto says the only sensible way to share the success is equally. Nobody should have more credit than anyone else. It's the only *moral* way.

Claims of intellectual property often require a more precise calculation. Although a molecule cannot be patented, the many techniques by which it is discovered can be; and the practical applications can be highly profitable. I asked Kroto whether the chances of receiving a patent encouraged or affected his work. He answered, no. He has no liking for entrepreneurs who buy up new products, putting their financial interests above the interests of society. 'Intellectual property is a can of worms.' It is practically impossible to say who should benefit commercially from research, especially the pure research that Kroto does. How does one quantify the value of ten years' worth of thinking; or the value of a bright idea at the lab bench one afternoon? How does one calculate the work of a student who, as part of their Ph.D. research, makes a contribution as valuable as anyone's?

Kroto's interest continues to be pure science. A few years ago, he launched the non-profit Vega Science Trust to produce programmes for TV and the Internet to 'reveal the excitement of discovery and reflect science as a cultural activity'. This could be seen as riposte to those who still believe science is somehow not creative. It certainly illustrates the true nature of the creative spirit.

WHAT IS CREATIVITY?

Kroto's discovery, which was triggered by a hint of a possibility of a new molecule, led to the development of other new ideas and new products. He is interested in the former; he leaves the latter to others. There are two kinds, or stages, of creativity: Kroto's kind, which relates to our fulfilment as individuals, and is private and personal; and the kind that generates a product. The first is a universal characteristic of humanity and is found in all societies and cultures. It is found both in free societies, which encourage it, and in closed and totalitarian societies, which usually try to stifle it. When repressed for political or religious reasons, or constrained for economic ones, the result can damage individuals and weaken communities. This kind of creativity is found equally in indigenous peoples' villages, and in the West's academies and universities (like Kroto's University of Sussex), which were designed in part for this purpose. The second kind, which leads to the making of creative products, is stronger in industrial, Western societies, which put a higher value on novelty, on science and technological innovation, and on (intellectual) property rights. This kind of creativity also needs a marketplace and a smattering of legal rules. The first kind of creativity need not lead to the second, but the second requires the first.

While many people have offered descriptions of creativity, few have come close to a robust definition of its physical or chemical state. Like sleep, another basic human activity, it remains a mystery. We all sleep; we all know what it means to be 'asleep'; but there is no medical or psychological consensus about what actually constitutes sleep. The juxtaposition is ironic. One of the problems with defining sleep is its relationship with consciousness. It is generally believed that sleep is a special case of unconsciousness. Is there a gradation from being unconscious to being asleep to being awake and to being fully conscious? And is there a similar gradation from being awake through to being creative? In other words, is creativity a special case of consciousness?

The moment of creativity is sometimes accompanied by a sense of heightened consciousness, even an explosion of consciousness. When we are being most creative, we often feel most vividly alive, and more highly focused, even to the extent of becoming less aware of everything else. Yet there is a counter view that creativity involves a loss of control of consciousness and a move to a more dreamlike state.

The psychologist C. J. Jung differentiated between these states by describing one as 'moment of high emotional tension' and the other as 'a state of contemplation in which ideas pass before the mind like dream-images'. He described creativity as a release of 'energy-tension'. He was also well aware of the need for hard work, emphasizing the role of reason in the creative process. He was scathing about his contemporaries' inclination to link creativity and neurosis: 'Disease has never yet fostered creative work; on the contrary, it is the most formidable obstacle to creation.'

Neurologist Antonio Damasio, Van Allen Professor of Neurology at the University of Iowa, has followed Jung and other psychologists, including William James, in exploring this connection between creativity and consciousness. His analysis of his patients' feelings, emotions and consciousness leads him to suggest a circle of 'existence, consciousness and creativity'. He suggests that self-awareness is an important ingredient in the creative process, as is an ability to let the conscious mind generate its own patterns without becoming subservient to previous perceptions and knowledge.

There are echoes, here, of neurobiologist Charles Sherrington's description of the brain as an 'enchanted loom' which continuously weaves a construction, an image, of the external world. The aim is to match the image and reality; or at least to explore the differences. Psychologist Mihaly Csikszentmihalyi says the 'creative excitement of the artist at her easel or the scientist in the lab comes as close to the ideal of fulfilment that we all hope to, and so rarely do, achieve'. In his book *Creativity: Flow and the Psychology of Discovery and Invention*, he describes states of 'optimal experience' as where 'skill matches challenge'.

Recent experimental research has shown that the two different states of consciousness, which each fosters creativity in its own way, correspond to different brain states. Heightened consciousness and increased focus is associated with brainwaves in the beta range and the more dreamlike state with those in the alpha range.

Some scientists also regard creativity as a spiritual experience. Cognitive scientist Guy Claxton, author of *Hare Brain, Tortoise Mind: How Intelligence Increases When You Think Less*, says 'the core of creativity involves the popping into consciousness of a fruitful idea from "out of the blue" '. He asks, 'Why do we need to practise ceding conscious ego control in order to let this bubbling up happen more effectively? And is this state of receptive non-egoic cognition at all similar to the spiritual experience of "being still and knowing that I am God"?'

I suggest all kinds of creativity have three essential conditions: personality; originality; and meaning. The first condition is the presence of an individual person (the *personal*). People, not things, are creative. Creativity requires a person to see something, literally or metaphorically, and bring something into being. Sam Mendes, director of the five-times Oscar-winning film, *American Beauty*, refers to that moment in directing a play or a film 'when you discover something that only you can do, only you can say'. In artistic terms, if creativity is denuded of this personal spirit, it becomes kitsch.

It has long been a matter of debate whether a machine can have consciousness and whether it can create. For my purposes, machines cannot create; not even the fastest, most 'intelligent' computer can create. Machines can produce but they cannot create. 'Computers are useless,' said Picasso, 'they only give answers.' When they do produce something, they operate as we do when we discover something. The 'something' already exists and did not need us, the discoverer, to bring it into being. Computers have only the information that we allow them to have, directly or indirectly, which they manipulate only according to rules that we have given them. Dr Charles Jonscher, author of *Wired*

Life, says 'manipulation which is logical has the merits of precision and clarity but, by the very nature of deductive reasoning, cannot have a trace of originality . . . This is a very old theme: the logical versus the creative.'

The personality prerequisite does not mean the creative person always has to act on their own, or be self-sufficient. Some kinds of creativity tend to be done in private, even solitary circumstances, while others require and flourish in a group. Both situations can be equally creative. Whether one person thinks and works alone, and another in a group, has no more impact on their claim to be creative than the colour of their hair. The tendencies towards solitary working and group working spring from a mix of each person's inclination, the relevant processes and products, and the social arrangements. To discover C_{60}, Kroto sometimes needed to sit in a corner, sometimes to wander down the corridor to ask a question, and sometimes to collaborate with associates who knew how to build complicated machines. To make *American Beauty*, Mendes required many people, not least because he was a novice in film-making. Trevor Nunn, director of London's Royal National Theatre, enjoys what he calls 'collective analysis', saying that 'thirty opinions are always more valuable than one, so long as everyone knows they will be adjudicated'.

The point remains. When two or more creative people are working in a team, and could not succeed without the team, even to the extent of 'losing' their identity in the team, it is still their personal talent and individual contribution that generates the creativity and the product. It holds both ways. If someone who is part of a team is *only* part of a team, then they are giving nothing of themselves and they cannot be creative. This personal spirit of collaborative creativity is well summed up in the Talmudic saying, 'If I am not for myself, who will be for me? If I am for myself only, what am I? If not now, when?'

Second, creativity is *original*. It can mean either something completely new, which I describe as 'something from nothing', or the reworking of something that already exists, in the sense of 'giving character to something'. The modern belief that man could create something 'original' was a hallmark of the Renaissance and humanism. Writer Logan Pearsall Smith showed in *Words and Idioms* that Christianity used the Latin words *creator* and *creare* (to create) to refer exclusively to God and his actions. Only God could create, and whatever he created was original. Man could only rearrange what God had created. A poem that talked about God was original not because of its novel expression but because of its given subject matter. And a poem that talked about a building, however novel its expression, was not original for the same reason. The humanists took a different view. In the 1630s John Donne saw man as a creator when he said 'poetry is a counterfeit creation and makes things that are not, as though they were'. He meant to praise it, but in the climate of the Church of England's thinking at that time he was taking a risk. The word 'original' in the humanistic sense did not appear in Europe until the very end of the seventeenth century. The French word '*originalité*' first appeared in 1699. Horace Walpole and Thomas Gray were the first to use the English word 'original' in this sense, in 1742.

In his *Dictionary* of 1755, Dr Samuel Johnson gave several meanings of 'to create'. The first was 'to form out of nothing'. This happens, but it is rare. More often, a creative person takes and remixes existing ideas in a new and interesting way. Many dictionaries from the 1800s onwards prefer this latter definition. The new 'character' can be limited to an adjustment, a tweak, of the old or it can be something much more radical. The former displays its link with what went before, but the latter seems (and is) completely new.

Psychologist Margaret Boden, of the University of Sussex, distinguishes between ideas that are novel 'only to the mind of the individual concerned' (which she calls P-creativity for psychological creativity) and those that, 'as far as is known, are novel to the whole of human history' (which she calls H-creativity for historical creativity). Someone is being P-creative if they produce an idea that is new to them. A child can be endlessly creative in doing and making things that to adults are familiar and obvious. Children who behave like this are discovering and asserting their personality. Boden emphasizes that the 'H' stands for 'historical', not 'historic'. The criterion is not the idea's historic importance but its absolute novelty in time and space.

I see this as the difference between 'newness' and 'uniqueness'. Newness is novelty; the quality of being first. It is not an absolute measure. It can mean first in the mind of the creator, first in a group, or first in a particular period. Uniqueness is absolute. It means that the thing created is unlike anything else which existed previously. Of course, all things that are unique were once new; but all new things are not necessarily unique. The difference is reflected in intellectual property law. Copyright law, as I show in the next chapter, requires a work to be new but does not require it to be unique. Patent law requires it to be both new and unique. For example, if two people draw the same design at the same time, both their drawings are protected by copyright. But a person who wants to patent a new product must show that nobody has ever invented a similar one.

It is footling, for our present purposes, to burrow too deeply into the origins of creative processes. The world is too vast and too mobile – too full of ideas – for us to be able to say definitely in all cases if one thing is truly original and another thing is not. We use our stored memories, often unconsciously, even when we are asleep. But the principles still stand and affect the question of ownership.

These two criteria (personal and original) are necessary elements of creativity. But they are not sufficient. We jib at calling something creative unless it expresses our creativity in a meaningful way, even if the meaning is personal or trivial. Naming an idea or invention gives it a bit of meaning, if only to create a relationship between namer and named. But we may still feel something is lacking. So the third condition is *meaning*.

There are strong psychological arguments in favour of this. When we have been creative we commonly feel that we have accomplished something; we have made or produced something with identity and character. This emotion does not depend upon other people giving their approval or even their understanding. It would be absurd to say that someone's creativity depends on another person's understanding; that van Gogh was not being creative when he painted his canvases in the 1880s because nobody understood him, and that he only became creative retrospectively when people began to buy his paintings. On the contrary. He was astonishingly creative in terms of the creative process and the number and scope of his created products.

There is support in law. Copyright laws distinguish between an 'idea', which cannot be copyrighted, and its 'expression', which can. They require an author to use skill and effort to take an idea and create an expression or a work. Patent law goes further, and requires the inventor to carry out an 'inventive step'. Without such a step, no patent is awarded.

As we move from the personal to the industrial, and into the realms of economic transactions, so the role of meaning shifts. Teresa Amabile, Assistant Dean of Research at Harvard Business School, says that, in business, originality isn't enough: 'To be creative, an idea must be useful and actionable.' To be useful, the meaning must be communicated to the customer.

SIX CHARACTERS IN SEARCH OF AN AUDIENCE

Creativity has several other characteristics which are not necessary or always present but which round out the picture. First it is a *basic element* of life. People may disagree about many fundamental matters – morals, social behaviour, sex, politics – but most cultures and religions acknowledge creativity's primal importance as a generative power. They feel that it enlivens and makes distinctive what would otherwise be routine and repetitive. Socrates said the unexamined life is not worth living. When Shakespeare's Lear wants to express complete futility, he says 'nothing will come of nothing'. We admire creative people because they do make 'something from nothing'; and we may fear them for the same reason. When people stop being creative, in an important sense they stop living. As Bob Dylan sings, 'He who's not busy being born, / Is busy dying.' The Egyptian lawyer and economist Kamil Idris, who became Director-General of the World Intellectual Property Organization in 1997, says: 'It is a simple formula: to live, we must create.' Without creativity, we could not imagine, discover or invent anything. We would not have fire, language or science.

Creativity is also self-sufficient. We do not need outside resources to be creative (although we do need them to manufacture creative products). The second law of thermodynamics says that within a closed system organization becomes disorganized and energy runs down. This process is described as entropy. Entropy is the natural state of things unless energy is brought in from outside the system. Henry Margenau, Emeritus Professor of Physics and Natural Philosophy at Yale University, says the 'creative act', insofar as it consists of the organization of ideas into new states and patterns, 'frequently violates' the second law of thermodynamics that entropy always increases. I can start with one idea and generate three or even thirteen depending on how creative I am. Creativity exists and grows within its own domain. Being creative is analogous to negative entropy.

Second, creativity is a *universal talent.* Everyone is creative to a degree. Children are instinctively and openly creative. All children draw. It is only when people grow older that some say they cannot draw. All children dream, and talk about their dreams. Adults are more likely to say they cannot remember their dreams.

Scientists have not discovered a gene sequence for creativity (and it is unlikely that a single gene or sequence is responsible) but recent research by clinical psychologists tends to confirm this universality. Psychologists Allan Snyder and John Mitchell at the Centre for the Mind at the Australian National University, Canberra, who have researched infant prodigies and idiot savants, suggest that everyone has inherent creative skills, even including 'prodigy' and 'savant' skills, but very few know how to exploit them. Their experiments with electronic scans show how our brains process sense data very quickly, before we become consciously aware of it. For example, when we hear a piece of music the brain immediately searches the memory for patterns of similar music in order to categorize and compare it. In this way, the brain's cognitive processes swamp our instincts. Prodigies and savants 'fool' their brains and make no such search. Prodigies are abnormal not because they have a facility that is very rare but because they do not have a block, a filter, on a talent that is universal. The researchers conclude that the physiological make-up of creativity is common; what is rare is our ability, or natural physiological disposition, to use it.

This intrinsic universality applies to creativity but not to the making of creative products. Anyone can dream and have an idea. Fewer people can produce a creative product. That depends on technical skills, physical resources, and possibly on environmental factors. Professor Michael Howe of Exeter University suggests that creative achievements depend largely upon common behavioural and environmental factors. He agrees that everyone has a basic aptitude for creativity, but suggests few people have the necessary attributes to develop it fully. They need a long-term commitment, a firm sense of purpose, a strong motivation to succeed, a capacity to focus efforts towards specific goals, and often a supportive home environment.

Third, creativity is *fun*. It is 'play' in the sense that the Dutch historian Johan Huizinga uses the word in his book, *Homo Ludens*. Play is light-hearted and enjoyable; when it stops being fun, people stop playing. It is voluntary yet operates within given rules which everyone obeys absolutely, even though the penalties and sanctions may themselves be 'fun'. It is trivial although the outcomes may be highly significant (other people observing creative people at work are often puzzled – 'they don't look as if they're working'). In spite of being light-hearted and inconsequential, it is completely absorbing. It is uncertain and chancy; the opposite of routine and repetition. It engenders a strong sense of team spirit and thoroughly enjoys its own insider jargon and loyalties.

Samuel Johnson said that 'It very seldom happens to a man that his business is his pleasure.' But many creative people make their business out of their pleasure. They would agree with Noël Coward that 'Work is much more fun than fun.' For many, their work is their life and they do it naturally and as if inevitably. Ideally, they have a high quality of work and a high quality of life and these two qualities intertwine and support each other.

Richard Feynman, Nobel laureate, and probably the greatest physicist of the late twentieth century, decided early on while at Cornell University that

I was only going to do things for the fun of it. Only that afternoon, as I was taking lunch, some kid threw up a plate in the cafeteria. There was a blue medallion on the plate: the Cornell sign. As the plate came down, it wobbled. It seemed to me that the blue thing went round faster than the wobble and I wondered what the relationship was between the two. I was just playing; it had no importance at all. So I played around with the equation of motion of rotating things and I found out that if the wobble is small the blue thing goes round twice as fast as the wobble. I tried to figure out why that was, just for the fun of it, and this led me to the similar problems in the spin of an electron and that led me back into quantum electro-dynamics which is the problem I had been working on. I continued to play with it in this relaxed fashion and it was like letting a cork out of a bottle. Everything just poured out and in very short order I worked out the things for which I won the Nobel Prize.

From this story, with its echoes of Archimedes, we learn three things. One, have fun. Two, always have a problem at the back of your mind. Three, don't skip lunch.

The fourth characteristic is a sense of *competition*. Creative people can be vigorously competitive: some for themselves, some for their work, and some for both. Some creative people set themselves very high standards. Often, these are personal, and known only to themselves. The psychologist Erving Goffman spent a lifetime thinking about 'those existential moments of truth when character is gambled'. His book *Where the Action Is* describes situations in which 'people take risks sometimes wildly unjustified both to prove themselves right and, more profoundly, to prove themselves'.

If they want to make a creative product, creative people must also compete commercially in the marketplace. Here, the sole purpose is to produce something which is new and which works. James Dyson, inventor of the Dyson floor cleaner, says he had to build 5,127 prototypes before he could start to sell his first model to the public.

Fifth, creative people, as they engage their creative talents, tend to exhibit several recognizable *personality traits*. Anthony Storr, one of the most articulate analysts of the creative spirit, believes that creative people are characterized by a greater division of opposites than are other people and, equally important, that they are more aware of those opposites. Creative people do not close off possibilities. Physicist Nils Bohr said that one of his father's favourite maxims was that 'Profound truths are recognized by the fact that the opposite is also a profound truth'; and writer F. Scott Fitzgerald said in *The Crack-Up* that 'The test of a first-rate intelligence is the ability to hold two opposed ideas in the mind at the same time, and still retain the ability to function.' Creative people, says Storr, are more determined, and have the skill, to explore or reconcile these opposites and tensions. They have a strong ego, tend to be more creative in their domestic arrangements and, if so minded, surround themselves with beautiful homes and gardens. Compared to the average person, they tend to be more independent; to have a greater concern with shape and form; to have a greater preference for complexity and asymmetry; to have, in Goethe's words, a 'love of truth'; and to be more overtly bisexual.

Peter Bazalgette, Creative Director of Endemol Entertainment UK, part of Europe's largest TV production group, says creative people have six characteristics. The first is open-mindedness: 'It means allowing your mind to wander in an almost dream-like way.' The second quality is independence of mind: 'Creative people are rule-breakers, not rule-makers.' Third is not being afraid of change. Fourth is 'the blank sheet of paper test . . . Creative people are challenged by a space and want to put something in it.' Fifth is a well-developed sense of humour. Last, he says that creative people are competitive and ambitious.

Also, in spite of these generalizations, creativity is *surprising*. It is not preordained; it follows few rules; it evades most categories. This might seem obvious, but it needs to be said at a time when creativity is becoming a management nostrum. Creative people may exhibit typical characteristics, as Storr suggests, but one of these is idiosyncrasy. They are hard to sum up. T. S. Eliot is a case in point. He wrote harsh, elegiac poetry; worked competently in Lloyds Bank; wore rouge; enjoyed bird-watching; and loved boxing. Eliot was aware of the incongruities, according to his biographer Peter Ackroyd, but had no special interest in making them consistent with his literary work. Creative people may instinctively understand scientist and Nobel prize-winner Ilya Prigogine when he says that complexity and chaos are the natural order of matter; that, given enough complexity and chaos, a new life and a new order will emerge; but only to tip into more complexity and chaos. Salvador Dali advised: 'You have to systematically create confusion, it sets creativity free.' Creativity isn't *easy*.

Many creative artists, even the most proficient and self-aware, do not fully understand their own talent. One evening Laurence Olivier gave a majestic performance in *Henry V* which reduced his fellow performers to wide-eyed admiration. After the final curtain, Charles Laughton and others went to Olivier's dressing room to congratulate the great man only to discover him weeping. 'But, Larry,' said Laughton, 'you were marvellous.' 'I know,' Olivier said, 'but I don't know why.'

Finally, it must be said that, while creativity is generally a positive virtue, there is no guarantee. The conditions of being personal, original and meaningful have no intrinsic moral quality. They can be good or bad. Creativity can be used for mischievous purposes. The good is no more creative than the evil. Our conception of Satan is of a grand creator, even if he created in Hell, and humans have not stopped using their talents in ways he would admire. Many contemporary dictators such as Hitler and Stalin, and cult leaders and criminals like Jim Jones and Crippen were and are creative, and their numbers or their creativity do not lessen. Creativity flourishes in the torture room, in crime and in petty meanness. Fortunately, if we include 'meaning' as a condition we have the language to make moral judgements about creativity.

RIDERS ON THE STAGE

The catchphrase of creativity is 'Eureka!', a sudden upsurge of emotion and joy. 'Eureka' is the Greek word for 'I have it' or 'I have found it' which modern Greeks still exclaim when they discover something, whether a new theory or a lost key. The use of the word is originally attributed to Archimedes, who had been asked by King Hieron to test whether a crown was made of solid gold or included silver alloys. He had puzzled about the problem for several months until, one day, stepping into a bath and seeing the water run over, he perceived a relationship between an object put into water and the mass, or weight, of the overflow. A solid gold crown would displace more mass than a composite one. According to legend, Archimedes was so excited that he leapt naked from his bath and ran into the street.

How can we generate our eureka moments? There's a nice story of a young film-maker walking along a beach near Los Angeles one evening and seeing Steven Spielberg sitting on the sand looking at the sunset. He paused, watching and waiting. When the great man got up and left, the new arrival went and sat in exactly the same place and looked in exactly the same direction. 'I know it was silly,' he confessed afterwards, 'but I just wondered if I could imagine myself into Steve's head and pick something up.' The *Paris Review* had a long-running series in which it asked famous writers how they wrote – with a pen or a pencil, on paper with or without lines, early in the morning or late at night, at a desk or at a table – in an attempt to reveal a secret trick, an alchemy, that would help the readers to extract their own creative capital. Of course, they couldn't, just as the young film producer could not become more creative simply by sitting where Spielberg sat.

Many companies have devised systematic tests of creative and innovative thinking in an attempt to recruit people with creative talents. The majority of systems test people's creative thinking but not their ability to follow through. One attempt to combine both facilities is an Innovation Potential Indicator devised by psychologist Fiona Patterson at Nottingham University. It centres around four criteria: the motivation to change (indicated by a low boredom threshold); challenging behaviour (assertiveness and non-conformity); adaptation (a preference for tried and tested approaches); and a consistency of work style (efficiency and orderliness). Creative people are those who score high on the first pair and low on the second pair.

My own analysis of the creative process is a five-fold mix of dreams and analysis, intuitive jumps and cold-blooded calculation spelled out in a list which I call 'RIDER'

- review
- incubation
- dreams
- excitement
- reality checks

Review is the process of taking stock of things. It is noticing what is curious; making connections; asking 'what was that?' and 'why?' It is the conscious evaluation of raw materials (which economists call 'factors of production'), including the attributes of our mind (which economists tend to ignore). It encompasses both ideas and things.

Incubation is letting our ideas sort themselves out; it can last a few hours or several months; it is a time of rest. The creative person must recognize when incubation is necessary, and have sufficient resources (money, time, whatever) to provide it. One of the delights of the Christian and Jewish creation myths is that even God became tired after creating the world and had to rest on the seventh day.

Dreams are unconscious wanderings, the explorations and tastings of myth and symbol and magic and stories. In night dreams and daydreams we can be free of human constraints. Francis Bacon called it 'drifting', allowing his mind to be open to outside influences and unknown energies. Somerset Maugham said, 'Reverie is the groundwork of the creative imagination.' And, as J. R. R. Tolkien said, a few years later, 'Not all those who wander are lost.'

Excitement is the adrenaline that powers intuitive jumps and half-calculated sideways movements. It is close to Jung's moments of 'high emotional tension', letting the mind loose to ask 'what if . . . ?' without wondering whether the answer is sensible or crazy. The trick is *not* to look before you leap.

We need reality checks to ensure our dreams and intuitions have not taken us too far away. We need to analyse and measure where we are, checking back to the problem and investigating the answers on offer. The rigour and timing of these checks, and how harsh we should be, need careful management.

There are several points about this list. The most obvious is that some steps are the direct opposite of others. Dreaming and checking are diametrically opposed, requiring different mind-sets and thought processes. Creativity is a balance of opening and closing, tightening and letting go. Accelerating, as Trevor Nunn says, and slowing down. The skilled creative recognizes when to take each step, and for how long.

There is no magical order. Actually, there is no order at all. I have listed them in what might appear to be a rational order solely to make them more memorable. But there is no rank, no hierarchy, no better beginning or worse end. We can start anywhere. Sometimes we need to start by dreaming and other times by analysing. Whatever; the important thing is to start, and take control, knowing when to dream and when to calculate. Each person should choose his or her own process. Someone who wants a ready-made process, who waits for the whistle, who waits to be *told*, will create nothing.

FROM MIND TO MARKET

Creativity on its own has no economic value. It needs to take shape, to be embodied in a tradeable product, if it is to accrue commercial value. This, in turn, needs a marketplace with active sellers and buyers, some ground rules on laws and contracts, and some conventions about what constitutes a reasonable deal. By requiring these conditions I do not imply that creativity outside the market is any the less creative; but only that it has not produced an economic product.

In the next two chapters I describe the legal and commercial nature of these creative products.

2

THE BOOM IN INTELLECTUAL PROPERTY

LAW 2: PATENTS AND COPYRIGHT ARE THE CURRENCY OF THE INFORMATION AGE

'Intelligence is the new form of property.'
Charles Handy, writer

ANDREW WYLIE

New York-based Andrew Wylie has been described as 'the world's most famous literary agent' as well as the most vociferous and ferocious. It is a truism in the publishing industry that literary and commercial values are in conflict. Wylie believes the opposite: that the highest literary standards and the most aggressive business behaviour are completely compatible. His attitude flatters clients and irritates his competitors. It sums up the tension that lies at the heart of intellectual property; the balance between private ownership and public access.

Wylie is scornful of the majority of publishers and booksellers, who have been sucked into the mass market at the expense, he believes, of their clients' best interests and ultimately of their own interests too. He criticizes them for treating all books as identical commodities, merely trying to sell as many copies as possible in the shortest possible time. The result is that an increasing number of bookshops display only a very small selection of titles, albeit dozens of each title, while many good books published over a year ago are out of print and unavailable. This strategy, while suitable for the most popular books, is now applied to an ever-increasing number of titles. It brings hefty short-term revenues for the few but squeezes out the majority of the other 60,000 books published annually in America and the many others that might be imported. Wylie says publishers believe 'the most fleeting is the most valuable'. He disagrees emphatically.

He believes people should be able to own their copyrights as robustly as they can own their physical property. Owners of trademarks and brands own them totally and for ever. But owners of literary rights do not.

As a result, he says, the Walt Disney Corporation, which operates a trademark business, can invest in its intellectual properties as confidently as someone investing in their own home. But people who own a copyright business, or a patent business, cannot. Lewis Carroll's *Alice in Wonderland*, which is a copyright business, has no permanent existence. Its owners, he says, cannot justify an investment in a Wonderland.

When the estate of P. G. Wodehouse complained about the 'AskJeeves' website, which benefits freely from the name of the author's famous valet, its reliance on a copyright was a disadvantage. A trademark business called Jeeves could have stopped the website in its tracks, but a copyright business based on Jeeves could do little. Wylie says that, if William Shakespeare had been able to protect himself by trademarks, the Shakespeare business would be bigger than the Microsoft business. He relishes the idea of representing Shakespeare.

Trademark businesses are also more skilful in raising capital finance and in marketing, and so can often squeeze extra value from a copyright. Wylie describes how companies like Microsoft and Getty Images are buying up reproduction rights to the world's pictures, and creating many times more value than the original owners. Trademark companies are also buying non-exclusive rights to picture libraries in the hope they can exploit them more successfully than do the existing owners. Wylie says Picasso is the most valuable artist of the twentieth century not only in terms of his paintings but for the reproduction rights. One car company even reproduces his signature on a 'Picasso' model. He asks, 'How much would a trademark company pay to own the rights to Picasso and be able to charge licence fees for ever?' He answers his own question: '*Huge* amounts!'

He regards the limits on copyright as a failure of economics and a black hole in the law. He has made it his personal mission (twinning his love of literature with his rumbustious business acumen) to give authors the same legal protection and the same chances of long-term capital accumulation as are currently enjoyed by owners of trademarks and designs. He points out that the copyrights in James Joyce and William Faulkner are diminishing assets and will become worthless (the latter ironically summed up his life in the phrase, 'He made the books and died'). Wylie says this discourages a proper business attitude to investment, not only in the famous but in the unknown.

IN THE MARKET

Andrew Wylie is talking about the heart of intellectual property. What is its nature? Where does its economic value lie? Where *should* it lie? In publishing, what is the right balance between paying an author more and enabling the rest of us to have cheaper access to his books? Wylie takes an extreme view: that rights should be stricter. Others like Hugh Laddie, a leading British judge, take the opposite view: that copyright already lasts too long and the penalties for infringement are too severe. The patent industry faces similar tensions. What is the prime function of a patent? And should the same rules that apply to mechanical gadgets also apply to human genes? In this chapter I look at the laws of intellectual property and their treatment of the balance between economic reward and social welfare.

Intellectual property has been described as a 'subtle and esoteric area of law'. The speaker was not a despondent plaintiff in one of Dickens's more tortuous stories, but Bruce Lehman, Commissioner of the US Patents and Trademarks Office, and the author of a US Green Paper on *Intellectual Property and the National Information Infrastructure*, published in 1994. Lehman was echoing Supreme Court Justice Story, who had said 150 years earlier that copyright and patent cases come nearer than any other kind of law 'to what may be called the metaphysics of the law where the discussions are, or at least may be, very subtile and refined and sometimes almost evanescent'. He was in good company. Mark Twain, who believed writers should be allowed to own their literature as securely as their house, wrote, 'Only one thing is impossible to God: to find any sense in any copyright law on this planet.' When Kim Howells, UK Minister for Competition and

Consumer Affairs, set up an advisory group to try to raise public awareness about copyright and creativity, he said, 'Few laws have such wide effect and yet are so little understood by the public.'

Not only the public. Many governments that are quick to promote the Internet have been slow to adjust their intellectual property laws to cope with digital copying. Many companies that have become dependent on their trademark and designs have been slow to exploit their full value (the growth in patent licensing revenues in recent years is due more to companies becoming better at exploiting existing patents than to the registering of new ones). There are many business people, adept at negotiating contracts for all other resources, who believe intellectual property is not for them; that copyright is just for print publishers and patents cover only mechanical inventions. They are wrong. In the same way as successive generations of managers have needed to learn about computers and the Internet, so they now have to learn about intellectual property.

While the possession of land and financial capital is enshrined in a thousand years of law and custom, like the ownership of most physical goods, owning and protecting ideas is fraught with complexity and confusion. Landowners sleep comfortably because they know the law (which their ancestors likely wrote) will protect them. But the marketplace of intellectual property is a more crowded and confusing place. In one corner are millions of people with ideas and inventions that they want to sell or distribute almost regardless of any law and whether or not they make any money. They want to share their ideas with anyone who wants to listen and, though technically property owners, happily waive their rights. They might want to claim what lawyers call 'moral rights', such as the right to be known as the author, but not their 'economic rights', which would bring them money. In another corner are a milling crowd who want legal protection and to make money but do not know how. They may be excellent creators but they are amateurs at the law and business (and many cannot afford professional advice). In a third we can see a smaller group of people who are professional at both creating products and protecting their rights. In a fourth, a fortunate few sit, like prosperous farmers and bankers, atop their intellectual capital. And in the middle there is a vast crowd of agents and intermediaries who want to buy and sell, negotiating with lawyers, investors, government policy-makers, accountants and publicists. It is a volatile mix of legal nicety and skippy negotiation. Tidy it isn't. They are buying and selling words, music, pictures; gadgets, computer software, genes; copyrights, trademarks, patents; proposals, formats, fame, faces, reputations, brands, colours. The goods on sale in this noisy marketplace are the rights to use – or, in the lawyer's phrase, to exploit – intellectual property.

I begin my analysis with some general principles. Then I look at the main variants of intellectual property, starting with patents. I describe the way in which the American Patent Office is widening the scope of what can be patented from purely technological matters to business procedures and biology. Next I look at copyright and the threat of the Internet. Next I describe trademarks, brands, designs and trade secrets. Then, after a section on theft, I review the global market in intellectual property. I finish by asking if the 'property contract' which regulates deals between rights-owners and consumers needs to be redrafted. I suggest it does.

SEVEN PRINCIPLES OF INTELLECTUAL PROPERTY

Property

First, the determining fact of intellectual property is that it is property. Property is defined as 'belonging to someone'; i.e., it gets its character not in terms of the thing or idea itself but in terms of its relationship to someone. Thomas Raleigh, author of *An Outline of the Law of Property*, said physical property is a 'complex whole made up of many rights' including 'ownership; possession; the right to use and destroy; and the right to sell, lend and give away'. Intellectual property delivers ownership, certainly, but seldom guarantees or even offers possession, by which I mean sole physical control over the property. With physical property it is reasonable to say, 'possession is nine-tenths of the law'. With intellectual property, 'relationship is nine-tenths of the law'. Some cultures are less possessive. Islam's Sharia says the property of the brain is the property of God; Hindu societies assume that mental work is shared with the Divine and cannot be privately owned.

Intangibility

The ideas that lie at the heart of intellectual property are often hard to possess and to keep (and also, perversely, hard to give away) because they are intangible. They are a public good. This commonality was paramount in all early thinking and still persists in some legal systems. Thomas Jefferson described these qualities in a letter to Isaac McPherson in 1813, and nobody has said it better:

> If nature has made one thing less susceptible than all others of exclusive property, it is the action of the thinking power called an idea, which an individual may exclusively possess as long as he keeps it to himself; but the moment it is divulged, it forces itself into the possession of everyone . . . Its peculiar character, too, is that no one possesses the less, because every other possesses the whole of it. He who receives an idea from me, receives instruction himself without lessening mine; as he who lights his taper at mine receives light without darkening me . . . Inventions then cannot, by nature, be a subject of property.

It is a persuasive case. But Jefferson was a prolific author and also knew what happens when an intangible idea is embedded in a tangible product (like words in a book, or the idea for steam power in a boiler) and was not averse to exceptions, as we shall see later.

The tangible and intangible can overlap awkwardly. Consider a book. It has two intangible elements: the literary contents, which are purportedly its chief value, and the rights to those contents. It is also a physical object, over which one or more people may have rights of ownership. (I said the literary contents were purportedly a book's chief value; but of course in some cases it might be more valuable propping up a broken table leg or holding a door open.) So a book has at least four constituent parts: the physical object; the rights to the physical object; the intellectual property like the story of which the book is a physical form; and the rights to this intellectual property.

Government

Third, intellectual property exists only insofar as a government or a law court says it does. No law, no property. That is why there are so many government policy-makers in the intellectual marketplace. Consider the term of a patent, which is generally twenty years. The reason is not inherent in inventions, or the market for inventions, or their cost. Patents last twenty years because governments say they should.

Each government has its own mix of legal statute, regulations and case law. In Britain, the main statutes are the 1977 Patents Act, the 1988 Copyright, Designs and Patents Act, and the 1994 Trade Marks Act. America has the 1970 US Patents Act, the 1976 Copyright Act, the 1998 Digital Millennium Copyright Act and the 1999 Intellectual Property and Communications Omnibus Reform Act. In all countries, the judicial courts play an important role interpreting statute and adjudicating on common law rights; in addition, some countries have a special appeal court for patent infringements. Britain and America share strong traditions of common law, although in many areas these have been replaced by statutory rights (one major exception is the law of 'passing off', by which a company can prevent a competitor from 'passing off' goods similar to its own). The difficulty in fitting the idiosyncratic, one-off nature of intellectual property into statute and common law means that the courts play an important role in determining which ideas we can own and which should stay public.

These laws define the various kinds of property that qualify for protection, and spell out the owner's rights, notably their scope and their term, or lifetime. It is a peculiar attribute of rights that their scope is mainly negative; that is, the right to stop somebody from doing something. Copyright prevents others from copying. A patent prevents others from making. As for the term, it varies widely for each kind. There was historically a principle that terms were shorter for property with an industrial application and longer for property more expressive of artistic expression, but the quasi-permanent state of most trademarks tilts the balance. The term of a patent used to vary between about fifteen and twenty years (American patents lasted for seventeen years) but nowadays almost all countries have a standard term of twenty years. The basic copyright term is the author's lifetime plus seventy years. During their term, patents and most copyrights can be 'assigned' – given or sold to another person. Moral rights cannot be assigned, but in Britain and America they may be bequeathed in a will like any other kind of property.

International Conventions

Fourth, the ease and quickness with which creative products travel and can be copied or used in another country have encouraged governments to establish international conventions to protect their nationals' intellectual property wherever it may be traded. Someone writing a book or making a scientific invention needs to know that it will be protected not only in their own country but worldwide. When I travel to a foreign country, nobody questions that my luggage remains mine at my destination. But intellectual property has to be protected anew wherever I go. The first global convention, covering patents, trademarks and designs, was signed in Paris in 1883, and the Berne convention on copyright followed three years later. All conventions are periodically reviewed and amended to take account of technological change.

The copyright conventions have proved the most troublesome because of the need to keep pace with technological change. France was long the most friendly towards foreign nationals' works, and America the most xenophobic, saying for many years that only books 'manufactured' in America merited American protection. Nowadays, copyright protection is more standardized.

The laws on patents operate differently. An inventor must register his invention country by country. Someone who registers a patent in country A thereby gains protection only in country A, and must register it anew in country B, C, etc. for protection there. As the patent-holder in country A, he is the only person allowed to register it elsewhere (because he is the only person who can claim it is novel). So a competitor can make and sell a rival product in country B, C, etc., but cannot claim patent protection and, once the original inventor sees what is happening, he can claim a patent and stop the competitor forthwith.

The two organizations that administer these global arrangements have a major, and increasing, impact on national legislation and consequently on international trade. The World Intellectual Property Organization (WIPO) based in Geneva administers the Berne and Paris Conventions. It also administers the 1970 Patent Cooperation Treaty (PCT), which provides one-stop shopping for those seeking to establish patents based on local checks by the American, Japanese, Australian and Russian patent offices and by the European Patent Office. The

PCT started slowly but by 2000 covered over 100 countries and was receiving over 7,000 applications a month. Its members have signed a global treaty ensuring standardization and mutual recognition, so that every country recognizes a PCT patent, which may prove the first step towards a single global patent. Separately, the much newer World Trade Organization (WTO) operates a regulatory system for Trade-Related Intellectual Property Rights (TRIPS). The WTO is a very different kind of organization from WIPO. Whereas WIPO operates as a secretariat, merely coordinating its members' meetings, the WTO has independent powers of policing and can impose penalties.

In the past ten years the European Commission has taken the lead in reforming the law of European states. Britain and other EU members seldom bother to revise their own copyright laws except to implement European Union directives. The Commission would also like to introduce a single European-wide patent. Meanwhile, and separately from the European Commission, the European governments have established a European Patent Convention and a European Patent Office (based in Munich, Germany), and a Community Trade Mark Office (based in Alicante, Spain). They have also passed a Community Plant Varieties Convention (Union Internationale pour le Protection des Obtentions Végétables, UPOV).

Justifications

Fifth, the justifications for intellectual property can be summarized under four headings as: incentive; reward; disclosure; and human rights.

The *incentive* of owning what I create, of obtaining private property rights, is believed to encourage innovation. However, the evidence is quite complicated. Individuals and companies are creative for many different reasons, both internal (because they want to) and external or environmental (such as market competition). There is also a counter argument that property rights, especially patent rights, inhibit competition and operate as a drag on innovation. In general, though, the net effect is positive, especially in the case of patents and industrial property. The incentive justification is weaker in the case of copyright.

More certain is the law as a basis for *reward*. Authors and inventors need a mechanism for recouping their investment and making a profit, whether or not the law encouraged them to innovate in the first place. These rewards operate very differently in each industry. A patent is a block monopoly and, once granted, the patent office has little interest in its future development. In contrast, the reward to a copyright-holder is a collection of rights which are subject to amendment as technology evolves.

The benefits of *disclosure* are specific to patents. Patent offices publish every application for a patent so that others may understand how it works and take it further. Without disclosure, inventors could keep their inventions secret.

These first three points are primarily economic. There is also a moral presumption that people have a *natural right* to own whatever they create. Natural rights are strongest in products of human expression and weakest in industrial property. The theories of Thomas Hobbes and John Locke about the rights of man in the seventeenth century gave an unassailable moral push to the introduction of copyright. At the beginning of the twenty-first century, new ideas about natural rights are a factor in the debate about how far human and animal matter should be privatized.

Property Contract

Sixth, the basis of all intellectual property law is what I call the 'property contract'. It is an abiding principle of intellectual property law that it takes account of ownership's effect on social welfare. It tries to balance two principles: the principle that people deserve to be rewarded for their creative efforts, and will only work if they are rewarded, and the principle that society as a whole benefits if the resulting creations and inventions are put into the public domain and made freely available. All laws, in all countries, strike this balance between ownership/control and use/access. Of course, they tip the balance at different points, favouring either the creator or the public. People who favour the creators and rights-holders are often called 'maximalists', because they want to maximize property rights, and those who believe property rights should be restricted are called 'minimalists'. Paul Goldstein of Stanford Law School describes the former as 'optimists' who always want more and expect to get it, and the latter as 'pessimists' who believe authors and inventors should be rewarded the bare minimum necessary to enable them to continue to work. In their comprehensive survey, *Intellectual Property Research*, Peter Hayward and Christine Greenhalgh say, 'The knife edge on which the law tries to balance the system is that of defining enough private property rights to generate adequate incentives for creating knowledge, whilst avoiding the gift of monopoly power which leads to overpricing and complacency.' The 'property contract' is a major theme, and a controversial one, of the creative economy.

Each country draws up its own contract to reflect its cultural attitudes to the ownership of ideas, albeit within the general ground rules set by the WTO and global and regional conventions. Countries fall into four main camps. The US and Japanese take a 'utilitarian' approach, favouring commercial exploitation over the creator's rights. They like to pay authors or inventors just enough to buy them off; and no more. Most of Asia's newly industrial economies that take their business models from America follow its lead in these matters. In contrast, most European countries, notably France and those countries whose legal systems are also based on the Napoleonic Code, put a greater emphasis on protecting a creator's 'natural' rights. The UK stands somewhat awkwardly between the utilitarian and natural law approaches. Economically it favours America's commercial approach (and the two countries share a tradition of common law); but as a member of the European Union, it is politically obliged to harmonize its laws with its Continental neighbours.

The difference between the Anglo-American and European approaches is symbolized by their attitudes to 'moral rights' (the French '*droit moral*') and the similar 'personal rights'. The rights discussed so far are economic rights, regulating commercial exploitation. Moral rights spring from the belief that the author has a personal claim on his work irrespective of what deals may be done. Immanuel Kant wrote in *The Critique of Judgement* in 1790, 'Every artistic work consists of the creative spirit in a physical object. People can buy the physical object but the spirit, the soul, cannot be bought.' He believed copying was acceptable only on condition it admits and does not disturb the writer's integrity. Moral rights are in part protection against unscrupulous agents. Authors have a right to be identified as the author ('paternity'), a right to prevent derogatory treatment ('integrity'), a right to prevent false attribution, and a right to privacy in relation to photographs and films of them and their work. In France these rights are everlasting and inalienable. If I mock a nineteenth-century French novel long out of copyright, the writer's heirs can sue me. America has little truck with such sensibilities. Britain, likewise. Both countries only adopted moral rights under international pressure in the 1980s.

But there is an even greater disparity between these three Western camps and the fourth camp, which is composed of all rural, developing and still-emerging economies. It is a division between exporters and importers, between sellers and buyers, between 'commerce' and 'culture'. Sellers want their products to be protected in all countries (as I want my luggage to be mine everywhere). They want their domestic rules to be enforced worldwide. The film, music and drug companies are reluctant to sell their products where they are very likely to be copied or stolen. The importing countries, with little to protect in terms of their own equivalent intellectual property (which is why they are importers) seldom bother to have their own laws or, if they do have them, are slack at enforcing them.

India, for example, has very weak patent rules on drugs, which means that few global companies risk selling their drugs in India, and India's own R & D is minimal. But it also means that Indian drugs are cheap, whether local inventions or imported (stolen) varieties. Many non-proprietary drugs on sale throughout Asia and Africa are 'made in India', contributing to a profitable export surplus. Under WTO pressure, India has promised to recognize Western pharmaceutical patents as from 2005. The result will be a dramatic shake-up of local industry and research. Many companies will go out of business; retail prices will rise. The prize, according to the WTO and the World Bank, will be a more innovative, legitimate industry that can compete on the world market. But many Indians fear their own companies will disappear or be swamped by WTO-protected Western conglomerates.

There is an additional complication. Many developing countries (not only those following Islamic and Hindu principles) regard creativity as part of the public commons, and do not treat creative products as private property. They define authorship loosely and provide minimal levels of protection. They regard Western rules as an unwarranted, quasi-colonial tax on the import of ideas, knowledge and technology. These countries resist the WTO's policies on stricter intellectual property rules. However, they dare not complain too strongly, for fear of being shut out of Western markets in retaliation.

Opting Out

Finally, these laws are voluntary in the sense that everyone can create and invent outside the property contract. There are many creative people who do not enter the marketplace at all, and do not sign the contract. They opt out. They do not claim their rights. Some people accept that their work has little or no economic value and that to ask for money would stifle it at birth. There is another group of people whose work is valuable but who refuse financial gain on moral grounds. Some software programmers are opposed to copyright on moral grounds, which is why most Internet protocols are not copyrighted or patented. I return to this abnegation, which has important implications, later in this chapter. And there are others who simply make mistakes, like the music companies who said copyright in the Beatles' songs wasn't worth a candle, and like Xerox, who decided not to patent its graphical user interface (GUI), thinking it valueless, and so let Apple and Microsoft copy it for free, and make substantial profits from it.

The next section discusses the four main types of intellectual property in detail. An author or inventor cannot choose which he prefers. The product determines the category. A book falls within copyright law, an industrial process falls within patent law, and a person's name falls within trademark law. Some products fall into more than one category. A written description of a scientific idea qualifies as a literary work and wins copyright protection, while the idea may (or may not) qualify for patent protection. Similarly, a film, as well as qualifying for copyright, will include many other qualifying works with their own rights. It will almost certainly include music; and the music rights will probably involve copyright, performance rights and recording rights. The last, by the way, are called 'mechanical' rights. Subtle it is.

Andrew Wylie is not alone in wanting to choose his rights. Many creators want to move from the weaker copyright forms to the stronger forms of patent and trademark ownership. Society has approved different bundles of moral and economic rights for artistic expression and industrial innovation. As artistic expression becomes more industrial, so the division of rights becomes more difficult. In the late 1990s, an artist in London cut a sheep in half. The result qualified for copyright. Some scientists in Scotland cloned a sheep. They won a patent for the method. If Damien Hirst had been as radical or far-sighted in legal terms as he was in aesthetic terms he would have applied for a patent for his cut-up sheep. The art of the patent.

PATENTS

Patents are the clearest example of intellectual property as property. Patents are not merely property, they are monopolies, and deliberately so. Jefferson's fine and compelling words about the impossibility of owning ideas did not stop him from being one of the three people who set up America's first patent office. He was Secretary of State at the time and his fellow examiners were Henry Knox, Secretary of War, and Edmund Randolph, Attorney-General, their eminent status indicating the seriousness with which the new government took its role.

Patents vividly demonstrate governments' and industries' fondness for the privatization of creative products. By privatization I mean the process of extending private property rights over creative products, particularly over products that previously were not treated as private property at all, or only to a limited extent. This process started in the fifteenth century and grew slowly and haphazardly through successive centuries until, in the late twentieth century, it became the dominant paradigm in our attitudes towards new ideas and inventions. In the last few decades, many more creative people have put a higher priority on the monetary value of their output; many businesses that were ignorant of intellectual property have begun to value it highly; and there is a worldwide trend towards the extension of private property rights to matters that had been regarded as part of the public commons (such as genetic material). Although inventors often bemoan the difficulty of getting a patent, it is becoming easier day by day. In their first year, Jefferson and his colleagues gave out three patents. Now, the US

Patent and Trademark Office gives out three patents every twenty minutes of the working week. Western governments encourage their patent offices to award as many patents as possible in order to support their international competitiveness. International league tables showing agricultural output or miles of railway track have been replaced with lists of new patents.

Of the four justifications for intellectual property, the arguments for patents rely mostly on innovation, reward and disclosure. There is a broad assumption that the likelihood of a patent does encourage people to spend time and money on research and development, searching for technological innovation. The American and British offices make this link explicit in their instructions to their patent offices. The Japanese government welcomed its new patent system in 1998 by saying, 'Japan is in dire straits . . . but the new patent system will offer important protection and incentives to people to innovate and thus generate a variety of new technological advances.' It pointed out that 'In the forty-five years from 1947 to 1992 the Japanese life span has grown twenty years and it is estimated at least half of this growth is due to newly developed pharmaceuticals which exist only because pharmaceuticals are patent-protected.' Companies involved in R & D would support this contention in general terms, although marketplace competition is at least as strong a factor. The disclosure point, while often relegated to a minor role, is also significant because it requires a patent-holder to publish the tricks of their trade, and thus open up the possibilities for further innovation by others.

A patent is concerned with how things work; what they do and how they do it. It protects an idea and its implementation or 'embodiment' in a device. Anyone who wants one must make a detailed application which will be measured against three tests: novelty; non-obviousness or inventiveness; and usefulness as measured by a technical effect. A patent is usually given to the first person to file an application (assuming the three tests are met) rather than the first person to invent (unless they publish their invention first, and thereby establish 'prior art'). A patent does not oblige the patent-holder to do anything; it merely prevents anyone else from doing it. Once awarded, regular renewal fees must be paid up to the maximum of twenty years, after which the invention goes into the public domain.

The word 'patent' comes from the Latin word for 'open', and is short for 'letters patent' – documents that could easily be opened and inspected – the mechanism by which privileges are traditionally granted. The first recorded patent was awarded by the City Council of Florence in 1421, for glass-making, and patents became common throughout the northern Italian states during the early fifteenth century. They were a tangible, demonstrable piece of property, and a valuable business asset. In the 1460s, when John of Speyer crossed the Alps to bring one of Germany's new printing presses to Venice, he applied for 'letters patent' to protect his business. Otherwise, the locals could have built a similar press and gone into competition. The city council agreed, and gave him a five-year patent to publish books in the city. The writers had no such protection; copyright was not yet thought of.

A few years later, when William Caxton, another successful European trader, brought a printing press to London, he set up shop in the precincts of Westminster Abbey in order to claim the Church's patronage and increase the chances that Edward IV would award him a similar monopoly. Both Caxton and king did well out of the deal. For the next few centuries, monarchs and guilds manipulated patents as a source of revenue and as a means of exercising political and religious censorship. In England, France and other countries they were also a means of keeping out foreign competitors, a principle that continued for a long time.

Slowly, as trade and commerce developed, inventors won the right to patents that more precisely protected their business interests regardless of royal whim. Modern patent law originated with Britain's 1624 Statute of Monopolies, which restricted the award of a monopoly patent to new inventions of a 'new manner of manufacture'. No longer could rulers and politicians award patents to suit their own domestic needs. Still less could they do so on a continuing basis, allowing the recipients to pass them to their heirs. It was the beginning of the property contract.

But the definition of what constituted an invention was hazy, and the procedures for registration were informal and uncertain, and so the overall impact of patenting on science and manufacturing, even during the Industrial Revolution, was less than it might have been. W. R. Cornish of Cambridge University points out that although it is claimed that strong patents encourage innovation, the Industrial Revolution cannot be used in evidence. It was not until the late nineteenth century that most countries began to establish strong patent offices and to impose systematic rules for registering patents, including a proper search to see if the invention already existed. Cornish recounts the Fry committee's discovery in 1901 that 40 per cent or more of British patents were for inventions that had been mentioned in earlier applications and, for that reason, were invalid. The first British Patent Office opened for business in 1883, and the system of testing applications was extended from the single test of 'novelty' to today's additional tests of the 'inventive step' and 'technical effect' or practicality.

America, unusually, included intellectual property in its Constitution. It instituted its first registration system in 1790 and a formal system of testing in 1836. The first Japanese patent law was passed in 1885, at the very beginning of the Meiji period of modernization and even before the country's new constitution was approved, so important was it seen to be. An American who was helping Japan reform its educational system told his interpreter that Americans put a high value on original research, creating new patents and registering new trademarks, but that Japan was a nation of copiers. The interpreter, Korekiyo Takahashi, said he did not have the 'slightest idea what all of this was about' but determined to learn. He set up the Patent Office, became its first commissioner and later became prime minister, playing a critical role in encouraging companies to register and protect their intellectual property.

Since then, the majority of countries have established patent offices or signed up to an international treaty, and many apply the same tests before giving a patent. The busiest offices, reflecting the countries that spend most on R & D and have the biggest consumer markets, are the US Patent and Trademark Office, followed by the Japanese Patent Office and the Munich-based European Patent Office. (I give further information on these offices in Chapter 3.)

Registration

The registration of a patent has evolved from a simple entry in a register to a full application process, complete with the examination and searches necessary to prevent a patent office from finding itself in the embarrassing position of granting two monopolies for the same idea. This burden of proof reveals a key difference between patents and copyright. Inventors have to file an application to win protection; they have to prove that their new invention really is new. Artists have no such burden. Their work is protected regardless of whether someone else is doing the same work, so long as there is no element of copying.

The 'priority date' on which an applications gets made is critical. In Britain and most countries, the priority date is when the application is filed (a system known as 'first to file'). America operates a 'first to invent' system and an inventor may use an idea for up to one year before filing, which tends to favour private inventors with fewer resources. In principle, inventions should not have been used in public before being filed, but rules differ from country to country. Applications are published either on filing, during investigation (most countries publish eighteen months after filing) or on award. Knowledge that is available before the priority date is known as 'prior art'.

An important if mythical person throughout the whole process is a 'person skilled in the art'. This phrase is used in many countries' patent laws in the same way as the concept of a reasonable man is used in common law. Unlike the reasonable man, however, who is held to be average, the skilled person is a specialist in existing knowledge or 'prior art'. He is used as a benchmark. An application, when disclosed, must be comprehensible to a 'person skilled in the art' but, conversely, if it is obvious to such a person, then it will not be awarded a patent. The same skilled person would not be expected to understand a patent for mechanical engineering and for DNA fragments like nucleotides. Although this assumption is reasonable, due to the specialist nature of many patent applications, it can allow people to entertain different ideas about what is novel or inventive. In theory, the patent examiner ensures standard principles are followed. In practice, this can be difficult.

The cost of applying for a patent is negligible in terms of the patent office's own charges (the UK Patent Office abolished most filing charges in 1999) but quite high in terms of what the applicant has to pay to prepare the application, especially if it is complicated, lodged in more than one territory, or challenged. A complicated application, complete with supporting research, may cost many thousands of pounds, and a successful award will incur annual renewal fees. Many private inventors and small businesses are reluctant to pay these costs; and some are unable to do so. The European Patent Office and the Patent Cooperation Treaty have helped to cut cost and speed the vetting process, but the applicant's costs remain substantial. It is mostly a European (and Japanese) problem. In the US, applications from private individuals and small business are increasing faster than those from large corporations, and there are fewer complaints.

To qualify, an application must fall within the category of patentable matter. Some things cannot be patented. The British Act has four sets of exclusions: 'a discovery, scientific theory or mathematical model; a literary, dramatic, musical or artistic work or any other aesthetic creation whatsoever; a scheme, rule or method for performing a mental act, playing a game or doing business, or a program for a computer; the presentation of information'. The exclusion covers these things only 'as such' or on their own, the meaning of which is a rich source of debate.

The first test is novelty: whether the idea or invention already exists, or whether something similar exists from which a 'skilled person' might reasonably deduce the idea in the application; if so, then the application is rejected. Here, the priority date is crucial.

The second is the inventive step. The invention must be truly inventive in the sense of being 'non-obvious'. This is defined as not being obvious to a normally educated person who is 'skilled in the art' and has some expert knowledge and experience of the subject. The need for an 'inventive step' is used by patent offices and the courts to dismiss applications that are happenstance and meaningless, and confirms meaning as an essential requirement of creativity. It is akin to copyright's requirement that a work must involve skill and expertise (discussed later in this chapter).

These two tests are made by reference to 'prior art', the body of existing knowledge deemed relevant. Prior art is used to demonstrate not only cases where existing inventions have anticipated the new one, but where they have not. For this reason, the larger the amount of prior art the stronger the application. It shows a proper search has been done and exhaustive inquiries carried out. The patent office will then do its own research, in order to support or reject the application.

The aim is to gather enough prior art to show that, while other inventions might come close, they do not cover the new applicant's 'inventive step'.

Third, it must be useful and have what is usually known as a 'technical effect'. It must have, or be capable of, an industrial use. The technical effect need not be very dramatic. The British Patent Office has granted a patent to a blue squash ball not because it admired the colour but because players could see a blue ball better than the traditional black ball, and it felt the difference constituted a 'technical' difference. The Americans require an invention to have 'utility'. This criterion was easy to evaluate when inventions were chiefly of mechanical devices and other physical objects. It is much harder when the idea or invention involves a process, and especially if the process is microscopic or intangible. When the examiners have to test an idea of an idea.

The bare bones of patenting are well established and, thanks to recent international treaties, common to many countries. Patent offices defend them strongly. However, they are now being put under severe stress by technological change and commercial ingenuity. I have selected the three areas of current patenting policy where the property contract faces the greatest pressure. In two, at least, our concepts of property are ambivalent. I will start with computer software and business methods, which are connected, since patenting a piece of business software is very close to patenting a business method involving software; and then I will move to genetics. I will show how America approved the patenting of biotechnology in 1980, computer programs in 1981 and business methods in 1998. Europe and Japan are not so generous, but I expect them to follow suit. We have come a long way from John of Speyer and his printing press.

Owning the Shopping Basket

The early computer programs were not treated as intellectual property at all, and received no protection outside the laws of contract and confidentiality. Then the US 1976 Copyright Act and the European Union's 1991 Directive on computer programs, which is implemented in British law, both categorized a program as a literary work and gave copyright protection. Most other countries have followed suit.

But the protection may not be worth much. It is an effective method for inhibiting an end-user from literally copying a program in its entirety, but it is powerless to stop another developer from copying its main features and producing another product. When Microsoft 'copied' Apple's desktop, and when Borland 'copied' Lotus's spreadsheet in the early 1990s, both Apple and Lotus sued and expected to win. They lost. The courts found in favour of the 'copiers'. They said Microsoft had not copied Apple's code line-by-line but had only picked up Apple's 'look and feel'; and that Borland had not slavishly copied Lotus's entire code but only some of its principles. Under copyright law, a qualifying work has to be new but it does not have to be unique. Microsoft and Borland were able to assert that, far from copying someone else's work, they had actually produced their own, and could claim their own copyright. The courts' decisions alerted industry to the weakness of copyright law in protecting computer programs and the need for something stronger.

If copyright was too weak, could a patent be the answer? Companies as diverse as banker Merrill Lynch and retailer Wal-Mart argued that their computer-based programs for providing customer services were patentable. Merrill Lynch had a system for managing share transactions, Wal-Mart for controlling inventory. Both companies, and thousands like them, realized these systems were valuable commercial assets and they wanted to protect them as much, if not more so, as they protected their buildings and their equipment. They wanted their ownership to be recognized in law. As they locked their warehouses at night, so they wanted to put patents on the intellectual processes inside.

The Supreme Court, in *Diamond v. Diehr*, 1981, found in favour of patenting computer programs so long as they fulfilled the three criteria (novelty, inventive step and technical effect). The case arose because the Patent Office had refused an application for a computer-based device to develop synthetic rubber. Patent laws expressly exclude mathematical formulae and algorithms, including computer programs, 'as such'. A computer program 'as such', or 'on its own', cannot be patented, but a computer program that fulfils an inventive function may be. In other words, the presence of a computer program does not debar a patent. The court distinguished between a program's underlying algorithms, which could not be patented, and their use in a specific system, which might be.

The extension of patenting from a computer program to a business method (albeit a business method delivered by a computer program) was confirmed in 1998 when the US Court of Appeals decided, in *State Street Bank & Trust Co. v. Signature Financial Group Inc.*, that a computer-based 'business method' does fulfil the criteria for a patentable product. The Court said the principles of novelty, non-obviousness and utility worked the same way here as elsewhere. The Court was fully aware that it is difficult if not impossible to distinguish between the mathematical code of a business method and the business method itself. In computer code, the software is the method. There is no external, physical, bricks-and-mortar reality.

The *State Street* case marked a watershed in American patenting policy. It changed the link between a patent and technology. Up till then, patents were centred on technology. What's more, a patent required the technology to be novel, non-obvious and with a technical effect. From 1998, the technology was optional. The seeds had been sown back in 1991, when the courts had said technology encompassed both hardware and software; in other words, both equipment and the ideas that drive them. The *State Street* decision took this argument to its logical conclusion.

Although the American Patent Office was initially reluctant to cut the link with technology in the sense of physical apparatus, it was emboldened by the *Diamond v. Diehr* and *State Street* cases to do so. It has since given Dell Computers more than seventy patents for its business processes. Dell is the largest computer seller in the world, selling about $35 million worth of computers every day, and its success depends on being more flexible in personalizing each computer to the customer's specification, and delivering it more quickly, than its competitors. Understandably, it wants to protect the computer processes which allow it to be so successful.

Patents for business methods are now being awarded thick and fast. The name of Peri Hartmann is not well known in the publishing world. But Peri Hartmann has won a patent (which also has the give-away name of Jeff Bezos, CEO of Amazon.com, attached) for a 'method and system for placing a purchase order via a communication network'

(US patent no. 5,960,411). The 'method and system' enables a customer to click once on the shopping basket in order to confirm an order. Bezos calls it his 1-Click system. It is hardly non-obvious and, according to James Gleick in the *New York Times*, the patent examiner initially had some doubts. But after discussion and revision she awarded the patent. Amazon.com immediately sued one of its competitors, Barnes & Noble, and forced them to change their online ordering system into a two-click process.

Hartmann and Bezos have grand ambitions for their baby. The patent's full text includes this phrase: 'Although the present invention has been described in terms of various embodiments [based on Amazon.com as it now operates] it is not intended that the invention be limited to these embodiments. Modifications within the spirit of the invention will be apparent to those skilled in the art.' Patent offices allow patents to cover as-yet unspecified applications if, as in the Amazon case, they might be imagined by such a person. The purpose is to ensure that a patent is not too narrow, and that applicants do not have to apply for a separate patent for each (minor) variation. Patent offices are liberal in allowing one patent to cover possible future uses. In the Amazon case, Hartmann and Bezos said that people who were 'skilled in the art' and likely to see future modifications could expect to find Amazon's 'No Trespassing' sign. This liberal policy encourages speculative patenting.

Priceline.com took the same approach with its software program, which provides a kind of reverse auction. Would-be buyers offer a set sum of money for a specific product without knowing if the product exists. They might offer $50 for an airline ticket from New York to Miami at 6 p.m. on Wednesday without knowing if any airline has such a ticket (airline tickets seemed the basic commodity of many early Internet businesses, which gives the lie to those who say computer nerds never leave home). In 1998, the US Patent Office awarded Priceline patent no. 5,794,207 for 'buyer-driven conditional purchase offers'. One of the main investors in Priceline.com was Jay Walker, who set up Walker Digital, a 'patent farm' which has generated a number of patents in business methods.

Another company, Open Market, based in Massachusetts, has received a patent for its technique of analysing the ways in which people go into a website and move around (measuring its 'hits' and 'stickiness'), which provides valuable information to the owner and advertisers. Critics argue that this is akin to patenting the way we read or browse a book. Sightsound.com has received a patent for the sale of digital audio and video over the Internet and consequently sued CDNow.com, MP3.com and others for a 1 per cent royalty on every transaction involving the download of CD to a customer. It says its reward would be merely similar to the royalty that Sony and Philips, co-inventors of the CD, receive for every CD sold.

The business methods now being patented are comprehensive and diverse. James Gleick says 'companies have gotten patents for keeping calendars on the World Wide Web, for downloading pages at regular intervals, for storing documents in databases, for "real-time" shopping, for auctioning cars; for creating profiles of users; for search engines, for payment systems, and for every other fundamental gear and lever in the theoretical machinery of online business'. Since he made his list, the Patent Office has awarded patents for club buying (where a group of buyers can negotiate a discount), offering professional advice, and generating footnotes in a text. It has awarded a patent for a system that 'lowers your price if your customer asks about a competitor's lower price'. Gleick quotes Lawrence Lessig, Berkman Professor of Constitutional Law, Harvard University, who advised the federal government in its anti-trust suit against Microsoft: 'This [granting of patents] is a disaster, a major change that occurred without anybody thinking through the consequences. In my view, it is the single greatest threat to innovation in cyberspace, and I'm extremely sceptical that anyone is going to get it in time.'

Faced with this 'marked increase in public attention', the US Patent Office published a White Paper, *Automated Financial or Management Data Processing Transactions (Business Methods)* in 2000 to explain its new policy. It began by saying that nothing much was new; it had given the Tabulating Machine Company, the forerunner to IBM, its first data-processing patent in 1889. But it did protest too much. It had given IBM a patent for a technical device that others purchased to use as the basis for their own business processes. What is happening now is that the US Patent Office is directly patenting those business processes. Its own description of suitable candidates for patenting (in the relevant business classification no. 705) include such common commercial activities as '(1) Determining who your customers are, and the products/services they need/want; and (2) Informing customers you exist, showing them your products and services, and getting them to purchase.' The White Paper also admitted that 'This Class no. 705 is transitioning away from technology towards the end result the inventor is attempting to achieve with that technology.' It confirmed that, following the *State Street* decision, the technology, or technical effect, is being replaced by pure business. It quotes a recent patent for a sales team (no. 6,070,149), 'The present invention relates to virtual sales personnel, and more particularly, to software which is capable of assisting a computer user to complete an online sales transaction in a substantially similar manner as a human sales representative.'

According to Keith Beresford, a leading patent attorney, an inventive business method not involving any novel technology, while it may be patentable in America, is almost certainly not patentable in Europe. European patent offices take the view that inventions that lack a technical or practical input or output, or an industrial use, do not qualify. However, we should not exaggerate the differences between America and Europe on this point. America's more active approach is caused by social factors which Europe has already begun to import. Johannes Lang, a German patent attorney, says, 'Today in Europe the emphasis is put on the technical character . . . while in America the discussion focuses on its useful application; i.e., a useful, concrete and tangible result.' The American office is simply responding to its own customers. In the coming years, it will be hard for Europe to withstand the trend towards patenting business procedures, and many American software companies have already filed applications at the European Patent Office in the expectation that European attitudes will change.

The options for the European Patent Office were spelled out in a European Commission report, *The Economic Impact of Patentability of Computer Programs*, in 2000. The report says the main difference between America and Europe is that 'in Europe the invention has to be of a technical character whilst in America the fact that an invention uses a computer in any way is enough to qualify' (assuming, in all cases, that the criteria of novelty and inventiveness are met). It acknowledges Europe must follow America's path. A few months earlier the EPO had already voted 10:9 to liberalize its rules. The only question is, how quickly? The report offers three options. Even the first, minimalist, option would remove the phrase 'as such' from the European Patent Convention, which would have the effect of bringing computer processes to the centre of the patenting fold. The second option would allow the mere use of a computer to enable the invention to qualify as 'technology' (even if the use of the computer itself were neither novel nor non-obvious, nor had a technical effect). The report says this would be 'highly controversial'. The third option is to alter European law 'to have no requirement that patents be limited to technology'. This would cause 'great controversy'.

Patenting computer programs and business methods gets close to patenting the heart and soul of an organization. W. R. Cornish says, 'Computer programs lie exactly at the boundary of what previously has been thought to separate the patentable from the non-patentable.' A policy that conjures up the further possibility that business processes may be patented and privatized even if they do not involve technology has implications for economics, regulation and social equity. If you cut the link with technology the way is open to the privatization of every process so long as it is new, inventive and useful.

Private Genes

Equally awkward and even more publicly controversial is the patenting of biological matter. It is said scientists are patenting life itself, though we should be careful about what we mean by 'life'. Many countries have allowed people to own and register plant varieties for decades. America took the lead, starting with the 1930 Plant Patent Act, followed by Germany and other European countries. Britain passed its Plant Varieties and Seeds Act in 1964, awarding a full monopoly right to the owner of any plant variety that can be shown to be novel, distinct, uniform and stable. The test of novelty is much looser than that for an industrial patent (who knows what plants may be growing in the wild?). So a plant qualifies for protection even if it has a history of growing wild, so long as it has not been sold commercially for more than four years.

At the time, patenting a seed or a plant for agricultural purposes was regarded as being no different from patenting a chemical or biological recipe for pharmaceutical purposes. Western farmers and horticulturists were eager to increase yields as their own costs grew (especially farm wages) and they had to compete with imports from low-wage countries. They were also keen to grow new varieties that could be picked and brought to market a few weeks sooner. The huge investments in faster-growing and more disease-resistant seeds over the past forty years might not have been made if the seed companies had not been able to protect their work. (In the same period, home gardeners, faced with weeds in their flowerbeds, and the modern curse of too little time, also enjoyed the benefits of buying huge quantities of glyphosate in Round-Up and other patented weedkillers.)

The number of applications for plant and genetic patents has increased with extraordinary rapidity. Technological advances in biotechnology have extended scientists' ability to exploit biological matter from whole plants to their various elements; from whole animals to parts of animals; and from animals to humans. Developments in DNA and in cell technology have allowed scientists to identify, nurture and remix cells so that they can create living material. The identification of the human genome, which contains the genes that control the design of each human (how and what the human reproduces, and how it builds and maintains itself, or not) will need a new property contract.

Should the genome be public property in the same way as, say, the knowledge of blood types is public property, or the structure of DNA itself? Or should it be private property? The American Supreme Court famously said in 1952, 'Anything under the sun that is made by man is patentable'; implying that everything that was not made by man was not patentable. Since then, its position has shifted. In *Diamond v. Chakrabarty* in 1980 it was asked to rule on a patent application by Anand Chakrabarty for a genetically modified bacterial micro-organism designed to gobble up oil spills at sea. It decided to shift the dividing line from between 'inanimate things and living things' (the former patentable, the latter not) to between the product of nature, whether living or not, and human-made inventions which may, of course, be living; and it approved the patent. In 1987 the US Patent Office issued new guidelines which said that all bio-organisms except humans could be patented. It said humans were protected by the

Thirteenth Amendment to the Constitution, which prohibits slavery (it was silent on the possibility of artificial masters).

The Patent Office later issued a patent to Harvard University for an experimental mouse known as Oncomouse, into which an oncogene had been inserted for the purpose of cancer research. The European Patent Office, after initially demurring, did likewise. It said Oncomouse was such a considerable manipulation of genetic material as to be new and unique. It was protested on ethical grounds that the mice would suffer during the research, but the EPO decided the benefit to society outweighed the loss to the mouse; a neat variation on the 'property contract' that balances the creator's reward against the social gain. This rapid shift over seven years from saying 'nothing, never' to 'everything but slaves' was a breathtaking expansion of private property and a massive shift in our (or, rather, the patent offices') attitude towards the ownership of life.

Another odd case, reinterpreting the property contract against our common instincts, occurred when a Californian university medical centre managed to own and patent the cell line found in a spleen that had been taken from a man, John Moore, who had hairy-cell leukaemia. The doctors had discovered that Moore's T-lymphocytes were extraordinarily rare and potentially of great medical value. Without telling him, they carried out intensive tests that ended with the removal of his spleen. The cells were indeed as valuable as they had expected, generating products worth hundreds of millions of dollars. When Moore discovered how the university had privatized his cells, and made its profits, he sued; but he lost. The Supreme Court of California decided that we do not own our cells after they have left our body.

The two rival organizations that are mapping the human genome are conveniently taking completely opposite approaches to patenting the results. I say 'conveniently' because it makes the alternatives very clear, in a way that seldom happens in science or patent policy. The publicly funded $3 billion US–UK Human Genome Mapping Project (HGMP) is publishing all its results so they become public property. John Sulston of the Wellcome Trust, which sponsored the British research, said, 'Our basic information, our "software", should be free and open for everyone to play with, to compete with, to try and make products from.' The commercially funded Celera, on the other hand, is publishing the majority of what it discovers (since the majority is scientifically unproductive) but retaining the productive and valuable parts. Both the HGMP and Celera agree in principle that genes may be patented but they disagree on the criteria, especially the 'what', the 'when' and the 'why'.

What is the what? The words 'invention' and 'discovery' are problematic. The public generally understands discovery to mean finding or identifying something that already exists, and an invention to be something that did not previously exist. But science, and patent offices, eschew such simplicity; or, rather, they have looked and found it unworkable. Thomas S. Kuhn, who introduced the idea of the 'paradigm' to scientific evolution, says in *The Structure of Scientific Revolutions*, 'We must ask how changes of this sort can come about, considering first discoveries, or novelties of fact, and then inventions, or novelties of theory. That distinction between discovery and invention, or between fact and theory, will, however, immediately prove to be exceedingly artificial.' He gives many examples, starting with the discovery of oxygen, whose authorship has been contested for over two centuries. He argues convincingly that Joseph Priestley may be said to be the first to have discovered something new, but that he did not know what it was; while Antoine Laurent Lavoisier, who followed Priestley, was the first to invent a new concept of something that might have been oxygen but which in fact was not; leaving others to identify it correctly. The US Patent Office says with some bravado that 'invention means invention or discovery'. American companies who apply for biotechnology patents use the words interchangeably, although they seem to prefer the word 'discovery'. The European Patent Convention says discoveries cannot be patented at all (they are 'excluded matter') and the UK takes the same view.

Is it sensible to ask if identifying a gene is a discovery or an invention? Given that the property contract is a social contract, in which society has half share, and that the popular meaning of both words is quite clear, the question seems worth considering. The HGMP asserts that the identification of a particular gene is a 'discovery' not an invention, and cannot be patented. It says the raw genetic data is 'obvious'. Every half-qualified scientist knows it is there. But merely knowing it is there has no practical value. The HGMP believes that scientists must apply further skill and intelligence before they can justify a claim for a non-obvious, practical use. A patent is granted to stop others from making, selling or using the patented product, which must be novel. It cannot therefore be granted to a naturally occuring gene.

On the other hand, Celera and many other companies argue that their techniques for identifying a raw gene sequence are so difficult and out-of-the-ordinary (i.e., so novel and non-obvious) that they constitute an invention as popularly understood, and qualify for a patent. They also say that they have a large and sufficient number of ideas for industrial applications. It is a reasonable approach. To get a patent you have to show that your idea has a practical application but you do not have to prove you can deliver the practical application yourself. The Supreme Court judgement in *Diamond v. Chakrabarty*, and the US Patent Office's more recent policy statements, support Celera's case. The Patent Office has said it will award patents to genes only if the use is 'substantial, specific and credible'. But the gene grabs continue.

Cloning raises another question. The cloning of plants, fruit and vegetables has been going on for centuries (most apples and potatoes are cloned). Gene cloning has been possible for over twenty-five years. But animal cloning is new. It involves taking a donor's single cell, extracting the DNA, injecting it into a fertilized egg cell from which the DNA has been removed, and stimulating the new-cell-with-its-DNA with a burst of electricity. The resulting embryo contains embryonic stem cells that will generate specialized cells for each body function. Animal cloning, and the potential for human cloning, came to public notice when Ian Wilmut at the Roslin Institute near Edinburgh cloned Dolly the sheep by recreating, via an easily obtained body cell, an egg cell and thence an embryo which was compatible with the host. Since then, PPL Therapeutics, which has a licence from the Roslin Institute, has cloned Polly the sheep, which (or should that be 'who') contains a human gene; as well as cows, rabbits and mice. It has also cloned five piglets, including one called Dot.com. PPL has produced a compound called AAT, based on a protein in the milk of genetically altered sheep, to treat cystic fibrosis and breathing disorders.

The Roslin Institute, the UK Ministry of Agriculture and the UK

Biotechnology and Biological Research Council successfully applied for two patents (no. 2,318,578 and no. 2,331,751) to protect their techniques for cloning. The patents are mainly for animal cloning but they also cover the 'cloning of human cells'. Whether or not Roslin or its licensees will use its techniques in humans depends more on political decisions than on patent procedures.

These political pressures were expressed in March 2000 when Prime Minister Tony Blair and President Bill Clinton responded to public concern by what they called a 'moral exhortation' in support of 'unencumbered access' to the genome sequence. They said, 'We applaud the decision by scientists working on the human genome project to release raw fundamental information about the human DNA sequence and its variants rapidly into the public domain, and we commend other scientists around the world to adopt this policy.' Overnight, shares in biotech companies in London and New York fell by an average of 12 per cent.

Both leaders noticeably failed to take any action to put their words into effect, not wishing to permanently damage the biotech industry. Rather, the opposite. In 1998, the British government had voted in favour of a European Directive (no. 98/44) on the legal protection of biotechnological inventions. It did so against opposition from the Dutch government which later, supported by the Italian government, appealed to the European Court of Justice. The Council of Europe has called for the Directive to be immediately 'renegotiated', yet a month after the Blair–Clinton statement, the British Patent Office began the official implementation procedure by issuing a consultation paper which confirmed the Directive fitted with existing British law. It stated that the 'human body, at the various stages of its formation and development, and the simple discovery of one of its elements, including the sequence or partial sequence of one of its elements cannot constitute patentable inventions' (Article 5.1) but that 'An element isolated from the human body or otherwise produced by means of a technical process, including the sequence or partial sequence of a gene, may constitute a patentable invention even if the structure of that element is identical to that of a natural element' (Article 5.2). The same Article emphasizes that the application must disclose how the sequence may be used in practice. The Directive requires the applicant to list some practical applications, but these may be quite general. In America, the Patent Office declared its policies in favour of patenting genes were 'unaffected' by the Blair–Clinton statement. Business as usual.

The Central Banks

The American, European and Japanese patent offices are the 'central banks' of patent property. They sit in the middle of a comprehensive network of researchers, inventors, entrepreneurs and corporations who increasingly believe that they must patent not only what they sell but how they sell it. For them, patents and trademarks are the core of their business: their main product and competitive advantage. For compelling reasons, they are driven to privatize as much as they can. They usually have the support of their shareholders, who want healthy balance sheets, and of their governments, who want strong industries. The 'central banks' issue the currency.

Their chief purpose is to award as many patents as possible. The first objective of the British Patent Office is to 'stimulate innovation and the international competitiveness of British industry through the promotion and understanding of intellectual property rights'. It has a 'clear focus on customer satisfaction'. To that end, it provides a range of educational and advisory services. It leaves Parliament to settle the social and moral framework within which it operates, although Parliament has shown little interest, discussing patents only twice in twenty years. The mission of the US Patent Office is to 'promote the use of intellectual property rights as a means of achieving economic prosperity'. Its internal noticeboards are more punchy: 'To Help Our Customers Get Patents'.

It is a profitable business, this banking of ideas. The US Patent Office had revenues of about $830 million in 1999 and profit, depending on how the government allocates the overhead, of $90–190 million. The British Patent Office recorded revenues in 2000 of £52 million and profits of £13 million. Its accumulated surplus was £113 million.

Meanwhile, the customers are banging on the door. The gold rush has become too general a metaphor to have much meaning, but we are seeing a gold rush in the search for patents, both old and new. It is not the first time. In 1882 the US Supreme Court, faced with a rush of applications, said, 'An indiscriminate creation of exclusive privileges tends to obstruct rather than stimulate invention. It creates a class of speculative schemers who make it their business to watch the advancing wave of improvement, and gather its foam in the form of patented monopolies, which enable them to lay a heavy tax on the industry of the country, without contributing anything to the real advancement of the arts.' Looking at the advancing waves in Washington, Tokyo and Munich, not much has changed.

There is a boom in specialist advisers who encourage companies to apply for more patents (for instance Aurigin, QED, BTG and other 'patent mining' companies). Aurigin provide 3-D maps of industries showing where patents are crowded close together, which appear as hills, and where they are scarce, which look like valleys. They advise prospectors to head for the valleys and to take out speculative patents. Kevin Rivette of Aurigin is a specialist in maximizing a company's patent assets, including searching for patents the company has forgotten (as described in his enticingly named book, *Rembrandts in the Attic*). Many technology-based companies have a storehouse full of their own patents that are not being fully exploited. Aurigin has developed a technique for a company's patent strategy called 'patent mining' which determines which it should grow, reinforce or sell. Aurigin has many examples of companies that do not know what patents they have, and how they might help their future business. Ben du Pont, one of the heirs to the Du Pont fortune, has started a company called Yet2.com which provides a business-to-business exchange for patents and rights. Launching the company, du Pont was quoted as saying, 'I worked at Du Pont for fourteen years and hadn't the foggiest about what we had for licensing.' For a small fee, Yet2.com will list a patent and seek buyers. IPNetwork.com does the same for copyrights and trademarks, InterDigital for wireless patents.

Usually, their deals are confidential, but occasionally they become public news. BT applied for patents for its hyperlink technology in the 1970s. Most offices awarded a patent which expired over the next 15–20 years. The American patent was appealed and so not effective until 1986. By that time, BT had lost interest. Then in 2000 BT suddenly discovered its patent (no. 4,873,662) rusting somewhere in its Suffolk research centre, and started the difficult process of charging licence fees to companies which had been using the technology in the belief that it was free. BTG, a company that assists people to find their 'Rembrandts', estimates that companies like BT are losing up to $100 billion worth of licensing revenues. It describes its own staff as 'merchant scientists'.

The strains are beginning to show. Rivette has criticized the US Patent Office for 'serious deficiencies in staffing, resources and examination procedures'. A hint of the scale of the problem came in 1999 when it appointed an extra 1,000 staff, including 850 examiners, bringing the total to 3,500, an increase of 40 per cent. The British Patent Office's examining staff rose more modestly over the same period by ten; from 205 to 215. According to Greg Aharonian, whose Internet Patent News Service provides an invaluable 'reality check' on patenting policy, the US Patent Office's staff turnover is high at 20 per cent a year, and over 50 per cent of the examiners have been there for less than two years. He gives persuasive evidence that their technical knowledge and legal expertise is not good enough.

These examiners are the heart of the patent process. They are the front-line people, usually working on their own, who decide whether a patent should be awarded. They should justify each decision by reference to citations either from the office's own archives, centred on previous applications, or in relevant science and technical journals. These sources are sufficient if a technology is developing slowly. They are not adequate if the technology is developing very fast; if its inventors operate outside conventional research or academic circles; or if they are spread over many countries speaking many languages. The Internet Patent News Service estimates that over 50 per cent of American software patents do not cite any 'prior art', which patent experts have criticized as being sloppy and probably illegal.

The US Patent Office is the most powerful central bank of all. The American patenting system, comprising Congress, the Patent Office and the courts, has an exceptional influence on global policy on what should and should not be patented. The Patent Office has dealings every day with the world's largest corporations and R & D organizations; it is literally at the defining edge of what is new and innovative. Its decisions affect where the line is drawn between public and private, and thus influence corporate fortunes in America and worldwide. Although an American patent is enforceable only in America, it automatically becomes 'prior art' and the idea cannot be patented elsewhere except by the holder of the original patent. If one office is quicker and more generous with its patents then it tends to set the pace worldwide. Other countries follow America's policy for reasons of economic self-interest. They admire America's ability to turn ideas into profitable invention. They wish their own national companies were similarly profitable. They know that American corporations will not invest abroad where their rights are not protected.

Creating wealth through patents is as reasonable a business proposition as drilling for oil or making cars (or writing a book). Patent offices and patent holders can reasonably claim the current system fits society's general view about what should be public and what may be private, without too many upsets or changes of direction. But the critics are becoming more vociferous. All patent offices are technology-neutral; in other words they apply the same principles of novelty, inventiveness and technical effect regardless of the technology, whether it be a mechanical device or a business method. This principle, which served well for over a hundred years, is too general when technology's meanings and effects are so wide. In terms of computer programs and business methods, the lines of demarcation are very blurred, and the differences between America and the rest of the world are awkward. In terms of plants and animals, moral questions are unanswered. Industry wants to dismantle the barriers between what Mother Nature is and what companies are free to make. Some countries, unconvinced that they should hand out twenty-year monopolies on such matters, have revived ideas for a 'minor' or 'petty' patent which provides a lower level of protection for a few years and which can be provided more cheaply and quickly.

The patent system is both conceptually troubled and administratively overburdened. The US Patent Office has the most problems; although, to its credit, it is also the most open about them, publishing a White Paper on the patenting of business methods, as we have seen, and setting up quarterly forums in business methods and biotechnology. The system is unlikely to break down. Equally, the decisions taken now in Washington and elsewhere are rewriting the property contract. The deliberate effect is to privatize a wider range of ideas and knowledge in ways that we cannot fully grasp but which, if misguided, will be hard to change.

The public needs to state its claims alongside those of the commercial prospectors, and it needs to do so forcefully. At present, patent offices deal daily with their customers and the courts; seldom with politicians; and hardly ever with the public. They regard themselves as functionaries, deliberately keeping away from the moral, social and political complexities of the creative economy. As a result, the public is not being well served.

The first step is for each country to ensure its national patent office serves not only its customers but the public as well. Second, all offices, not just the trilateral club of Washington, Tokyo and Munich, should work more closely together. In a global economy, the rules of ownership should be democratic and consistent.

COPYRIGHT

Copyright offers a different version of the property contract. It exists only in 'qualifying' works which can be grouped into three categories: literary, dramatic, musical and artistic works, films and TV programmes; performances and broadcasts; and the typographical arrangement of published works. Literary and artistic works are not limited to what the public might regard as such; for example, the law treats a wiring diagram as an artistic work.

The work must fit the category, must be original, and must have involved the author's skill and labour, although the test of originality and skill is lower than the similar tests for a patent. A qualifying work does not need to have any 'novelty or aesthetic value'. However, it does have to be the result of 'independent intellectual effort'. The resolution to this seeming contradiction is that a work has to be original not in the sense of the idea but the expression. The idea can be a copy; but the expression must be original.

In some ways copyright provides a less substantial reward than a patent. Instead of giving monopoly protection to an idea, albeit an idea with a technical application, it gives no protection at all to an idea and protects only a work. But it does have its advantages. All 'works' that qualify are automatically protected and do not have to be registered (uniquely, America does maintain a vestigial registration system but all qualifying works are still assumed to be copyright). Instead of a patent's twenty-year monopoly, copyright provides longer-term protection, usually the author's lifetime plus seventy years. Copyright is not a right to do anything, let alone a monopoly right; rather, it is a right to stop others doing something.

The economic case for patents can be easily stated. I invest my time and money in developing a new scientific process or product which has practicality, usefulness and economic value (so I hope). Society wishes to enjoy the social and economic benefits of my inventiveness and grants me a temporary monopoly so I can make a profit. The case for copyright is less clear-cut and remains unclear to many people.

The problem is twofold. One, societies that are open and democratic assume that individual expressions of a literary and artistic nature should be freely shared as part of ordinary discourse. We do not 'own' our contribution to a conversation. We do not own wit. We do not own insight. So why should people own their literary and artistic expressions merely because they write them down, or perform them? Two, whereas an inventor almost certainly does incur some economic costs, and his invention will have an economic value, an author may incur no cash costs and his product may have no economic value. In turn, the author protests: my works are as valuable as any machine (if not more so, he may think privately); and I have worked hard and long and I must eat (and not only eat, he thinks, but have the chance to be as rich as anyone else).

This uncertainty is evident throughout the history of human expression. Many early societies treated artistic and creative expression, notably writing, painting and music, as belonging to the whole of society rather than to the individual. In Asia, many languages associated with the Islamic and Hindu religions have no word for artist. Concepts of individual authorship and individually-owned expression began to emerge in classical Greece but withered away in the early Christian period and the Middle Ages. Martha Woodmansee of Case Western Reserve University, and author of *The Author, Art and the Market*, says that writers and artists believed themselves to be vehicles for divine inspiration, and thus not entitled to benefit personally from their work. 'Freely have I received,' Martin Luther said of his writing, 'freely given, and want nothing in return.' Authors' rights emerged as one of the characteristics of secular humanism during the Renaissance, from the fifteenth century onwards. According to the Whitford Committee's Report on Copyright in 1977, English case law recognized an author's rights over his work from the fifteenth century onwards, but only later did Parliament approve a legal code to protect those rights; and only much later did copyright provide a major source of income to authors.

The invention of printing in the mid fifteenth century was a prime stimulus of individual authorship, but for many years the 'stationers', as Britain's printers and publishers were called, benefited more than did the writers, and it was the same in other countries. Under the terms of a royal patent the stationers exercised exclusive guild privileges and operated a register and licensing system for every new book. Throughout the sixteenth and seventeenth centuries many writers were content with these arrangements. They were less concerned with protecting their work than having it published in the first place. Most received the bulk of their income not from sales but from state or private patronage. The commercial rewards for writing were not great; John Milton's publisher paid £10 for *Paradise Lost* in the 1660s, though his wife received a further £8 after his death.

Around the time of the Civil War the political mood changed. The stationers' guild lost its exclusive privileges. Authors began to assert their economic rights. Most of the writers lived in London and knew each other (an early example of an economic cluster becoming a successful pressure group) and when the printers' increasingly intemperate demands for new work exceeded the writers' wish or capacity to write, they found themselves in a strong negotiating position. They lobbied for an act of parliament to stop printers and publishers who 'have of late taken the liberty of printing, reprinting and republishing books without the consent of authors'. Writer Daniel Defoe argued splendidly that 'A book is the author's property, tis the child of his inventions, the brat of his brain.' Queen Anne's parliament duly passed the world's first Copyright Act in 1710. The Act laid down the fundamental principle that the author has 'the sole right and liberty of printing books'. Defoe, whose *Robinson Crusoe* was published in 1719, was able to say proudly, 'Writing . . . is become a very considerable branch of the English Commerce.'

In America, the business of printing was also protected by patents before its works were protected by copyright. The General Court of the Massachusetts Bay Colony granted a nearby printer the exclusive patent to print its General Laws and Liberties as early as 1672, but the federated states did not pass laws on author's copyright until the 1780s. Thomas Paine, Noah Webster and other writers based their demands for copyright on the natural law of Hobbes and Locke, given a twist by their own political independence and belief in free speech. As copyright historian Ronald Bettig puts it, the laws assumed 'an inherent connection between creativity, profit and social welfare'. In spite of the states' anti-colonial fervour, most modelled their laws on the English Act. Congress passed the first federal law in 1790.

Following Queen Anne's Act, the English (now British) parliament progressively widened the number of qualifying works and invented new rights, chiefly as the result of new technology. Engravings won protection in 1734, textile designs in 1787, sculpture in 1814, musical performances in 1833 and paintings, drawings and photographs in 1862. It might seem odd that paintings had to wait so long. But copyright is exactly what it says: a right to copy. Paintings have always been protected as private property, and they won protection as intellectual property only when the technology produced copies that were attractive to buyers.

Some of the nineteenth-century reforms of intellectual property caught the public's attention in ways that are difficult to imagine today. The five-year debate in Parliament on extensions to the duration of copyright, which led to the 1842 Copyright Act, attracted 500 petitions with over 30,000 signatures, and many public meetings. The majority attacked copyright as a tax on knowledge. Thomas Babington Macaulay called it a 'tax on readers for the purpose of giving a bounty to authors'.

Today's copyright laws in Britain and elsewhere follow the general principles of Queen Anne's. There is still no copyright in ideas, or in creativity. Creativity is the fuel of the process but it is not itself protected. As I mull over the writing of this next sentence, the various phrases in my head are not copyright works and have no protection. But, once written, the sentence does. When the idea is fixed on to a medium then the law kicks in; lawyers talk of the act of 'fixation'.

The standard term, as we have seen, is the author's lifetime plus seventy years, but there is very little that is standard or clear-cut about copyright terms, coping as they must with a wide variety of works that may have different, multiple or even unknown authorship. Literary works (including plays, musical compositions, artistic works, films and TV programmes) qualify for the author's lifetime plus seventy years. Performances such as sound recordings and broadcasts qualify for fifty years from when they were made. Typographical settings qualify for twenty-five years. The spread of electronic distribution by satellite, cable and the Internet has stimulated a radical reassessment of these rights.

There are five logical stages to the concept of copyright as a force in the creative economy. The *author* comes first, a term which includes not only writers but other creators of a work. Second, the author's *action* on an idea creates a work. This action must involve skill and effort. It cannot be accidental or thoughtless. Third is the *work* – the text, image, performance, publication, broadcast, etc. Fourth, the law specifies the kinds of *rights* that are protected. Each work has a large number of different rights that may be sold or licensed in terms of different media, territories, languages, time periods, etc. Fifth, a *transaction* takes place in which the rights-holder allows, or prevents, others from making copies. A transaction may be an agreement between author and intermediary, intermediary and intermediary, or intermediary and user. Again, the variations are almost infinite.

These five stages have an internal logic in business and legal terms. I create something; and I let you copy it, or not. The logic works in all media. The twin peaks are the author's work (however defined) and copying (however defined). The main forms of work are straightforward, and the idea of copying is familiar from school and everyday life.

The Digital Flip

Digital information ignores this traditional logic. It subverts the familiar principles of creation and copying. A digital binary digit, or 'bit', keeps its unique characteristic for ever. It can be endlessly moved, copied and edited without being at all damaged or degraded. It can be merged and converged without losing its individual meaning. A bit stream can also be compressed to a fraction of its size without appreciable loss, which increases the speed of transmission.

The traditional five-stage logic of copyright is outmanoeuvred: the essence of computer processing is to reduce words and images to data, manipulate them in whichever way is desired, and then reproduce them as perfectly as the original; the essence of the Internet and other networks is to move these data around the world and reproduce them irrespective of national laws and local business structures. Together, these two processes redefine the nature of media. In its 1994 Green Paper on *The Internet and Copyright*, the US Department of Commerce said, 'The distinctions between authors, producers and performers are becoming irrelevant.' The basic definitions of 'original' and 'copy' imply a hierarchical master/servant relationship between the original and a copy. Digital flips this assumption on its head.

The US National Academies, reporting on *The Digital Dilemma* in 1999, said:

> The problem is illustrated simply enough. A printed book can be accessed by one or perhaps two people at once, people who must, of course, be in the same place as the book. But make that same text available in electronic form, and there is almost no technological limit to the number of people who can access it simultaneously, from literally anywhere on the planet where there is a telephone (and hence an Internet connection). At first glance, this is wonderful news for the consumer and for society. The electronic holdings of libraries (and friends) around the world can become available from a home computer, twenty-four hours a day, year-round. They are never 'checked out.' These same advances in technology create new opportunities and markets for publishers. But there is also a more troublesome side. For publishers and authors, the question is, How many copies of the work will be sold (or licensed) if networks make possible planet-wide access? Their nightmare is that the number is *one*.

John Perry Barlow, a former cattle rancher and Grateful Dead lyricist who is a co-founder of the Electronic Frontier Foundation, an Internet body committed to free speech, argues this case vividly, with approving nods to Thomas Jefferson: 'We're going to have to look at information as if we've never seen the stuff before . . . The protections that we will develop will rely far more on ethics and technology than on law . . . Encryption will be the technical basis of most intellectual property protection . . . The economy of the future will be based more on relationship than possession.' He welcomes this. 'Most of the folks who presently make their living by their wits do so not under the protection of legally instantiated methods of 'owning' their own intelligence or expertise but by defining value on the basis of a continued and deepening interaction with an audience or client base.' In the creative economy, these relationships (personal, original, meaningful) are the main enduring source of value.

Some people say it is not necessary to own creative property in most media outright. Jeremy Rifkin, author of *The End of Work* and *The Age of Access*, says we are turning from a society of sellers and buyers to one of suppliers and users. Ownership is being replaced by access. The critical question is not who owns something but who has access to it, who can use it. Intellectual property law has close similarities with landlord–tenant relationships; for example in the tension between a landlord's absolute rights and a tenant's partial and temporary rights. In terms of intellectual property, we are moving from a society of owner-occupiers to tenants; we are becoming nomads.

Esther Dyson, publisher of an Internet industry newsletter, *Release 1.0*, and author of a book, *Release 2.0*, assumes the collapse of intellectual property is inevitable. She foresees a new business model in which, while the formal kinds of intellectual property lose economic value, the surrounding add-on elements, such as service and support, gain in value. She believes the latter will more than compensate for the loss of the former. She believes that intellectual property is becoming less protectable, and that more money may be made by giving it away for free to entice customers to spend money on contingent goods and services. She writes, 'The likely best defence for content providers is to distribute intellectual property free in order to sell services and relationships.' Her theories echo the traditional marketing principle followed by Gillette, for example, which sells its razors at well below their marginal cost in the certain knowledge it will be able to charge a high price for its blades (in economic theory, to charge an excess rent). She extends the principle into the realm of intangible products and copying. She says, 'In the new world it will be easy to copy information but hard to find it . . . Creativity will proliferate but quality will be scarce and hard to recognize.' Dyson is right that original (copyright) products may become less valuable than the subsequent (trademark) goods and services. But few companies can afford to take this risk, if only because they cannot be certain they will retain control of the revenues.

The Music Goes Round and Round

The National Academies' nightmare of the single copy seems closest in the case of music. Music takes to digital technologies like a duck to water. Sound is pure physics and occupies no material space. In digital terms, it has little information and requires little bandwidth or storage space. It may be objected that the quality may be patchy, but we accept scratchy sound much more readily than indistinctly printed words or murky pictures, and the quality will improve. Other industries are hovering at the water's edge. Books and magazines need more bandwidth, especially if they incorporate a high level of design, and we have become more aware of their convenience and fond, as ever, of their social status. Books are powerful symbols of learning and knowledge (as Anthony Powell wrote, 'books do furnish a room'). These connotations could fade away, but people have been predicting the end of the book for decades and sales continue to rise. Films and TV programmes require another order of magnitude of bandwidth as well as big, high-quality screens. So music leads the way. Ben Keen, executive editor of *Screen Digest*, said in 1999, 'Within five years the world's top music publishers (Warner, Sony, Bertelsmann, Polygram and EMI) will either have reinvented themselves as Internet companies or they will be in danger of withering away.

When I asked Rupert Perry, president and chief executive of EMI Europe, in 1999 whether he saw the Internet as 'friend or enemy' he answered 'friend'. One year later the industry answer might not have been so warm or confident. The record companies' attitude to the Internet varies between interest, anger and opportunism. They initially saw it as a marketing medium and encouraged artists to design their own websites, keeping music clips to the industry maximum of thirty seconds. They welcomed the growth of online CD sellers because they made available the backlist of old CDs and LPs that bricks-and-mortar shops cannot afford to keep.

Then a few artists began to break the thirty-second rule. The Beastie Boys, licensed to Capitol, put some of their rare and out-of-print songs on the Internet against Capitol's policy. David Bowie launched an album on the Internet before selling the CD. Elvis Costello started to put all his work on the Internet. The problem escalated when MP3 player-recorders began to be an even smarter urban accessory for the streetwise techie than the most silver-tongued mobile phone. MP3 refers to Motion Picture Experts Group, Layer 3, and is the industry standard for a music file (the MPEG has separate standards for video, etc.). Its first promoters used MP3 to distribute new music that had not been signed to a record company and was not protected by copyright. Like John Perry Barlow, they saw the Internet as a democratic, copyright-free zone.

Jeff Patterson was a computer science student at Santa Cruz, California, in 1993, when he began to post songs by new bands on to a website which, with considerable aplomb, he called the Internet Underground Music Archive. It was a typical Internet start-up. Anyone could contribute ('post') a song. Listeners could listen for free by downloading a file on to a hard disk or MP3 player, or pay to buy a CD or tape. Today IUMA has over 4,000 bands and about two million visits a month, and makes its money by charging a commission on CDs and tapes sold through the site.

As IUMA and other sites flourished, and as the technology became cheaper and easier, the realization that anyone can put music on the Internet began to terrify the major music companies. The Recording Industry Association of America (RIAA) tried to ban the first MP3 player. Then it pushed its own Secure Digital Music Initiative (SDMI), an encryption system, which allows someone to download a CD but prevents them from making further copies. Jay Samit of EMI said, 'Most people are not going to hunt around for poor-quality pirate copies when they can get the real thing.' But several commercial websites, including MP3.com, continued to make music files available without charge. The RIAA started a legal action against MP3.com, who settled out of court with two RIAA members, Warner and BMG, by paying them $20 million each. Another member, Universal/Polygram, went to court and received damages of $53.4 billion; they also acknowledged MP3.com's business case by buying shares in the company.

The comparative cost of distributing a CD through a traditional retailer (like Virgin Megastore), an online ordering website (like CDNow) and a web download (like MP3) strongly favours the latter, according to Forrester Research. A sixty-minute piece of music has an average retail price in America of $15 but the publisher's income ranges from a low of $6 from the over-the-counter sale to $9.50 from an online sale and a high of $11.50 from a download. So MP3 websites, both commercial and non-profit, continue to grow (http:/mp3.lycos.com lists the sites where you can help yourself, including www.real.com, which has a RealJukebox, and www.winamp.com). By the end of 1999 one in five CDs bought in America were bought online. In the UK the figure was one in ten. The International Federation of the Phonographic Industry (IFPI) reckoned that during the Christmas period in that year 4 million MP3 files were being downloaded every day.

The RIAA was soon back in court, together with AOL Time Warner, against a new competitor. In 1998, eighteen-year-old Shawn Fanning developed a file-sharing program called Napster which allows a user to search for all MP3 files held by all other users with the same software, and transfer selected files to his own hard disk. Its principle is 'share and share alike'; because by searching other people's computers you also allow them to search yours. Other programs called Gnutella and FreeNet did the same. Whereas IUMA offered material deliberately made available, with a 'Look Here' sign attached, the new generation of file-sharing systems allow explorers and trespassers to wander at will into private property. Type in the name of a band or a track and Napster searches not only websites but the hard disks of all connected users for a music file containing that track. If a music executive has put a demo recording of a new unpublished track on to his hard disk, Napster will identify it, copy it, and deliver it home. The use of these search-and-find technologies caused an outcry on a number of fronts: breach of copyright, breach of privacy and breach of confidentiality. In 1999, they became so popular that several American universities' networks were clogged and the authorities banned their students from using them; the students responded with a nationwide campaign for free speech.

It must be acknowledged that these systems do enable people in their millions to find, identify and copy music. Each does so in a slightly different manner. Some operate a centralized directory (as does Napster, which makes its owners more directly responsible for their traffic and more openly liable in law) while others operate a peer-to-peer system whose owners can genuinely say they have no knowledge and no control over what the system is being used for (as do Gnutella and FreeNet). Some (like Napster) can only handle audio files while others (like Gnutella) can also handle video. But all the systems have a single purpose, which is to enable people to get free access to material, and to copy it. In most cases, this copying is illegal.

Napster's defence was that it merely provides a system for copying files which is no different in essence from the use of an audio cassette to tape music or the use of a video-cassette to tape a TV broadcast. Certainly, the record companies' cries of outrage and fear about Napster and other file-sharing systems echo their earlier protests when faced with audio cassettes and cartridges, and the TV and film industries' outrage when faced with videos and DVDs (not to mention cable retransmission and satellite direct-to-home delivery). Technically, Napster had a point. Copyright law allows exemptions for private copying as 'fair use' or 'fair dealing'. There is nothing intrinsic to these file-sharing systems that favours theft over legitimate usage. They can handle encrypted or copy-protected files just as well as 'open access' ones. On this point, we cannot blame Napster any more than we could blame the manufacturer of a ladder which a burglar uses to gain access to an upstairs window. But in 2000 a US district court decided the sheer scale of Napster file-sharing undercut its defence of 'private copying'. The decision had precedents. US courts have long been active in punishing print shops who carry out large-scale copying, especially for university students. In 1991 a New York district court fined Kinko's copy-shops damages of $510,000 (for copying twelve books published by Basic Books) and ordered them to pay the plaintiffs' legal fees, which were ultimately set at $1,365,000. In 2000, when the number of works copied had grown to 12 million, the court found Napster guilty, and the company changed its business model.

It is hard to calculate the impact on the industry's revenues. Because some people steal one piece of music does not mean they will not buy another piece. There is evidence in both directions: that people use

Napster instead of buying CDs, and that they use it to discover new music which leads them to buy more CDs. If a person copies a news item to friends, he places a higher value on the publication, not less, and has more incentive to buy it; as well as indirectly promoting it to the recipients. Demographic factors play a part. A young student with little money but lots of free time may enjoy downloading a MP3 file; as he or she gets older and has more money and less free time, and a desire for top-quality sounds, they may prefer to buy a legal CD.

The film industry faced a similar challenge in 2000 when Jon Johansen, a sixteen-year-old Norwegian schoolboy, broke the encryption code at the heart of the Content Scrambler System (CSS) used to protect DVDs. By some circuitous but entirely predictable route, the hacked decryption code, or DeCSS, was placed on the Internet for everyone to download. The film industry cried 'foul', and sought injunctions in the courts, although there was some confusion about the extent to which the industry's CSS actually protected copyrights, and also how far DeCSS undercut it.

It is in the nature of the Internet for codes and systems to be hacked (as we shall see in Chapter 6). The Internet is an organism that avoids obstruction, whether bad code or obstructive censorship, and navigates around it. As networking and file-sharing becomes easier (more transparent; more effective; faster; cheaper) so it changes the economics not only of distribution but also of production. This is because digital copies of a product are intangible and the marginal costs of distribution are so low.

Industries do not collapse because their existing business models are threatened but because they fail to find new ones. This is true of all industries, but it is especially true of industries based on the technologies of copying, like music and film. I expect to see, over the next few decades, a continual outpouring of new and improved devices for exploiting the Internet's instinctive capacities for copying and delivering copyright material. At the end of 2000, the Internet users had the initiative. The question remains whether the conventional music and film industries will reinvent themselves and regain it. Whether they do, and *how* they do, will affect the future of all creative products, and all industries, that depend on digital copying.

Mixed Reforms in Geneva

The principles of copying were addressed at a WIPO diplomatic conference in Geneva in 1996. It approved separate treaties on copyright and performing rights, which Europe implemented by means of a 2000 Directive on Copyright, and discussed but postponed a treaty on the protection of databases. Vigorous arguments took place between the major rights-holders, especially of music and films (led by America, Europe and Japan) and the rest of the world who buy their products and consume their rights. In this debate, countries split along familiar North–South, rich–poor lines. There was a second debate, only slightly less passionate, between the global corporations who invest in rights and therefore want to protect them as much as possible (especially on the Internet) and individuals who want to publish them as widely as possible (especially on the Internet). In this, Americans faced fellow Americans.

The conference did not question the need for a 'property contract', but adopted a new approach. It replaced the old logic, whereby every copy required permission unless it was given a specific exemption, by a differentiation between the unavoidable 'technical' copying that occurs when data is moved around within a closed system, with no obvious economic significance, and the kind of copying that is made with the purpose of, or that enables the action of, adding economic value by making a new transaction. Purely 'technical' copying can be ignored; it has no more significance than a snatch of music heard through an open window. The new rules also continued the rights-owner's control of copying with, as now, exemptions for private copying under the American term of 'fair use' and the British term of 'fair dealing'. These allow the public to copy something for private use (such as education) and public use (such as criticism or review) if it is only a small or 'insubstantial' extract and, if appropriate, proper credit is given. These two principles were redefined for the digital age, although the Europeans disagreed amongst themselves about how much private copying should be allowed, with the British and Dutch being most in favour and the French, Spanish and Belgians being more hostile. Everything else still requires the rights-holder's permission either before or after a copy is made.

Enforcing these rules requires 'rights management' systems, which enable rights-holders to exercise their rights in electronic form. They include Microsoft's Document Rights Management System, Softlock and Adobe's PDF Merchant, which ensure no file is released until the rights-holder's specified conditions are met, such as payment being made. The development of rights management systems for music and films is highly important, and will shape the industry's future structure and economics.

Other systems put an electronic 'watermark' into every file that contains a piece of copyright work (text, sound, image). When a rights-owner discovers a website is illegally using its material, and provides the evidence, the thief will normally stop whatever he was doing. There is big business in digital detective agencies that surf the Web checking for stolen music, pictures and fashion, such as the IP Warehouse Inc. in Palm Beach, Florida, which operates its (patented) DragNet system, and GrayZone Inc. in New York. But even they are helpless against peer-to-peer file-sharing.

Copyright material is best protected by two factors: a mixture of good law and bad technology. By good law, I mean law that is fair and effective, and whose remedies are proportionate to the mischief. By bad technology, I mean technology's inability to make good copies. The best protection is a legal copy that is cheaper or more easily available than the illegal one. The challenge of digital is that the *technology* for creating and copying (or recreating) material is now cheaply and widely available and the users and consumers are minded to take what they can. That puts more pressure on the *laws*, which are not certain of coping. The technology is leading the race, with the users close behind, and the laws a distant third.

It is much easier, and more fun, to make new technology than new law. But the whole point of a property contract is to reconcile these two forces. We need copyright rules that recognize the public's feelings of right and wrong; provide appropriate incentives and rewards; cope with new technologies; and support sustainable industries.

TRADEMARKS

The eighteen-year-old daughter of a friend of mine likes the Nike logo. One evening, she is wearing a Nike T-shirt, sweater, cap, trousers and socks. When I ask why, she responds slowly, believing the question to be dumb, but because she is polite and bright (having that week been offered places at Oxford and five other universities) she does give it a little thought. The answer is obvious. I like it. It's cool. It's there. No more need be said.

The growth of brands and other trademarks is the most noticeable symptom of global consumerism. It is loved by some, disdained by others. Actually, the word 'symptom' is no longer appropriate. Trademarks have become the core factor in most marketplace competition, successfully communicating across diverse languages and cultures. The Nike corporation is not in the business of selling any particular objects like shirts or socks or even shoes (with the partial exception of its special Air system which cushions an athlete's feet). Instead, it sells its brand; it sells itself. The T-shirt is a means of wearing a brand. It is the only sensible strategy. Any large global corporation could compete with Nike in terms of its physical goods; they could design similar shoes, find similar workers to make them at similar prices and create a similar global marketing campaign. Its versions of these products would be commodities, like everyone else's, with no inherent distinguishing feature. But nobody can compete with the Nike trademark. It is registered in every country in the world. Physically, its goods are vulnerable to competitors on design, technology, materials, colours, style, fashion and price. Intangibly, in terms of intellectual property they are almost impregnable. I say 'almost' because another company could build another brand to challenge Nike, just as Nike built its own. The aim of modern branding campaigns is to instil the brand in consumers' minds so that the consumer simply cannot imagine buying anything else.

A trademark does not require any unique inventiveness, as does a patent, or any intellectual or artistic effort, as does a copyright work (which is why the description of 'intellectual' property is grandiose). Any word, name, image, sound or even smell that identifies a good or service and distinguishes it from others can be a trademark. (In the US services have 'service marks' rather than trademarks.) The mark must not be descriptive. It cannot be a word that other traders might reasonably expect to be able to use, nor must it indicate the product's quality, purpose or value. Anything else is acceptable.

Trademarks are probably the oldest kind of intellectual property, although the last to be fully enshrined in written law. The word 'brand' comes from the Anglo-Saxon verb 'to burn', and the first trademarks were the brands used to mark domestic animals, either by burning the hide or by clipping an ear. Potters, carvers, furniture-makers and stone-masons incised their names, initials or marks into their creations. The growth of industrial manufacturing and trade, especially international trade, gave fresh impetus to corporate branding, as manufacturers wanted to promote their goods worldwide and buyers wanted to know what they were buying.

Today, brand names can be protected in two ways: by trademark registration and by common law actions against 'passing off'. The most common method is registration, although the mere fact of registration may not deter unfair use and the plaintiff may have to apply to the courts. The British Patent Office has had a registration system since 1875, although it was selective in coverage and not much used until the 1994 Trade Mark Act widened the scope and gave more protection. In 2004 the Patent Office received 61,900 applications for trademarks and registered 49,900.

The laws against 'passing off' are an inheritance from common law, and protect property against wrongdoing. They prevent someone from passing off his goods as someone else's. The courts ask a practical question: is the public likely to be confused and to mistake this product for that product? According to copyright expert Michael Flint, there are five tests. The passing off must (1) consist of a misrepresentation that is (2) made by a business in the course of trade (3) to prospective customers (4) which is calculated to injure the business or goodwill of another business and (5) which causes actual damage to the business' trade or goodwill.

A prosecution for 'passing off' is the most common action against trademark infringement, whether or not the mark is registered. It can also be used against any other mischief or unfair dealing. For example, a book publisher might lose a copyright action against a publisher of another book that had the same or similar title to his own. No copyright would have been infringed. But, if his case met the five tests, he might win a 'passing off' action.

DESIGNS AND SECRETS

The fourth major form is industrial design. Britain's first law protecting industrial design was passed in the 1830s, a few decades before copyright was extended to paintings, indicating design's importance in manufacturing industries then and now. Today, a design can be protected both by registration, rather like a patent, and by a 'design right', which is like copyright.

Registration gives the strongest protection. In order to qualify, a design must be the result of 'skill and effort', which must be evident in its inherent aesthetic independently of its natural shape. Purely functional designs, which involve no skill, are not eligible. This criterion is equivalent to the need for an 'inventive step' in patenting and 'skill and effort' in copyright, and demonstrates the need for a creative product to have 'meaning'. There are four further criteria for registration: shape, configuration, pattern and what is called 'ornament'. Britain's unregistered 'design right' which, like copyright, accrues automatically to every new three-dimensional design, is a relatively new invention and lasts up to fifteen years from when the design was first created. It extends private property rights to functional objects like crafts, toys and furniture, which fall outside copyright law and which might fail to win patent protection.

There are, finally, the general rules of commercial secrecy and confidentiality. Secrecy may seem the antithesis of the creative spirit, whose instinct is to shout from the rooftops in order to reach as many people as possible. But climbing to the rooftop is best done in secret. These laws allow people to own information, and to stop others from using it. America defines a trade secret as a 'formula, pattern, device or compilation of information which is used in a business and which gives the business an opportunity to obtain an advantage over competitors who do not know it or use it'. It is a wide-ranging category.

STEALING BEAUTY

The point of these laws is to prevent theft and misuse. But there is, stuck deep in our psyche, a feeling that the concepts of ownership and possession that we use in terms of physical property are not so compelling when applied to intellectual property, and that stealing intellectual property is not so injurious as stealing the 'real' thing. The intangible nature of intellectual property evades precise definitions of ownership and possession and causes problems when we try to define its theft. Even rights-holders are reluctant to mention 'theft' and prefer to talk about piracy, conjuring up images of likeable rogues in distant lands with parrots on their shoulders.

The evanescent nature of intellectual property, to quote Justice Story, is evident in our different attitudes towards its various states. Buying a fake may result in social obloquy but seldom in legal distress. In some circles, it would be indicative of a breach of social etiquette more than of a legal tort; in others, an indication that one knows what is fashionable (a positive virtue) without being able to afford the 'real thing' (only slightly negative). The possessor of the real thing may feel socially superior to the possessor of a fake, but seldom suffers any direct or indirect economic loss. It is fairly obvious that the cost of a legal bottle of Coca-Cola is not affected by the sale of a fake bottle, unless the fake sold in high volumes and affected Coca-Cola's margins. In fact, it is to many companies' advantage for their products to be known to be worthy of fakery and theft, although naturally they would prefer everyone to buy the real thing.

Patents, by their nature, are seldom stolen or infringed by consumers. They are however regularly infringed by companies, and the penalties can be enormous. Litton Industries won damages of $1.2 billion in 1993, and damages of $200 million are not uncommon. Legal damages are only part of the cost, as Kodak discovered in 1990 when the courts ruled it had infringed Polaroid's patents in instant photography. Kodak had to pay $873 million damages, shut down a $1.5 billion factory, and spend nearly $500 million to buy back 'illegal' cameras; as well as lawyers' fees of say $50 million and uncounted millions on wasted management effort and R & D, and its damaged public image.

Copyright is stolen regularly and substantially. But here again attitudes are ambiguous. If you steal a chair from your neighbour, everyone (State, Church and your neighbour) will agree you have committed an offence and should be punished; make a habit of it, and you will go to prison. Steal a book (or 'forget to return it') and that is still theft but you are unlikely to go to prison. Steal what's in the book and who cares? Copy a video. The neighbour says, 'Can I watch, too?'

The person who steals a book or video will feel more guilty about the physical property than about the words and pictures that make up the intellectual property. People are deeply offended by plagiarism, which they regard as cheating, but less troubled by stealing the final product. People feel more guilty stealing a hardback than a paperback. We have not rid ourselves of the notion that a physical book (the design, the covers, the paper pages; the thickness of it) and the video of a film (again, the heft of it) have more economic value than their contents, and that it is this physical value, not the intellectual value, which determines the offence. It gets worse (or better, according to your view). People who feel guilty about stealing a paperback do not feel so guilty about stealing the same words printed out from a computer hard disc or downloaded from the Internet. It is true that the likelihood of being caught is less, but the feeling of guilt is less, too.

Digital technologies encourage us to treat music and pictures as we have become accustomed to treat words. They reduce all three formats to the same bit data, so that a music file and a text document look alike on a computer's electronic desktop or when attached to an e-mail. As a result, a person accustomed to copying a text file for free sees little reason why he or she could not similarly copy a music file for free. The same confluence of attitudes happened when mobile telephones were enabled to receive music. People who were accustomed to listening to a radio station broadcasting music for free expected an MP3 file delivered to a mobile telephone to be free. The next generation of data compression files squeezes a digital file to about a five-hundredth of its original size, so that a short film can be downloaded in a few minutes. Naturally and inevitably, the file of the film looks like a text file.

People who steal computer software (for instance, by installing office software with a single-user licence in a second computer at home) perceive little damage is done. Indeed, they know that companies want their software to be as widely networked as possible, and often give it away. The success of many modern brands, from software to shoes, depends upon their rapid dissemination to create a network effect, a buzz of 'street cred'. So, it is said, theft is helping the company, not harming it. There is more than a shred of common sense in all these attitudes.

Nobody knows how many of those who buy stolen copyright material might otherwise have bought legal material. Nobody knows whether the theft of computer software, although against the terms of the licence, actually damages the copyright-holder. Many people who steal material would not have bought their own copy, either because they could not afford it or because it was not available locally. Nobody knows how many times a stolen video or music cassette may be re-copied and reused.

The trade associations do try to quantify the loss, in order to support their lobby for stricter laws. The Global Anti-Counterfeiting Group, which represents major brand owners, estimates theft at about $250 billion a year, of which copyright theft is about $20 billion. According to the International Intellectual Property Association (IIPA), which monitors copyright theft, the worst countries are Brazil, where 95 per cent of music recordings are reported to be stolen, followed by Russia (75 per cent) and China (56 per cent). The safest are America (5 per cent) and Britain (1 per cent). Overall, music theft runs at $4.5 billion a year. The International Federation of the Phonographic Industry (IFPI) estimates that one in three CDs is stolen. The IIPA says $2.2 billion worth of filmed entertainment is stolen. The worst countries are China, Russia and Turkey, where over 90 per cent of films are stolen. Video copies of major Hollywood films are usually available in Asia one week after their American release, which is why Hollywood tries to open its movies very quickly in those countries. The figure for the theft of books is much lower; say $1 billion. Theft of computer games runs at $3.3 billion. Bulgaria and Israel are notorious for the theft and re-export of scientific instruments.

The Business Software Alliance reckons that half the world's software is stolen, costing manufacturers $7 billion a year, with theft in America running at 25 per cent and in Britain at 29 per cent. The result is what one Singapore judge has called 'flagrant and massive plunder'.

The level of theft is increasing in almost all categories and in all countries. Of the worst offenders, Russia and China, which do have some laws, seldom bother to enforce them. Worldwide, consumers' leisure spending is increasing faster than the rights-owners' ability to enforce local laws. The growth of the Internet adds massively to the problem. The Internet is intrinsically hostile or evasive to people who want to restrict the passage of material.

The question facing the OECD countries is how to liberalize trade (so they can sell more products overseas) while protecting their property rights.

THE GLOBAL MARKET

America, springboard of globalization, was the first country to realise how greatly its exports, and therefore its entire economy, depend upon its trade in intellectual property. It wanted to liberalize international trade, but it also wanted to protect its exports. As the world was reeling from OPEC's increase in oil prices in 1973–4, the US Senate Committee on Foreign Relations held an emergency session on whether the country could be 'held to ransom' in other areas of the economy. The committee decided that ideas and information might be next. It asked percipiently, 'If information and its communication represent a strategic resource in international affairs, whose value may approach or exceed that of energy, will appropriate US Government policies be formed only after there is an energy-type crisis?' A few years later, President Ford set up a Task Force on National Information Policy which concluded:

> Property concepts have been central to legal theory and social and economic activity in our society, but concepts of property were formulated to deal with tangibles, primarily land and chattels. When information, ways of dealing with information, or information products are treated as property, issues arise which differ from those resulting from the application of property theories to tangible matter.

The wording is awkward but the thinking is clear: we need a new foreign policy not only for information but for intellectual property, for the ownership of ideas and information. The subtext was equally clear: we need a policy that suits American interests.

That did not mean a one-sided bargain. All exporters of creative products, whether selling a brand or licensing a copyright, need both a *high* level of protection everywhere and the *same* level everywhere. America wanted to collaborate with other exporting countries to hike up the global levels of protection so they were the same in Peoria and Penang. It appealed to its fellow members in what is known as the Quad (consisting of America, Europe, Japan and Canada), which forms the main negotiating bloc in international trade. But few paid much attention. Britain continued to give priority to its dwindling manufacturing industry. As late as 1994 the Department of Trade and Industry was stating, against the evidence, that Britain's electronics industry was economically more important than its creative industries. Its view did not change until New Labour won the 1997 election and, amongst other initiatives, set up the Creative Industries Task Force. Germany agreed with Washington about patents, though not about copyrights, and anyway its voice in international affairs was muted. The French have always given a high priority to authors' rights, but they export mostly to a few Francophone countries, and they instinctively disliked America's treatment of 'culture' in purely economic terms. The Japanese, exceptionally gifted at designing TV, video and music equipment, wanted to ensure their patents were protected in all countries, and sided with America. But it was not enough. Washington wondered what to do.

It knew that the global copyright conventions were wrong for its purpose. There was and is a wide gap between its own legal traditions and those of most countries that buy its goods, and it had always been a reluctant member of such conventions. Moreover, WIPO and Unesco, which administered the major conventions, had no brief for trade (and America was at the time extremely hostile to Unesco, as a result of the organization's spirited promotion of Third World interests). Instead, America turned to the international regime for trade, which perfectly suited its interests. In 1986 the General Agreement for Trade and Tariffs (GATT) started its eight-year Uruguay Round for the overhaul of global trade rules. It had twin aims: primarily, to liberalize trade by the abolition of national restrictions on imports and, secondly, to maintain the value of these imported goods and services in the country of destination. America used the time to lobby intensively for stricter rules on copyright and patent protection. It was supported by the major film, music and pharmaceutical companies. Slowly, other governments came to take its line.

In 1994 over 100 governments met at Marrakesh, Morocco, to replace GATT with the World Trade Organization (WTO), and also sign a Treaty on Trade-Related Intellectual Property Rights (known as TRIPS). The TRIPS agreement covers all creative products: patents; copyrights and related rights; trademarks and service marks; geographical indicators (for products whose value derives from the place of growth or manufacture); industrial designs; the protection of new plants; the layout of integrated circuits; and trade secrets. Unlike its predecessor, the WTO has a right to enforce its rules and apply sanctions.

The TRIPS agreement was not the first global standard for intellectual law and property; the Paris and Berne conventions had that honour, in the 1880s. But it was the first to treat intellectual property primarily as a trade issue. Before TRIPS, disputes on intellectual property were private matters of contract which were resolved, or not, behind closed doors or in the courts. Government trade bodies had no role to play. Afterwards, governments could seek, via the WTO, to enforce the rules, and mischiefs or malfeasance on intellectual property matters could lead to sanctions in other trade categories or, ultimately, to expulsion from the WTO.

The Quad's victory was not welcomed by all members. Some countries resented the Quad's enforcement of Western principles of private property in the rest of the world, whether with regard to plants, medicines or aboriginal art. These complained of TRIPS's adverse effects on a country's ability to protect its own culture and knowledge and therefore to sustain its capacity for creativity and learning. This critical view, hostile to Western privatization, was put by economist Jeffrey Sachs of Harvard University in *The Economist*:

> Just as knowledge is becoming the undisputed centrepiece of global prosperity (and the lack of it, the core of human impoverishment) the global regime on

intellectual property requires a new look. The US prevailed upon the world to toughen patent laws and cut down piracy. But now the transnational corporations and rich country institutions are patenting everything from the human genome to rainforest diversity. The poor will be ripped off unless some sense and equity are introduced into this runaway process.

In the 1970s Herb Schiller of San Diego University, who invented the term, and Jeremy Tunstall of City University, talked about America's 'cultural imperialism' in the media. More recently, Peter Drahos of the Queen Mary Intellectual Property Research Institute at London University, talks about 'information feudalism':

> There is a structural predicament of global dimensions. The outcome of this predicament is that the scope of patentability is expanding while the role of moral standards in the operation of the patent system is being increasingly limited. Ironically, this is happening at a time when the moral debate over patentability, at least in the field of biotechnology, has never been greater.

There is a delicate balance between the reasonable principle of owning what one creates and protecting those who are too weak, ignorant or poor to protect themselves; between allowing the richest and quickest to claim ownership by means of patents and copyright without allowing the inarticulate to be pushed to the margins. As Mahatma Gandhi said, 'I do not want my house to be walled in or my windows blocked. I want the cultures of all lands to be blown about the house as freely as possible. But also I refuse to be blown off my feet by any.' Standing upright becomes even more difficult if we have to contend with foreign scientific and technical patents on knowledge.

The growing intensity of negotiations over 'wild' plants and their biological derivatives symbolizes this conflict. There are countless examples. My favourite is the gentian. For centuries, Indians have used dogbane, a species of gentian, as a tranquillizer. In the 1950s, a Western company began to import it to the West (without paying for it), where it became so popular that the Indian government had to ban its export, because prices locally were rising beyond what Indians could afford. They also feared the roots would become extinct. Over in Africa, the chemical properties of another gentian, the Madagascan rosy periwinkle, which has pretty pink flowers with a deep red centre, were becoming highly sought-after. Its genetic properties seemed to limit the growth of cancer cells. From this discovery, according to the United Nations, Eli Lilly earns about $100 million a year, while the Madagascans earn virtually nothing. To them, Eli Lilly's actions have merely increased the price and restricted the supply to those who assumed either they owned it or that it was in the public domain. According to Dr Pennapa Subcharoen of Thailand's Ministry of Public Health, 'Drug companies come here, collect samples, take them away and say it is for the collective heritage of mankind. Then they study the samples, develop them, claim intellectual property rights and come back and make us buy them.' Subcharoen's point is that drug companies do not invent these plants but exploit local knowledge of their therapeutic qualities. The 1991 Rio Convention on Bio-Diversity puts some constraints on whether such plants may be traded, but it sets few rules on who should pay, or how much. The average royalty is about 1–2 per cent of revenues. The target for many developing countries is 10 per cent. This may seem high, but the US Park Service charges exactly that for bio-prospecting in the Yellowstone National Park.

The range of plant varieties now being studied for genetic value, whether for extracts or for genetically modified seeds, is very large. According to John Vidal, environment editor of the *Guardian*, many of the biological qualities inherent in maize, potato, rice, wheat, sorghum, cassava, millet, soybean and wheat have been or are being privatized. L'Oréal has patented the use of the kava shrub to reduce hair loss. An American company, RiceTec Inc., has obtained a patent for a gene sequence that mimics basmati rice. The patent does not prevent Asian companies from exporting their own basmati rice, but it does restrict the supply in America. Nestlé India has applied to patent a process for parboiling rice. Other companies have applied for patents on tea, coffee, soya, cotton and pepper seeds.

America achieved its aim. The economic value of intellectual property is now better protected than ever before, especially since China has wanted to join the WTO. But the question arises, in both Quad and other countries, whether the politics of trade is a satisfactory forum for moral subtleties.

A NEW CONTRACT?

Is the property contract, which emerged in the 1700s and whose fundamental principles have been unchanged for decades, the best way of regulating the ownership and transaction in ideas in the early 2000s?

There is a sharp debate between the maximalists and minimalists, between optimists and pessimists. The premise of the maximalists' case is the link between strong property protection and the rate of creativity and innovation. A recent WTO study reports that laws on tax and intellectual property top the list of factors affecting a multinational's decision to invest or to trade. Pfizer Inc. says, 'It is a major fallacy to think that the protection of intellectual property is the luxury of already prosperous economies. One of the most efficacious ways of building a strong economy is to insist on protecting intellectual property.' Of the four grounds for intellectual property (incentive, reward, disclosure and natural rights), companies put the strongest emphasis on incentives and rewards. The patent industries talk more about incentives (albeit incentives expressed in reward) while the copyright industries emphasize reward. Many artists create copyright works without calculating the economic return, but once the product is made, they rightly feel strongly about the need for a full and proper reward. The result is a trend towards privatization.

Intellectual property has become a factor in the global battle for competitive advantage. The effect is seen in almost every industry; not merely the traditional copyright and patent industries (which are expanding) but in all industries that depend upon trademarks, brands and designs, from food to sport. Companies want to maximize revenue from each idea and each creative product; and therefore create as many intellectual properties and as many rights as possible. From a company's viewpoint, there are many arguments in favour of privatization and few against. An increasing number of creative products have a property tag attached, and the tag says 'private'.

But the minimalist case, and the case against more privatization, has some powerful arguments, too. Many argue that the expectation of intellectual property rights provides little incentive. Others say that the prospect of an economic reward is not persuasive. Individuals and (less so) companies innovate for a number of reasons, and many would do so even if their ideas were not protected. As for the historical links between intellectual property and innovation, research by the United Nations and World Bank has shown that many countries flourished in the eighteenth and nineteenth centuries when their own legislation was minimal; the best-documented examples include America, Britain, France, Germany and Switzerland. There is a tradition of science being freely available, which universities and public research companies uphold jealously. Tim O'Reilly, a computer consultant, asks what would have happened if Isaac Newton, instead of publishing his discovery of the laws of motion, had patented their industrial application: 'No, I won't tell you what I know about parabolic trajectories, but I'll calibrate your guns for a fee.' Even rewards are problematic. It is axiomatic that monopoly rights tend to increase costs and are a restraint on competition.

The World Bank has spoken of the dangers of 'excessively strong intellectual property rights'. It cites many public and academic bodies which cannot afford to register their own inventions, nor to license the use of others'. The UN particularly criticizes the process of 'stacking', by which companies register patents for speculative reasons. Many developing countries have a tradition of communal ownership and lack the determination, as well as the legal and financial resources, to deal in the commercial market. Finally, the Internet's use of freeware and open source software gives some proof that the absence of copyright and patents, rather than impeding commercial progress, may hasten it (see Chapter 6).

The property contract is flexible, and continually evolving, which is partly why it is so complex and subtle. But it needs to be reformed. For example, patenting can hardly cope with the rapid moves towards patenting human cells, and copyright is baffled by the Internet's animal-like appetite for free copies. We need to work out a new deal.

There are some specific problems. On the patenting front, we need to review what is patentable and what is excluded. The British 'Statement of Patent Practice' says that its 'exclusions are directed to mental, intellectual, aesthetic or abstract matters'. But such intangible 'matters' make up an increasingly significant amount of Britain's economic output. We need a consensus about whether or not a patent requires a technological invention (as in Europe and Japan) or whether this is really immaterial (as in America). We also need to review the registration process. The three patent tests of novelty, inventive step and technical effect are being stretched beyond what patent agents and attorneys can agree on, let alone what the public or our elected representatives know about or, if they know, can understand.

In copyright, we need to reform existing copyright law to fit the Internet. The old master/copy relationship no longer holds. We need to redefine what we mean by private copying. In copyright, however, the lawyers can only go so far. The success of any new regime depends greatly on whether the music, film and publishing industries can devise new business models to exploit the digital technologies.

We need to review the nature of monopolies, whether public or private. As we have seen, intellectual property can be owned, possessed, rented and licensed in almost as many ways as can physical property. The salient points are the mechanisms by which the product is exchanged and traded. The most fundamental are whether access is open or closed; if closed, the nature and length of the restrictions; and, if payment is required, its nature (none; by negotiation; or by a non-negotiable, statutory licence).

The basic property contract still stands: a balance between the creator's private reward and society's public access. But each of its specific relationships needs examination: between creator and society; between private and public; and between reward and access. The public's concerns about patenting human genes and using Napster to copy music (or, in some circles, its lack of concern) are part of one single issue.

Above all, who should champion society's cause? The patent offices look after their customers, the patent-holders and rights-holders. Who should look after the patent offices? Who should examine the examiners? *Quis custodiet ipsos custodes?* Justice Story's description of copyright law as transcendentally subtle does not encourage outsiders to become involved. But they must, or the contracts will be one-sided and unfair, which is bad for all of us.

3

THE CORE CREATIVE INDUSTRIES

LAW 3: CE = CP × T

'Creativity is one of the last remaining legal ways of gaining an unfair advantage over the competition.'

Ed McCabe, copywriter

TERENCE CONRAN

We have looked at creativity and the laws of intellectual property. It is now time to look at creative products and to count the transactions. I have chosen Sir Terence Conran to illustrate this chapter because he is a hugely successful businessman who has built up two large, successful companies (and one not so successful) based on good design and craftsmanship in industries where large-scale commercial success is often elusive. He is best known for two achievements: the Habitat shops which he started in the 1960s, and which overnight became the supplier of choice to swinging London; and more recently for a string of fashionable home furnishing shops and smart restaurants.

He started young. When I asked him about his training at London's Central School of Art and Design, he said that his earlier teenage years at Bryanston School in Dorset were even more important because there he learnt practical skills in pottery, woodworking and metalworking. After Central, he turned immediately to designing and making furniture. The furniture business was slow to make a profit, and his commercial eye soon saw a gap in the market that had nothing to do with furniture: good, cheap food and coffee. Working on the principle, which drives everything he does, of bringing to others what he enjoys himself, he started a restaurant called The Soup Kitchen: 'Most of my efforts have been to put ideas that give me pleasure in front of other people for them to enjoy.'

Ten years passed before he opened the first Habitat store and by stages acquired a retail empire worth over £1 billion. But it came unstuck and in the process he sold the stores and the name too. He developed another furniture and furnishings chain under his own name, the Conran Collection. Then he saw another gap in the market. Not, as in the 1960s, for cheap sustenance but for more stylish and more expensive, grander places to eat and be seen. His group now includes the smart Bibendum, the smart and vast Quaglino's, Le Pont de la Tour, Mezzo, Bluebird, Orrery, Sartoria and Guastavino's in New York (they are all smart, of course, and most are vast). In 1999 Conran Holdings, of which he owns 62 per cent, produced revenues of £90 million.

For over thirty years he has manufactured, entertained and sold in abundance. Where I live in central London there are four Conran restaurants and two shops within half a mile. Each is completely different but each is unmistakably his. His first love is designing and making. When I ask him if he is a practical man he gently corrects me: '*very* practical'. In an age of global brands, which he is becoming, his business is still based on the individual's pleasure in making and shaping something. He much prefers making to selling. He sees the selling of his own products as a secondary part of the process, and dislikes selling other people's products. He is not a salesman. He tells me: 'I can get away with being a restaurateur, which is partly about selling, because we do manufacture the food in the kitchen. But I am somewhat ashamed of being a retailer.'

I met Terence Conran at his offices in Shad Thames, below Tower Bridge and next to Butler's Wharf and several of his shops as well as the Design Museum, which he founded. He lives above his offices. He was wearing his trademark blue shirt and round cufflinks. His office is typical Conran: comfortable, elegant, colourful, simple. He says he doesn't like the phrase 'well designed', preferring 'intelligently designed'.

He is a scavenger for pleasure. His talent is to notice something – a colour, a shape – and to recreate it and reposition it in such a way that other people enjoy it too. Before I met him I had focused on creativity in the absolute sense of 'something from nothing'. During our talk I realized repositioning is equally valid. He said, 'Creativity is hard to define. It's mostly straightforward but there's also something magical, almost spiritual, about the process.' And he comes back to the practical: 'You need to know the history of things and to be able to see a gap in the market.' He knows many people can have an idea but he also knows that few follow it through.

He recognizes from his own life that the creative person never moves in a straight line: 'I do believe that someone who is really creative is interested in everything that impacts on their life,' and deliberately searches out new experiences. But, having found what you want, 'You have to stick with it. You have to be absolutely determined, otherwise you might just as well write poetry.'

Does everybody have a creative talent? 'I always say to anyone who says, "I can't draw", that if you can write your name you can draw.' There is no special trick. The best education for children is to say, 'Look! Isn't that interesting?'

Conran reminds me of Warhol's description of an artist as 'Someone who produces things that people don't need but which he – for some reason – thinks it would be a good idea to give them.' But that rather apologetic remark (you don't really need this) obscures both men's steely determination to give it to us.

THE IDEAS BUSINESS

This chapter quantifies that 'steely determination' in the heartland of the creativity economy. It describes the 15 industries where creativity is the most important raw resource and the most valuable economic product.

Data on the creative economy are fragmented and elusive. Creativity and its products are found not only in factories and shops, as are traditional goods and services, but surround us almost everywhere. We are enmeshed by words and images, patented products, brands and trademarks. We talk of information overload in ways that we never talk of clothing overload or food overload.

Even once identified, creative products can be difficult to quantify and value. It is relatively easy to value a DVD or machine, but measuring and valuing the copyright or patent in them is more complicated. Government sources are patchy. In spite of their statements about the importance of the creative economy and the Internet's 'new economy', most governments remain fixated with traditional manufacturing and services. They have a reason for their bias. They depend mostly upon manufacturing, less upon services and hardly at all upon intellectual property for their tax revenues. This problem affects not only domestic output but also international trade. The export and import of creative products are virtually absent from the trade statistics because they are not subject to customs and excise taxes. This omission can be dangerous.

The criterion for inclusion here is whether the industry meets the definition of the creative economy given in Chapter 1: financial transactions in creative products, or CE = CP x T. The criterion of a creative product is a good or service that results from creativity and has economic value. The criterion of a transaction is that an exchange takes place with an economic value. All creative products qualify for one of the main forms of intellectual property (patents, copyrights, designs and trade marks) even if some accrue more value as a physical object (as do art and fashion). Conversely, I have excluded some forms of intellectual property, such as trade secrets, as being too general for my purpose.

I have included research and development into new processes and products that may lead to a patent, but I have not included the product that may result nor the sales that may follow. The same principle applies to trademarks. I have included the business of the creation of a trademark but not the resulting sales. The design of the Exxon logo is a creative act; but selling Exxon products to vehicle drivers is not. I acknowledge that this distinction is becoming blurred as more goods are treated as brands rather than commodities. But common sense requires it be made.

GLOBAL GROWTH

Worldwide, the creative economy was worth about $2,706 billion ($2.7 trillion) in 2005 and is growing at 6 per cent a year. Since, according to the World Bank, the world's gross domestic product (GDP) in 2005 was $44,385 billion ($44 trillion), the creative economy represents 6.1 per cent of the global economy.

The largest market is America. By 2004, American intellectual property was worth between $5 trillion and $6 trillion, which equated to 45 per cent of the country's GDP and exceeds the total GDP of any other country. A report using Federal Reserve Bank data found that US companies invested about $1 trillion a year in 'idea-related' intangibles, as much as they did in plant and machinery. The International Intellectual Property Alliance (IIPA) calculated that by 2000 America's copyright industries contributed more to the American economy than almost any other industry: more than chemicals, aircraft and aircraft parts, primary and fabricated metals, electronic equipment, industrial machinery and food and drink. During the 1980s and 1990s they grew at 6.3 per cent a year compared to the country's annual growth as a whole of 2.7 per cent a year. The American consultancy McKinsey added a new twist in 2006 when it calculated that 40 per cent of American jobs required people to express their talent, and even more significantly, over 70 per cent of new jobs did so. Gross exports of all IP industries exceeded $455 billion in 2004.

Over two million Americans described themselves as an 'artist' in 2000, an increase of 70,000 over the previous year, according to the Bureau of Labor Statistics. According to Americans for the Arts, there were 2.9 million people, 2.9 per cent of total employment, working for 548,000 organisations (4.3 per cent of US businesses). There were 30 per cent more writers and 50 per cent more musicians compared with 1970. Consumer expenditure on admissions to the performing arts increased at an average of 8 per cent a year through the 1990s. On the supply side, the American Patent Office issued 151,079 patents for inventions, 13,395 for designs and 816 for plants, a total (with 195 re-issues) of 143,396 (2005). It also registered 104,000 trademarks.

According to the World Bank, the next largest national economies measured by GDP are, in order, Japan, Germany, China, UK, France Italy, and Brazil. This ranking has been unchanged for several years apart from the extraordinary growth of China. The ranking of the countries' creative economies largely reflects their GDP but with some variations.

Japan has very high expenditures on R&D, as well as the world's highest per capita demand for newspapers, comics (its 'manga' comics had sales of over ¥700 billion, $5.9 billion, in 2005) and electronic entertainment. Germany also has high expenditures on R&D and mass media. However, both countries (as do France and Italy) have lower levels of production in other sectors, and a lower level of exports, compared to America and Britain. Brazil is still at a different (lower) stage on Maslow's 'hierarchy of desires' and a larger proportion of its GDP is spent on food and manufactured goods.

Overall, Europe is strong in creativity and innovation. A European Union study in 2006 found that Europeans are now much more likely to work in the creative industries than in a car assembly plant or other manufacturing processes. The creative economy employs no fewer than 5.8 million people, more than the working population of Greece and Ireland together. While jobs disappeared overall in the EU between 2002 and 2004, they actually rose by 1.85 per cent in the cultural and creative sectors. An even more important statistic is that people in the creative economy tend to be better educated than others. Almost half had a university degree, as opposed to about one-quarter of the total working population. They are also twice as likely to be self-employed which means they have to think for themselves not only about their creative talents but their financial and management skills.

China has embraced the ideas of creativity and innovation but its domestic markets are still small and fragmented. Nonetheless, the leaders of Shanghai and Beijing and a few other cities are moving quickly to encourage creative sectors and support local business people. The priorities tend to be design, crafts, publishing, electronic media and communications, especially those that appeal to young people. Most sources agree that in 2005 China became the world's third largest exporter of creative goods and services; quite an achievement for a country whose language most people cannot speak.

Britain's relatively high position, with a market size of £108 billion (nearly 10 per cent of GDP), is due to its substantial level of activity across all 15 industries, from art to video games. It has a reputation for originality and quality, which helps exports, although it has few major companies. It also has the two-edged benefit of speaking English which assists its exports (but also offers easy access to American exports). In 1997 Britain moved ahead of Germany and France into second place, behind America, in the exports of services, a large and growing proportion of which were creative products. Whereas America has shown continuous growth in both patents and copyrights, the British economy has always grown faster in copyright products. Its creative industries grew at an average of 7 per cent between 1997 and 2004, four times the growth of traditional manufacturing and twice as fast as traditional services. Over 1.8 million Britons describe themselves as working in the creative economy. The number has grown by 3 per cent every year since 1991, many times faster than the population. In 2004 the creative industries became London's second largest sector after financial services. Compared to financial services which are clustered in the City and Mayfair, creative industries are spread throughout the capital and have a more visible and perhaps greater presence.

Worldwide, the most remarkable phenomenon of the last few years has been the exponential growth of user-generated material in personal blogs and on Flickr, MySpace, YouTube and other online sites. These enable people to share their thoughts, words, pictures and music; initially with friends, then with like-minded communities and then with millions. Apart from making remarkable capital gains for those owners who sold out, and from providing some music bands with impressive launch pads for commercial success, these social networks have few financial elements. They are cheap to operate, and access is usually free. They are not a traditional industry. But that is the point. Their makers and users symbolise one of the most exciting developments in the new creative economy.

As the rich industrialized countries become more aware of creativity's contribution to growth, what are the still developing countries doing? In many, commodity prices are declining, populations are growing vigorously, and the US and Europe have used the open doors of globalization to either own or license many of the local assets. With very few exceptions, all the poor, developing countries of the South are trying to hitch a lift on the creativity express. They have tremendous strengths in national and ethnic cultures and arts and want to push and promote these for reasons of national pride and economic gain. It is not easy. They lack the business entrepreneurs, the familiarity with law and finance, the supportive politicians that are required. As fast as they establish their own sectors (India's R&D, Thailand's film industry, South Korea's video games) the rich West get even further ahead or simply move in to take control. In 1996, Brazil was the world's sixth largest music market; by 2004 it had dropped to twelfth place. As well as a digital divide, we are seeing a new creative divide, not in people's wish to be creative but in their ability to express their creativity in marketable products.

FIFTEEN SECTORS

This section gives data for each sector's (i) market size and (ii) industry earnings. The market size is the amount spent annually by consumers and businesses in a specific market; for example, the amount spent in America or Britain on film or fashion. The industry earnings give the industry's revenues; for example, the amount that American or British companies earn. The global totals will balance but individual countries will show disparities. For example, American and to a lesser extent British, French, German and Japanese companies often earn substantial sums overseas, so their industry earnings are larger than their domestic market. Conversely, countries which import a lot have a larger market than is shown by their national companies' earnings.

All data relate to 2005 unless stated. Currency conversions are based on exchange rates at 1 January 2007. The decline in the US dollar since 2003 results in non-US markets appearing to be relatively overstated when converted into dollars and the global market also appearing larger than if quoted in local currencies. The sources are given in the notes.

Advertising

Advertising has a love–hate relationship with creativity. In his seminal book *Confessions of an Advertising Man*, David Ogilvy, founder of Ogilvy & Mather, wrote, 'I tell new recruits that I will not allow them to use the word creative to describe the functions they are to perform in the agency.' He preferred the word 'remarkable'. Over 30 years later, Lee Chow, Chairman of TBWA Chiat/Day gave the opposite and more modern view when he said, 'I am an artist who happens to be in the advertising business'.

Today, advertising faces one great opportunity and three challenges. The opportunity is to widen its work beyond the traditional display media of press, TV and 'outdoor' (billboards) into the new relationships, both high-tech and low-tech, by which organizations now reach their customers, inserting logos, brand names and slogans into areas that have been ad-free. Already, some top agencies are making more money from the Internet and sponsorship than from display advertising. To achieve this, they face three challenges. The first challenge, almost solved, is to switch from charging their traditional 15 per cent commission on clients' media expenditure to fees or royalties. The second is to learn new skills (new to them, at least) of marketing and merchandising. The third is to compete with the many strategy and design companies, often younger and more nimble, which already have these skills and can focus on new concepts and ideas and sub-contract the rest.

Advertising is moving from being a copyright business to both a copyright and a trademark business. Agencies not only create new copyright works but are a major user of existing works; although ironically some of the most famous slogans, especially the simple ones, have been judged to lack the requisite 'skill and labour'. As they move into marketing, so they become more involved in the creation of trademarks and brands.

There are two ways to measure advertising. The industry itself prefers to combine the relatively small amounts that advertisers pay to agencies to create campaigns with the much larger amount the advertisers spend to buy media time and space on TV, newspapers, etc. This traditional approach made sense when the same agency both designed a campaign and bought the media. It does not cope well with the modern trend to separate these two functions. Today, a creative agency will devise the campaign and a separate company will buy the media outlets. Therefore, I give two sets of data: first, the amount spent on the creative work by the advertising agencies themselves; and second, the amount spent on both the agencies and the media. In calculating industry size, I use the former figure, since the latter payments appear as revenues of the other media industries, and to include them here would be double-counting.

The global market for the creation and development of advertising is worth about $55 billion. The two main centres are New York and London, followed by Tokyo, Frankfurt, Paris and Beijing. The US market is worth $22 billion and is growing at 6 per cent a year. American-owned agencies dominate the global business because American companies are the major advertisers. The top 25 agencies in America earn $4.8 billion domestically a year and the top 25 in the UK earn $4.5 billion (the top companies appear on both lists). The high value of London's agency work is the result of many advertisers using London agencies for European or worldwide campaigns. We estimate total US domestic revenues to be $22 billion and total UK industry's revenues to be £8 billion. The UK has a core workforce of 15,000 people (defined as those employed in member agencies of the IPA) and a total workforce, including media buyers, and freelance people, of 223,000 people.

These figures are dwarfed by advertisers' total expenditure on advertising (consisting of their expenditure on both agencies and media). The total amount spent on advertising worldwide in 2005 was $500–700 billion, depending on how much of the new media was included. Industry sources expected the 2006 total to be 6 per cent higher. Most of this growth is due to the increase in Internet advertising, up from $1.5 billion in 1998 to $33 billion in 2004. The largest national market in 2005 was America ($155 billion). The second biggest was China ($38 billion) followed by Japan ($37 billion). Together, these three countries account for well over half the world total (a pattern of dominance that occurs in many of the 15 industries). The next largest markets were Germany ($22 billion) and Britain ($19 billion). Outside these big five countries the sector is small.

Internet advertising is growing fast. Zenith estimated the Internet's share of global advertising to be 4.7 per cent in 2005 and forecast it to be 10 per cent by 2011. The company also forecast global Internet advertising would overtake global outdoor advertising in 2007 and radio advertising in 2009 (Internet advertising had already exceeded both media in the UK by 2005, taking 14 per cent of companies' spending, the highest proportion in the world).

National growth rates vary according to economic output. Whereas changes in spending in the arts and other creative industries generally follow broader economic trends, changes to advertising spending precede them. Typically, advertising budgets will slow 6–12 months ahead of a recession and recover 6–12 month ahead of other sectors.

China is growing by 10–15 per cent a year and America and Europe at 3–6 per cent a year but Japan's recession led to static figures for four successive years. Above average growth can be seen in Brazil and Russia. There is virtually no growth in the rest of the world. Media expenditure in Africa shows signs of growth but most of the advertising campaigns and most of the media outlets are owned by Western companies.

ARCHITECTURE

Architects provide the creativity that fuels the building and construction industry which is the world's fifth largest industry after defence, education, health and food. Their artistic and economic role varies widely from the top handful of prize-winning architects who design the world's most prominent buildings to the hundreds of thousands of architects, surveyors, builders and owners who design and construct the remainder.

Architecture is a copyright business as opposed to a patent or trademark business. An architect's sketches are protected by copyright, as are the scale drawings and models and all the artistic and literary works and designs up to and including the building itself. Architects often retain copyright in their buildings although they may license a contractor to make copies. The person who buys or rents a house does not normally acquire copyright in it.

It has the distinction of being the most truly international of the 15 industries, partly because it does not rely on words and partly because it has achieved its own global iconography that is independent of any single nation or culture. Even governments that restrict cultural imports in all other sectors are happy to appoint foreign architects to deal with buildings of the greatest national and cultural sensitivity. The French, probably the most culturally exclusive of all industrial nations after the Japanese, asked Briton Richard Rogers to design the Centre Georges Pompidou at Beauborg and the Chinese–American I. M. Pei to redevelop the Louvre. The Shanghai World Financial Centre which opens in 2007 as the world's tallest building was designed by Americans KPF Inc. Los Angeles-based Frank Gehry designed the new Guggenheim museum in Bilbao in the Basque country and Zaha Hadid, born in Baghdad but based in London, designed the Museo Nazionale delle Arti Dell XXI Secolo, MAXXI, Italy's first national museum of contemporary art. The German government asked Briton Norman Foster to design its new parliament in the Reichstag in Berlin, and Japan's Kisho Kurokawa designed the new wing for the Netherlands' prestigious van Gogh museum in Amsterdam.

Worldwide there are about one million professional architects who have combined revenues of about $45 billion. Of the top 30 firms in terms of revenues, America and Japan have 20 between them, with Britain in third place. The top five firms (2006) were Nikken Sekkei (Japan, with over 1,000 architects and fee income over $250 million), Genster (America, over $250 million), HOK (America, over $250 million), Aedas (UK, $180–189 million) and Skidmore Owings & Merrill (America, $180–189 million). Britain's Foster & Partners, which was voted 'most admired' firm by *Building Design* magazine in 2004, 2005 and 2006, had 584 architects and fee income of $90–99 million.

The size of a country's construction market reflects its national economy. However, architects' practices will flourish disproportionately in countries which have a flourishing private sector and private capital, and a sensitivity to corporate or civic pride.

In the US, members of the American Institute of Architects had gross revenues of $25.2 billion in 2002 and net revenues (excluding sub-contracted work) of $12 billion. There are 91,000 practising architects and 99,000 other people working in 16,500 firms. Since 2000, the number of architects has gone up but the number of firms has decreased. Total design, building and construction work in 2002 was worth $400 billion.

UK architects' revenues were £3.5 billion in 2005 of which slightly more than half came from British clients and the remainder from overseas. The Royal Institute of British Architects (RIBA) estimates there are 25,000 practising architects and a further 58,000 people working in architects' firms. Together, they account for about 3 per cent of all expenditures on construction.

The world's fastest growing construction market is China, which had about 32 million people working in about 700,000 construction companies in 2005, earning $30 billion. However, most Chinese architects have little status and are poorly paid and most of the new buildings in Beijing, Shanghai and Shenzhen are designed by foreign architects with the Chinese partner playing a secondary role. The government says there 11,000 architect firms earning a total of over $1 billion of which the biggest are Xian Dai in Shanghai, with RMB 1.144 billion revenues, and P&T in Hong Kong, with 500 architects and fee income of $40 million. Many new buildings are unimaginative, but Beijing and Shanghai have some striking designs including Rem Koolhaas's TV Tower and Herzog and de Meuron's Olympic stadium, and Xian Dai's Shanghai Museum and SOM's JinMao Tower.

Art

The art market is unusual in that it deals only in original works that are unique or rare. Whereas most industries try to multiply and sell as many new copies as possible, the art dealer's objective is to emphasize scarcity. Moreover, it is primarily a secondhand market, and old objects often increase in value. Astonishing prices can be paid for a single work that originally sold for little; in 2006, paintings by Jackson Pollock and Gustav Klimt were sold for $140 million and $135 million. Art is also one of the most stolen commodities.

As a result, even though artistic works do qualify for copyright, the purchaser of a work of art normally buys only the object and not the copyright to it. The artist retains the copyright. The priority given to the art object means that many artists do not encourage the copying of their works, even if they might gain financially. In addition, an artist's signature may be separately protected as an artistic work or as a design. A peculiarity of the European art market, originating in France, is the *droit de suite* or resale tax under which an artist (or the artist's heirs, for 70 years after the artist's death) qualifies for a percentage of the sale price, up to 4 per cent, each time a piece of work is sold.

By dealing in the same product over several years it is possible to accumulate an accurate record of its price as it goes up and down and demonstrates how the economic value of the same product can fluctuate. Paris-based Groupe Serveur's Artprice.com has a database of over 60,000 artists and 3 million works that have been traded since 1987. The art market also exemplifies the 'deal economy' because every transaction is unique. Even two identical prints sold consecutively constitute different transactions and may fetch different prices because the sale of the first will affect the market for the second. The very low barriers to entry and the low start-up costs allow many thousands of dealers to operate, and many individuals buy, sell and give away privately.

Determining the number of artists and their earnings is extremely difficult because of the difficulties of definitions, and the very large amount of private trading outside galleries and auctions.

Overlapping these markets is the stately world of museums and galleries which provide repositories and archives of high-quality or specialist art. Their main business (with some exceptions) is to guard heritage and celebrate new work. They do not normally buy and sell copyright except when they produce a catalogue which requires them to acquire rights, like any publisher.

Globally, the top of the market, consisting of work by high-end professional artists, is worth about $11 billion; this figure includes antiquities through to contemporary art as well as jewellery, fine furniture and some *objets d'art* (many of which might originally have been categorised as crafts). Whereas the buyers for art, especially for the more expensive contemporary work, are truly international, the actual purchases are done in a very small number of countries. The market is dominated by New York and London which together represent over 70 per cent of all sales both at auction and through galleries, and buyers from other countries often buy through a dealer in one of these two cities. The next largest market, Paris, has a mere 9 per cent, New York sees the largest turnover while London has the largest volume (in 2003 to 2004, 22 per cent of fine art auction sales went through the UK, compared to 20 per cent through the US). London has 60 per cent of the European market; the next largest centres are Paris and Geneva. This high-end market is very sensitive to macro-economic factors including stock market trends and currency fluctuations; in November 2006 the growth in hedge funds and the weak US dollar encouraged buyers to spend over $1.3 billion at auction in New York over two weeks, the highest two-week total ever. The two auction houses, Christie's and Sotheby's, dominate the market, with annual revenues around $3 billion. They are both about the same size, and operate similarly, though Christie's tends to earn slightly more. The world's most-visited art gallery or museum is the Louvre in Paris which attracted 7.3 million visitors in 2005 (partly helped by the bestselling novel *The Da Vinci Code*).

The US market is worth about $5 billion (the US and UK market data includes foreign buyers who buy through a US or UK agent). The New York art scene is the most active in the world and New York artists command the highest prices for contemporary art worldwide. The National Endowment for the Arts has a budget of $111 million and state, city and private donors provide many times that amount.

The UK art market is worth slightly over £2 billion, about one-third of the world total. Since 2000, the art market has boomed while the antique market has declined. The number of people describing themselves as visual artists is about 60–80,000 of which only a small proportion manage to live off their art. A further 60,000 people also define themselves as artists but typically work as illustrators and designers.

Museums and galleries attracted 42 million visits and had turnover of £900 million. The government provided grants of £369 million to arts organizations in 2005. National lottery funding for the arts, mainly for capital expenditure, reached £164 million in 2005 and has totalled over £2.17 billion since 1995. The opening of the fashionable Tate Modern in 2000 to complement the more traditional Tate Britain has meant the Tate (subsidy, £31 million) has the most visitors (6.4 million), followed by the British Museum (£39 million in subsidy and

4.4 million visits), the Natural History Museum (£39 million and 1.9 million visits), the Victoria and Albert Museum (£36 million and 1.1 million visits), the Science Museum (£32 million and 1.6 million visits), and the National Gallery (£20 million and 5 million visits). The private Royal Academy of Arts, which was set up by artists in 1768 and is still run by artists, had a turnover of £22 million in 2005, coming from exhibitions (£6.5 million), trading (£13.2 million) and donations (£2.7 million). It attracts about one million visitors.

Other important countries for the production and supply of art are France, Germany, Japan, Australia, Brazil, Italy and China. Demand is centred in countries with a high level of culture and a high level of disposable income. In recent years, the production and appreciation of Chinese art has expanded dramatically but most high-value sales take place outside China.

Crafts

Crafts flourish in two separate markets; in the art market, where they are exhibited in art galleries and sold at auction, and also in the much larger tourism and leisure markets. In the art market, artists work in the same way as in other media, and with the same imaginative skill. In 2003 the artist Grayson Perry won Britain's most prestigious art prize, the Turner Prize for his pottery (and his transvestite style). In the mass market, people make and buy crafts without much regard for authorship or formal aesthetic, and value them by price and utility as well as quality. Americans have a wide definition of craft and often include flower-arranging and house painting. Although crafts count as artistic works, if they fulfil the criteria of being novel and of requiring an element of skill, the majority of makers do not assert their intellectual property rights.

Some cultures have a chronic debate about the difference between arts and crafts. The British are deeply conflicted. They will happily treat an English silver chalice of the fourteenth century or a Sung bowl as a wonderful work of art but when they look at contemporary work they become confused and snobbery can set in. Most cultures are more open to craft's qualities, and Arab and Asian cultures often revere craft more highly than art, and consequently it is more expensive. The best response to this conundrum was given by an English gallery owner who asked Tobias Kaye, a wood-turner, whether he was making art or craft. Kaye replied, 'Well, the process is art but the result is craft.' 'Funny', said the gallery-owner, 'because I asked Richard Raffan [another leading wood-turner] the same question last week and he said, "The process is craft but the result is art."' Other countries do not have the same 'either–or' mentality. The Chinese, Japanese, Indian, other Asian, Aboriginal, African, Arab, Russian, Mexican, Peruvian, Amerindian, Aztec, pre-Colombian and Inuit cultures happily mix art and craft. Art critic Herbert Read said 'Pottery is at once the simplest and most difficult of all arts. It is the simplest because it is the most elemental; it is the most difficult because it is the most abstract.' It certainly fits the conditions of being creative. The best definition is that craft work has a function; and an individual work may be so well-made and beautiful to qualify as art.

The global market is varied and diverse. The high-end market, consisting of crafts whose authorship and provenance is identifiable, is worth about $2 billion. Based on industry reports, we estimate the mass market of works individually made for sale is probably worth 15 times as much, or $30 billion.

The US market is large and varied. The industry estimates the high-end sector to be worth about $1 billion and the total $3 billion. Total sales of craft materials to craft-workers are worth $11 billion, and are growing at the rapid rate of 10 per cent a year, although only a fraction of this material is used in crafts intended for sale.

Chinese production is traditionally strong, and worth $15 billion, with major sectors being jade, calligraphy, paper, costume, cloisonné, lacquer and pottery. China makes and exports more crafts in the widest sense than any other country. The Chinese market is estimated to be worth $1 billion.

The UK market is worth about £826 million. The Craft Council estimates there are 32,000 people working professionally (2003), mostly in textiles (23 per cent) and ceramics (21 per cent), followed by wood, metal, jewellery, glass, toys and musical instruments. Of these, 600 companies had a turnover in excess of £250,000 although the average annual turnover for a full-time craft worker is £35,000.

Design

The Industrial Design Society of America (IDSA) defines industrial design as the 'creation and development of concepts and specifications that optimise the function, value and appearance of products and systems for the mutual benefit of users and manufacturers.' Design as a 'process' has a much wider application, ranging from interior design to large-scale infrastructure, but this section deals only with the industrial core. It is not only responsible for the front end and the face of most products and services but a major input into all origination and manufacturing processes. Without some design element, most manufactured goods and services would either not exist or would fail to differentiate themselves in the marketplace. Research by the London Business School shows that for every 1 per cent of sales devoted to product design and development a company's sales and profits will rise on average by 3–4 per cent a year for five years.

Designers want their designs to be both eye-catching art and fit-for-purpose function. Their successes are world-renowned, although they themselves are hardly known to the public at all. The VW Beetle, the Coca Cola logo, the 'No Entry' street sign and the Nike swoosh are global icons that decorate our age. Yet few people could name their authors and the public is quick to blame designers for artiness and expense. Prime Minister Tony Blair admitted in 1997, 'If MPs pushed for a debate on ship-building they would probably get one but if they pushed for a debate on the design industry they would be dismissed as concentrating on trivia.' Britain's current lack of interest is a remarkable turnaround from the Victorian age when between 1839 and 1842 the British parliament passed four separate design acts. Since 2000 UK industry revenues have declined further. The market for industrial design has also declined in most other European countries and in America but has increased in Japan and China.

A design may qualify for three kinds of intellectual property protection. It will almost certainly qualify as an artistic work for copyright. In Britain it will also qualify for a 'design right' which is rather like copyright and intended for functional designs. In addition, a designer can register a design, obtaining a stronger level of protection, although this is available only to designs with a significant aesthetic element. The availability of automatic protection, especially the new design right, has led to a fall in the number of registrations. In all cases (copyright, design right and registered designs) the term of protection is shorter than for other copyright works, reflecting the traditional view that they are less a matter of 'artistic' expression and more a matter of industrial manufacturing.

The global industry is worth about $140 billion of which America, Germany and Japan generate nearly 70 per cent. The top five design firms are URS (US), SNC (Canada), Atkins (UK), AECOM (US) and Jacobs (US).

The US market is worth $49 billion, over a third of the global total. Turnover and fees grew 1995–2000 by 15 per cent a year but they have declined since then as they have in other countries. The IDSA's research into training and hiring suggest the four most sought-after skills for would-be designers are 'creative problem-solving; 2D concept sketching; verbal and written communication; and the processing of materials and manufactures.' Skills in information technologies rate fifth.

The UK industry is worth £11.6 billion a year divided about equally between companies' in-house budgets and independent and freelance consultants. The word 'designer' is used more loosely than in the US and it is difficult to estimate the exact numbers of people for whom design is a full-time or significant part of their work, but most estimates average around 68,000 full-time designers and about 120,000 other people working on design and product development. Two-thirds are men, and two-thirds are under 40 years old. According to the British Design Institute, which represents consultancies, their members' turnover, number of employees, fee income and margins declined significantly from 2000 to 2006. In 2004 the Patent Office received 4,174 design applications (of which British citizens made 3,273) and registered 3,874.

China's industrial design industry has grown significantly in recent years and by 2005 numbered about 800,000 people including support staff. We estimate the market to be worth RMB 30–40 billion. Student numbers were growing by about 20 per cent a year and many students are encouraged to study abroad. The government is committed to rapid expansion and, for example, has set a target of 20,000 shoe designers by 2010.

Fashion

Designer fashion is a small but intensely competitive business: a volatile mix of art, craft, design, manufacturing, retailing and publicity. It is the most visible tip, with an influence disproportionate to its size, of the global textile and clothing industry. Many cities try to copy the London, Paris, Milan and New York fashion weeks with their own events tied to tourism as much as to the fashion industry. The major brands and companies are headquartered in New York, Paris, Milan and Geneva and sell not only clothing but also accessories, watches, perfumes, etc. A fashion product is protected by copyright only if it is made with 'individual skill and effort' and thereby qualifies as an artistic work; so a handmade dress is protected by copyright but a mass-produced dress is not. Usually, copyright provides too narrow a protection to be effective, especially in such a fast-moving business (there are obvious similarities with computer programs). In practice, fashion designers rely mostly on trademarks, trade secrets and other forms of protection (including tight security, because several collections have been stolen hours before a show). Fashion is often quoted as an example of an industry that is wonderfully, endlessly, inventive without needing to use copyright.

The global market, strictly defined, is worth $12–20 billion (although a wider definition of what constitutes fashion brings the figure to nearer $60 billion). The largest national markets are America, France, UK and Germany. The major national producers are American, Italian and French. In all countries, sales of designer's accessories are growing faster than sales of the clothes themselves. The industry is dominated by a few major groups, such as Bernard Arnault's LVMH (Louis Vuitton, Dior, Givenchy, Kenzo, Pink, Donna Karan, Loewe, Marc Jacobs and Fendi).

The US market is worth $5 billion, consisting equally of American and imported goods. Top American names include Ralph Lauren, Brooks Brothers and Hilfiger. The best-known Americam-born designer is probably Tom Ford, who works mainly for Gucci. The UK market is worth about £1 billion and is dominated by American, Italian and French products. British designers are recognized for their creativity and quirky talent but few have built their own brands and they earn only a small amount: £250 million counter sales at home and £500 million overseas. The largest company is Paul Smith Ltd which had revenues in 2004 of £350 million and profits of £26 million (the value of the counter sales was considerably higher); the company makes most of its profits in Japan. There are about 2,000 British designers and about 9,000 other people working in the industry.

The Chinese fashion industry is dominated by Western brands. As yet, few Chinese companies have the right mix of style, publicity and distribution to attract local buyers, although as well as Wang Yiyang's Zuczug and Cha Gang a new generation of designers are emerging including Lu Kun and the brand Ya Ge'er. Like London, and unlike Paris, Milan or New York, Shanghai is best known for its street fashion: young people buying imaginatively and creating their own look. We estimate a total market of around RMB 3 billion.

Film

No architect can make a business from one building; no designer can survive on one frock, however beautiful. But film is one sector (music and writing are others) where success can come quickly and one success can be enough. The biggest selling film ever is Fox's *Titanic*, 1997, which has earned $1.8 billion. The lure of such riches attracts millions of people to be a player in the film-making game or to be close to those who are.

The industry consists of four main sectors: American production (Hollywood and independent); other national production (notably in Australia, Brazil, Britain, Canada, France, Germany, Italy, India, China and Hong Kong as well as, to a lesser degree, in some other 20 countries); American-owned global distribution companies; and the thousands of local companies which own cinemas, TV channels, and DVD outlets. The main trends are the growth of digital animation and the growth in home (as opposed to cinema) viewing, especially on pay-TV and DVD. According to *Variety*, the Hollywood studios earned $9.5 billion from American home entertainment in 2005: more than they did from American cinemas. In that year cinema attendances dropped by 9 per cent in America, 11 per cent in Europe, 21 per cent in Brazil, 10 per cent in Australia and 6 per cent in Japan. The growth of home watching was the major cause; another was the shortage of blockbusters.

A film is a qualifying work and protected by copyright. Most laws interpret the 'author' quite widely to include the author of the screenplay, the producer, the director and others as well as giving separate protection to the costumes, the design, etc. Once made, a film's rights will be sold or licensed to distributors within each territory, each medium (cinema, broadcast, etc) and in each language. There is a trend towards registering film titles as trademarks and registering merchandise as designs.

Globally, the film industry produces about 3,000 films a year worth $81 billion in terms of sales through cinema, video and TV. India produced the largest number of films (over 1,000 in 2005), followed by Japan (650) and America (611). But American films dominate all national markets except India and China (and North Korea). They dominate even in Britain, which has an active film industry, but whose consumers spend 70–80 per cent of their box office money to see America films. The world cinema market was worth $23 billion in 2005 of which America had $9 billion, 40 per cent of the total, followed by Japan ($1.7 billion), France ($1.0 billion), Germany ($0.89 billion) and the UK ($0.77 billion). The home DVD/video market is worth about twice as much as cinema, at $44 billion. Sales to TV are worth $10 billion.

Of the US average of 600 films a year, roughly 400 are released in cinemas and the remainder sold straight to video or TV. A Hollywood film cost an average of $63 million (the negative cost); however, a studio's budget always includes an additional marketing cost which averages $40 million. The average cost has declined slightly for three years in a row. Box office admissions in 2005 were 1.54 billion and box office receipts were $9 billion, of which the producer might receive one-third. Ticket sales are expected to decline between 2006 and 2010 but box office revenues are expected to increase to about $11 billion in 2010. In addition, video and DVD earned $11 billion and TV and cable spent $4 billion. The industry employs 359,000 people, divided into production (199,000), cinemas and video rental (132,000) and other areas (28,000).

India produced over 1,000 films in 2005, of which about 400 are Hindi-language Bollywood movies with their distinctive mix of film, romance and music, and the remaining 600 were more modest, local language productions. Cinema accounts for $1.91 billion annually, as much as 55 per cent of revenues, one of the highest proportions in the world, brought in by 2.7 billion admissions.

The UK market is worth £4.1 billion of which the consumer spent £770 million at the box office (representing 164 million tickets), £2.7 billion on video and DVD, and £600 million on pay-TV subscriptions. The BBC, ITV and other free-to-air channels spend an additional £100 million to buy broadcast rights. The figures for DVD and pay-TV are increasing rapidly while other sectors are static. Since 2000, between 75 and 90 films have been produced annually in Britain of which around 50 are pure British and 10 are pure American; the rest are co-productions. Almost all British films have budgets under £4.5 million, although *Casino Royale* (2006) cost £70 million.

The British industry is well-regarded for its creative and technical skills, and won an average of 21 per cent of the major Oscars through the 1990s, but for 40 years it has lacked the successful entrepreneurs that exist in advertising, architecture, art, fashion, publishing, theatre and music. As a result, the main financiers of British film-making are the Hollywood studios (who provide most of the finance for 53 per cent of British films) and the National Lottery and other subsidies which provide about £60 million a year. The first of the new wave of British films was *Four Weddings and a Funeral* in 1994 which cost $4 million and earned over $260 million; others include Fox's *Full Monty* ($250 million) and Polygram's *Mr Bean* ($235 million). Since 2000, the most successful films have been the Bond and Harry Potter franchises but US films still take 70–80 per cent of the box office each year.

The Chinese film industry produces about 260 films a year (2005), including many co-productions with foreign companies. Distribution remains a problem. Although cinemas flourished in the 1980s and 1990s, with 20–30 billion tickets and RMB 3 billion revenues (the average ticket price was 10 cents), the spread of DVDs has cut the cinema market back drastically. DVD sales reached 360 million legal copies in 2004 with many more pirate copies. In 2005 ticket sales dropped to 70 million, although price rises to RMB 50–60 in the big cities and RMB 10–20 in the countryside brought in box office revenues of RMB 2 billion (in the past 25 years, ticket prices have rised by 300 times but box office has still declined to one-third). In 2006, revenues rose to RMB 2.62 billion. By the end of the year, Zhang Yimou's *Curse of the Golden Flower* had grossed box office receipts of over RMB 270 million ($35 million), a record for a domestic film, enhanced through exclusive agreements with digital cinemas and China Mobile.

Music

Music is the most intangible of creative products. It is also, with publishing, one of the most pervasive. The industry has four main sectors: composition; performance; publishing/licensing; and sound recordings. This section deals primarily with music publishing and recording.

A piece of written music is protected by copyright and related rights at each stage of its life. The composition is protected for the composer's life plus 70 years; and recordings for the performer's life plus 50 years (95 years in America). The broadcast of a recording or a performance is protected separately for 50 years. Typically, a publisher will buy the rights and seek to exploit them by means of recording, performance, etc. The roles of a publisher and a recording company are traditionally separate (although, confusingly, most major companies carry out both functions). This separation may be ending as online delivery undercuts the role of the traditional stand-alone company.

The top recording companies are Universal (25 per cent of the market, $6.6 billion sales in 2004) Sony BMG (21 per cent, $2.5 billion), Warner Music (13 per cent, $3.6 billion), billion) and EMI (11 per cent, $3.8 billion). Together, these companies have over 80 per cent of the world publishing and recording markets. All four own both publishing and recorded divisions; generally, recording brings in the bulk of the revenue but publishing is more profitable. Since 2003 there has been continued speculation about mergers and Sony did acquire BMG Music in 2004 but several proposed mergers have been prevented by US or EU competition authorities.

Globally, the four sectors have a turnover of $80 billion. The main sector is recorded music which is worth $33.4 billion of which the US spends $12.3 billion followed by Japan ($5.4 billion), Britain ($3.4 billion), Germany ($2.2 billion), France ($1.9 billion), Canada ($730 million) and Italy ($670 million) Recorded music is one of the few creative sectors whose revenues are declining: having reached an all-time high of $39.5 billion in 1996 they fell to $33 billion in 2005. The underlying cause is that most households have now stocked up with CDs, including replacements for LPs and cassettes, and do not want to replace them or add to them. There has also been a dearth of new talent in pop music. And the companies have notably failed to exploit the new online delivery systems. Sony forecast in 2006 that CD sales would decline by 50 per cent over the next three years.

The actual sales will depend on the extent to which the audience turns to the Internet and mobiles for its music. Will music publishers exploit this form of distribution themselves or will they continue to license their rights to separate companies? George Geis, Professor of Information Systems at the University of California, Los Angeles (UCLA), expects the Internet to have a dramatic impact. He has remarked that the recording industry is a $100 billion business trapped inside a $40 billion body.

The Internet affects the way we make, share and listen to music in many different ways. It allows new musicians to distribute and promote their work; it provides social networks where people can share material; it makes copying much easier (both legal and illegal); and it provides companies with a new means of distributing their back catalogues. Above all, it provides a much larger range of revenue streams, from iTunes to ringtones, although the established companies are nervous of losing the established streams that have served so well in the past.

Digital downloads brought total revenues of $1.1 billion in 2005, according to IFPI, about half from online sources such as iTunes, mainly in America and UK, and half via mobiles (mostly in Japan). The market in ringtones flourished between 2000 and 2005, reaching $400 million a year at its peak, but then declined.

The US market is worth about $27 billion across all sectors. Sales of recorded music were $12.3 billion in 2005, or 36 per cent of the global market. It thus sells more than twice as much as Japan, the second largest market, and more than all the European countries combined. The industry consists of not only 150,000 professional musicians, but another 90,000 people who are aspiring musicians and another 300,000 who have jobs in the industry. According to the

National Endowment for the Arts, 20 million Americans, 10 per cent of the adult population, say they regularly sing in a choir or chorus.

The UK market is worth £5 billion. The biggest sector is the consumer market for recorded music, worth £3.4 billion. In addition, media companies (BBC, ITV, radio stations, etc) spend £200 million and the public sector spends £300 million. Consumers spend at least £850 million on performances (a major growth sector) and at least £400 million on instruments (2000). UK publishing and recording companies earn additional revenues of £1.3 billion overseas, made up of £1.5 billion from licences and the rest in direct sales. The industry consists of 53,000 people who call themselves 'musicians' on their census forms, another 29,000 people who are aspiring musicians and another 43,000 people who work in the industry in one way or another, totalling 125,000; as well as 600,000 people who participate in music-making and often pay small amounts of money to do so but are themselves unpaid.

Other major markets for recorded music include China ($211 million) and India ($152 million).

Performing Arts (Theatre/Opera/Dance/Ballet)

The 'performing arts' include all kinds of on-stage and site-specific performances. They involve the management of some of the world's largest and best-known landmarks buildings (including the Royal Albert Hall, Sydney's Opera House and New York's Lincoln Center) as well as many small local venues. Their activities include the skills of writing, producing, casting, directing and performing; design, lighting and sound; costume; set-making; marketing; and administration.

Dramatic works, like music, receive copyright protection when the original work is written down (as a literary work) and also when they are performed. However there are significant differences. Many contemporary works are not written down; and even a traditional work may contain elements that were not in the original script. Each of these elements is unlikely to receive protection unless they are subsequently written down or recorded in some way. For example, a play's lighting arrangement does not merit protection unless someone (not necessarily the lighting director) writes it down, whereupon it becomes a literary work and qualifies that way.

The global industry is worth about $50 billion although precise figures are not available. The main source of revenue is the box office but although venues do publish their box office figures, they do not differentiate between performing arts and other kinds of events such as corporate conferences. Moreover, in addition to box office revenues, many venues receive substantial funding from private sponsors and public subsidies which are seldom specified.

The English-language theatre arts are centred on New York's Broadway and London's West End. Broadway sold 11.9 million tickets in the 2005/6 season and London sold 12.3 million in 2005. Although the West End sells more tickets than Broadway, Broadway's average prices at $71 ($91, with service charges) are about 50 per cent higher. Plays and musicals that succeed on Broadway and the West End can have an exceedingly long life. Agatha Christie's *The Mousetrap* is now in its sixth decade in London. *Cats* opened in London in 1981 and on Broadway in 1982 where it had had 8,949 and 7,485 performances respectively by the end of 2005. The worldwide bestseller is *Phantom of the Opera* ($3.2 billion) which exceeds the box office revenues of *Titanic*, the bestselling film. Other high earners are *Cats* ($3 billion) and *Les Misérables* ($1.8 billion). *The Economist* once estimated Lord Lloyd-Webber's composing royalties to be over £2–3 million a week.

The US is the world's largest market. National box office revenues for theatre, musicals, opera, ballet and dance were $12.7 billion in 2005, slightly more than the box office revenues for film and spectator sports. Broadway earned ticket sales of $862 million and the 'Road', meaning all commercial theatres outside Broadway, earned $915 million (notably, women buy 75 per cent of the tickets for these shows and occupy 70 per cent of the seats). The Broadway box office has increased slightly year-on-year since 2000, but the Road, after rapid growth in the early 1990s, has declined in each of the past two years. Musicals account for 85 per cent of revenues. According to *Americans for the Arts*, theatres receive about $5 billion private sponsorship (half the $10 billion worth of sponsorship given to the arts overall), as well as federal ($300 million), state ($328 million) and city ($778 million) funding.

The UK market is worth £1.5 billion. The London theatres are flourishing but there is concern about the gap between the prosperous West End and the poverty of the regional theatres which, according to the Arts Council of England, have long been 'starved of finance' and are under threat of extinction. While Londoners can choose between 50 theatres, many people elsewhere may have to travel 30 miles to visit one. Some funding comes from the Arts Councils, Regional Arts Boards and other public funds (£121 million in 2004), sponsorship (£30 million) and donations (£30 million). Lottery funding provides a further £568 million a year for capital expenditure and increasingly for revenue funding as well. The workforce numbers 75,000 people (of whom 15,000 are likely to be not working at any one time). Most of these people are attached to one of the 300 professional theatres or to one of the 200 multipurpose venues in an administrative or technical capacity.

The Chinese performing arts industry, which ranges from Western music to Chinese opera, acrobats and dance, is large in terms of the numbers of artists (at least 140,000) but only attracts RMB 4.22 billion revenue made up of RMB 3.24 billion public grants and RMB 980 million ticket sales (2004). Successful Chinese productions in recent years have included *Impressions of Yunnan* and *Era-Intersection of Time and Space* (2005), a multimedia theatrical spectacular in Shanghai which had 497 performances and box office revenues of RMB 50 million.

Publishing

The Chinese invented paper and some elements of the printing process but the Europeans were the first to bring together paper, sticky ink, a press and reusable moveable type; Gutenberg and others in Germany printed the first, dated modern book, a Psalter, in 1457. The Americans printed their first document, a Freeman's Oath, in 1639. Printing and publishing is now the largest media industry in the world and the pre-eminent copyright industry, having given the world the two key words, author and copyright, that are the basis of intellectual property law in industries as diverse as film-making and computer software.

The industry is still based on this simple, universal process of direct copying, but over time has evolved numerous different formats and business processes to meet specific design needs and local cultural habits. In recent decades, while the local creative inputs of writers and editors have changed little, the technology of design and illustration have changed dramatically, as have the back-office functions of finance and marketing. Book and periodical publishing, like music publishing, has seen the emergence of global conglomerates, although newspapers have remained relatively local. Electronic publishing has grown rapidly, especially on the back of the Internet. It is unclear to what extent electronic publishing is an extension of magazine publishing, a part of the computer software business or an industry in its own right.

As a conveyor of human achievements from the awesome to the trivial the book has no peer. People appreciate the book not only as a packager of content but for its diversity of designs and for its solidity and respectability. The numbers of titles and of copies sold increases remorselessly, although the margins and profits on sales are ever tighter. Book retailing has undergone a recent transformation with the success of online selling and the introduction of large mega-stores that encourage browsing and often have cafés and sell music as well; like record shops, they are bright, busy and stay open late.

Books have one characteristic that distinguishes them from other created works. They are the most given of all creative products; their visual appeal, size, price range and cultural respectability make them a welcome gift in almost all circumstances and a new or bestselling book comes with the cachet of novelty and fashion. A CD has some of these attributes, but the music industry's smaller output and the CD's uniform shape, visual opaqueness and narrower price range are disincentives. DVDs, especially box sets, look more like books and are given more often than CDs.

Globally, the most active book markets are China, US and UK. China published 252,000 titles and sold 6 million copies earning $5.9 billion. America published 172,000 new titles and sold 2.5 billion copies of them. The UK published 206,000 titles and sold 460 million copies earning £1.7 billion at home (and another £1 billion overseas). Total book sales are estimated to be $220 billion.

The global magazine market was worth $135 billion in 2005, consisting primarily of advertising revenue of $75 billion with paid sales bringing another $60 billion. According to the International Federation of Periodical Publishers (FIPP), America publishes the most titles followed by China, Britain, Germany, the Netherlands and Japan. The advertising revenue earned by magazines rises every year in absolute terms but is falling as a proportion of total advertising expenditure.

The newspaper industry varies widely according to each country's social and economic factors. Japan, which is a highly centralized society, has six of the world's top 10 newspapers in terms of circulation, headed by the *Yomiuri Shinbun*. Between them, Japan, China, Russia and South Korea have 14 of the top 20 newspapers rated by sales. Of the remaining six, four are in Europe and only two (*USA Today* and *The Wall Street Journal*) in America. America has few big-selling newspapers because its newspaper industry is primarily city-based and local (as are its TV and radio stations). In total, the world's newspapers have ad revenues of about $130 billion and sales revenues of $60 billion.

The US market for books, magazines and newspapers is worth $126 billion. Books earned $25 billion. Consumer (trade) books earned $17.7 billion in 2005 and are expected to earn $18.5 billion in 2006. Professional and educational publishing, both print and online, earned $15 billion in 2005 (with internal and limited sales publications adding another $15 billion). The professional market is migrating to online publishing leading to a decline in print revenues. Americans spend more on buying books than on any other medium except cable TV. The magazine market is prolific, with 6,325 titles earning $22 billion composed of 55 per cent of advertising revenue ($12 billion) and 45 per cent of sales ($10 billion). The 2,400 daily and Sunday newspapers earned $59 billion consisting of $49 billion advertising and $10 billion sales. Online revenues are around $20 billion.

The British market is worth about £22 billion, and has grown at about 5 per cent a year in the past five years. Of this, print publishing has revenues of £16 billion and electronic information services £6 billion. The (printed) book market is worth £3.2 billion divided between consumer books (£2.4 billion), schools (£236 million) and academic/professional (£593 million) and employs 30,000 people. The number of new and revised titles continues to rise, almost doubling from 104,000 in 1998 to 206,000 in 2005, with the largest growth in school textbooks and travel. Although data is scarce, there are believed to be 50,000 local reading groups which, assuming that each group has about 10 members, means that 500,000 people are getting together on a monthly basis to discuss books. The magazine market is worth about £7 billion of which £5 billion comes from the magazines directly and £2 billion from spin-offs like exhibitions, books, special offers, etc. Newspaper publishing earns £6.5 billion and employs 55,000 people. The publishing market as a whole has about 253,000 jobs, of which 82,000 are writers, journalists and editors.

China's large population and its use of printed media for government and party information means its print media are among the world's largest. It publishes 252,000 books a year, printing over 6 billion copies, although prices are low. Book sales in 2003 totalled RMB 46.1 billion ($5.9 billion). Consumer, business and technology magazines started to take off in the 1990s and numbered over 9,000 by 2005. Revenues come primarily from sales (RMB 13 billion, $1.67 billion) with advertising bringing in only RMB 2.03 billion, $0.26 billion (2004). It has the world's largest newspaper sales, 94 million a day, outselling India's 79 million.

Research and Development

This section describes the scientific and technical R&D activities carried out by companies, universities and research organizations. It does not include academic research on non-scientific and non-technical subjects.

R&D is a patent business. Not all R&D leads to a patent (as we saw with Harry Kroto's discovery of C60), but almost all patents grow out of R&D or need an element of R&D to prepare a successful application. It is also, if secondarily, a copyright business. A researcher's notebooks are critical in telling the story of research; publication in journals no less so. The sector can be measured in several ways: the two most commonly used are expenditure on R&D; and the number of patents granted.

Globally, the leading markets in 2006 were America ($330 billion), China ($136 billion), Japan ($130 billion) and Germany ($53 billion). Other leading countries were France ($35 billion, 2003), Korea ($23 billion, 2003), UK ($21 billion, 2004), Canada ($18 billion), Italy ($17 billion), Australia ($9 billion, 2002), Netherlands ($8 billion, 2002), Austria ($6 billion) and Switzerland ($6 billion, 2000). We have used World Bank data to estimate that other countries (mainly India and Russia) spent about $50 billion in 2005. Of the OECD total, the private sector contributed 70 per cent and government and education the remaining 30 per cent. We put the total at £676 billion.

The world's 1,250 biggest corporate spenders, according to the annual R&D Scorecard published by the UK Department of Trade and Industry, were responsible for 70 per cent of corporate expenditure and 50 per cent of total expenditure. These 1,250 companies spent £249 billion in 2006, an increase of 7 per cent over the previous year. As might be expected, the list is dominated by American companies (which spent £103 billion) followed by the Japanese (£49 billion). Together, these two countries account for more than half the total expenditure. The next biggest market is Germany (£26 billion), followed by France (£14 billion) and Britain (£13 billion). Of the 10 biggest spenders, five are American: Ford Motor Company (£4.7 billion), Pfizer (£4.3 billion), General Motors (£3.9 billion), Microsoft (£3.84 billion) and Johnson & Johnson (£3.68 billion). The remaining six are Daimler/Chrysler, which is half American, (£3.88 billion), Germany's Siemens (£3.54 billion), Japan's Toyota (£3.73 billion), Korea's Samsung (£3.17 billion), and the UK's GlaxoSmithKline (£3.14 billion).

The three main patent offices in America, Japan and Europe (Munich) accounted for 75 per cent of all patents granted worldwide in 2004. They awarded 346,000 patents in the main industrial categories in 2004 (up from 299,000 in 2000). America awarded 165,485 in 2005, Japan awarded 147,000 and the European Patent Office awarded 39,000. The Trilateral Working Group, which consists of these three Offices, says 5.4 million patent registrations were in force in 2004. Patents have to be renewed either annually or every few years throughout their 20-year lifespan, and over 50 per cent of patents are not renewed within this period, so this is a net figure.

The growth in patents comes almost entirely from foreign applicants (i.e. a Briton applying for a patent in America, or an American applying for a British one). Globally, the number of domestic applications has remained steady at about 500,000 a year from 1980 onwards, although there has been a slight increase in American domestic applications.

Table 1: Patents registered by the US Patent Office, by country of applicant (2005)

Country	Number of patents	Percentage of total
1. US	85,238	52%
of which		
California	19,928	
New York	5,631	
Texas	5,660	
Illinois	3,352	
New Jersey	2,978	
2. Japan	34,079	20
3. Germany	10,502	6
4. Taiwan	6,311	4
5. South Korea	4,811	3
6. UK	3,745	2
7. Canada	3,368	2
8. France	3,355	2
9. Italy	1,706	1
10. Sweden	1,270	1
Others	11,100	7
Total	165,485	100

The US spent $330 billion on R&D in 2005. Its main corporate spenders in addition to the companies mentioned above include IBM (£3.1 billion). Although licensing data is often unreliable, it is reckoned that American licensing revenues are worth $200–250 billion a year and that IBM has the largest licensing revenues, averaging about 20 per cent of its profits. What is most remarkable about these licensing figures, as well as the absolute size, is that they have increased 200–300 per cent since 1994.

The company that registered the most patents in 2005, as in the previous year, was IBM Inc with 2,941. It was followed by Canon (1,828), Hewlett-Packard (1,797), Motorola (1,688), Samsung (1,641) and Micron Technology (1,561).

UK expenditure on R&D was £21 billion in 2004; we expect 2005 expenditure to be £22 billion. The main sources of funds were business

Table 2: Patents Registered by the UK Patent Office, by country of applicant (2004)

	Country	Number of patents	Percentage of total
1.	UK	3,780	36
2.	US	2,954	28
3.	Japan	1,101	10
4.	Germany	490	5
5.	South Korea	334	3
6.	Taiwan	291	3
7.	France	161	2
8.	Canada	149	1
9.	Switzerland	68	1
10.	Netherlands	54	1
	Others	1,159	11
	Total	10,541	100

(£9 billion), government departments, including the research councils (£5 billion), higher education (£2 billion), and non-profit organizations (£0.9 billion). A further £3.8 billion came from abroad. Of the total, £18.4 billion was spent on civil research and £2.6 billion on military. The 72 British companies in the global 1,250 list spent £13 billion in 2005, an increase of 8 per cent over the previous year. The drugs companies spent the most, a total of $6.8 billion.

In 2004 the British Patent Office registered 10,541 patents, compared with 9,761 in the previous year.

British expenditure on R&D is low in comparison with other industrial countries, and produces fewer patents. Its expenditure on R&D was 1.8 per cent of GDP in 2004 which is below that of other industrial countries (and a remarkable decline from the 2.4 per cent spent in 1981). These figures are especially dispiriting in the light of the research, quoted above, of the clear benefits of R&D to sales. Not only do British companies spend less but their research is less commercially orientated and produces fewer patents. In the two tables above, Britain scores below the State of Illinois. R without the D.

The Japanese have smaller R&D budgets than the Americans but, year after year, they make more patent applications. In 2004 the Japan

Patent Office granted 122,000 fully fledged patents and 14,00 utility patents, the overwhelming majority to Japanese applicants. This can be attributed to the Japanese liking for formailty and bureaucracy but a major reason is the sheer volume of high class R&D. The JPO estimated Japan's patent-based products to be worth over $1 trillion and its international trade in patent licences to be worth over $70 billion in 2004.

R&D in China in 2006 was RMB 135 billion, which was 1.3 per cent of GDP. It has set a target of 2.5 per cent of GDP by 2010. The number of researchers rose to 926,000. Priorities are energy, information, health and the environment. The State Intellectual Property Office (SIPO) said in 2005 it was listed among the world's top ten for patent applications; according to WIPO, it is the fifth largest. Applications in 2005 were estimated to be 110,000, about half from foreign companies.

Software

The design and writing of computer programs is clearly creative and Tim Berners-Lee, who invented the World Wide Web and Richard Stallman and Linus Torvalds who invented free software and Linux must be counted as some of the most creative people of the late twentieth century. It might make sense to include each kind of software in the relevant category; so the making and selling of software for an industrial process would be included in R&D and computer-aided design (CAD) would be included in design. But the people who work in computers see themselves as a separate industry and so I list them separately here.

They certainly produce intellectual property even if many programmers (hackers) prefer to make their code freely available. As we have seen, computer programs are recognized as a literary work worldwide and America awards patents to a program-and-its-effect. The European Patent Office is inclined to follow suit, in the interests of standardization, but the UK and many other national European patent offices are not convinced.

The global industry is worth $600 billion. The main markets are America and Western Europe which together account for 69 per cent of sales. The next biggest market is Japan with 10 per cent.

The US market is worth $410 billion. Since 2000 it has grown at 12.5 per cent a year, two and half times faster than the economy as a whole. It employs 1.1 million people who are remarkable for having average earnings of $85,000 a year, more than twice the national average of $37,000. US companies dominate the market in the US and worldwide and since 1997, when America began to show a huge trade deficit, the industry has continued to generate annual trade surpluses ranging from $13 to $24 billion.

The UK market is worth £13 billion and has an annual growth rate of 15 per cent. The leisure software sector is worth about £2.2 billion. About 350,000 people work in the industry, of whom more than half work as independent consultants.

China's spending on computer software was $3 billion in 2005 and is expected to reach $4 billion in 2006. Proportionately, China spends less on software (about 10 per cent of the total) than it does on hardware compared to other major economies. Most software is imported. However, the local industry is booming and 500,000 new software-related jobs were reportedly added between 2003 and 2005. According to the Ministry of the Information Industry, China's software and information industry market was worth RMB 390 billion in 2005 and is expected to reach RMB 1,000 billion by 2010.

One of the most dramatic phenomena of the past few years has been the growth of personal websites, blogs and podcasts. By the beginning of 2007 there were estimated to be over 100 million hosted blogs. Another has been the popularity of 'social networks' ranging from open platforms like MySpace (bought by Rupert Murdoch for $580 million in 2005) and YouTube (bought by Google for $1.4 billion in 2006) to more interactive role-playing situations like Second Life. All these depend on software to enable people to make and share words, images and sounds, to create avatars, and to create 'second' lives'.

Toys and Games (excluding video games)

The design, manufacturing and sale of toys and games has been affected by the growth of TV and video games. On the one hand, the new media provide a major source of new products as well as good advertising and merchandising opportunities; on the other hand, children want to spend less time playing with toys and more time in front of the TV or video screen.

A toy or a game qualifies for several kinds of intellectual property. Its name can be trademarked, and its design and artistic elements protected by copyright; for example, the printed design of a board game like *Monopoly*, and the characters of *Pokémon*, are protected as an artistic work. But the rules, even though they might seem to be the heart of the game, cannot be protected. British patent legislation specifically excludes rules for 'playing a game'.

The global market was worth $59 billion in 2005, about three times as much as the more visible video games industry, and it continues to grow.

The US market is worth $22 billion, about 40 per cent of the global market. The UK market is worth £3.2 billion, Europe's biggest, and it has shown 21 per cent growth since 2000.

The Asian market is worth $17 billion, slightly smaller than the European market, and is focussed on simple traditional games. China is a major producer of games, exporting $15 billion in 2005 (an increase of 27 per cent over 2004), and supplying 95 per cent of the toys bought in Europe and the US. It is also a major domestic market, currently about $3 billion but expected to grow to $12.5 billion by 2010.

TV and Radio

In technical terms, broadcasting is a highly specific and straightforward business, consisting of sending sounds and pictures through the air to household receivers. Over the years the means of distribution have changed from VHF to UHF, from analog to digital, from terrestrial to satellite, and expanded into cable, but the technical principle remains the same. It started with radio but TV is now the major form. In terms of content, TV has developed in half a century from a curious technical device to the world's most popular form of entertainment. Its living presence in every home (at least, in the rich countries) make it a powerful and affluent medium with substantial political and social significance.

The competition to create a new programme – even an old programme with a new twist – is formidable. The biggest growth in recent years has been in format shows, especially so-called 'reality' shows (e.g. *Big Brother*) and quiz shows (e.g. *Who Wants to be a Millionaire?*). These have several advantages. They can be produced in large quantities; they often involve audience voting, which brings in extra revenue from telephone calls; and the formats can be copyrighted and exported worldwide. According to Fremantle Media, a leading producer, sales of entertainment formats in 2005 topped $2.5 billion and are growing at 20 per cent a year. China's main trend is towards talent shows and big entertainment shows.

TV's future development depends on (1) increasing the capacity of the transmission networks, including digital and Internet protocol (IPTV) networks, and providing High-Definition TV, (2) interweaving broadcasting's traditional one-to-many services with the Internet's capability for one-to-one interactive services and (3) producing new content that can exploit all media. Most of these developments involve extra costs but are already bringing in substantial new revenues to the winners.

Radio and TV broadcasting started as a technical process and therefore as a patent business. The first broadcasts were live because there was no means of recording (copying) a programmes. It remained a patent business for several decades until first radio and then TV programmes could be recorded in advance for later transmission. Ampex Inc's invention in the 1940s of a recording tape powerful enough to handle moving pictures launched a whole new TV production industry and added a copyright business. All TV programmes count as a 'film' and qualify for copyright; and each broadcast counts as a performance. Recently, the growth of multichannel packages puts more emphasis on branding and marketing. So 'TV' has developed from being only a patent business to being mostly a copyright business and a trademark business.

TV makes up over 90 per cent of the revenues of the global broadcasting industry but radio is a minor success story, illustrating the principle that old media seldom die. American radio had advertising income of $11 billion in 1996 which grew to $20 billion in 2005. In Britain, BBC Radio receives £626 million from the licence fee and commercial radio earns ad revenue of £630 million. The BBC also receives a £200 million government grant to operate its worldwide radio services (the external services).

Global TV revenues are $237 billion, coming from advertising, subscription, viewer licence fees, sponsorship and government grants. Although TV viewing has declined as people spend more time online, revenues have gone up except on some American and European channels where advertising revenues have been weak. There are 1.1 billion TV homes, with the biggest markets being China (350 million in 2005), America (110 million), India (91 million), Russia (65 million) and Japan (48 million). Britain had 25.1 million TV homes in 2005 and is expected to have 25.3 million in 2006. In revenue terms, the biggest markets are America ($85 billion) and Japan ($20 billion).

The US TV market is worth $85 billion. Advertising revenue (spot advertising) for the four main networks and the 1,749 local stations totalled $36 billion in 2005. The networks lost audience share for decades until the 2003 season but their advertising revenues continue to increase as advertisers have to buy more spots in order to reach the same number of people. This oddity – that in a constant market, where supply is fixed, lower ratings may lead to higher revenues – is common in the broadcasting business. The cable-and-satellite channel operators earned $29 billion in 2005.

The British TV market is worth £10.5 billion, consisting of advertising (£4.1 billion), the household licence fee (£3 billion) and subscriptions for cable and satellite programming (£3.4 billion). About 95,000 people work in TV production and broadcasting (and about 3,000 in radio). Many are self-employed; nearly half the people working in ITV, the leading commercial network are self-employed.

According to China's State Administration for Radio, Film and Television (SARFT), national TV revenues were about RMB 45 billion in 2005 of which advertising brought in RMB 22 billion, subscriptions and carriage fees RMB 18 billion, and government grants the remainder. Employment numbered 581,000 (2004). CCTV's revenue in 2005 were RMB 12.4 billion, of which advertising provided about RMB 9 billion.

Video Games

The video games industry consists of three sectors: console-based games with proprietary consoles and software; CD and DVD games that can be played on any computer; and online games. As the consoles become more sophisticated, with faster processors and Internet connectivity, so the PC-only sector has declined. Overall, the market is extremely volatile, and heavily dependent on new consoles often given as presents at Christmas. America's Atari was the first major producer but was soon trumped by Nintendo, a Japanese manufacturer of playing cards, which launched Game Boy in 1989 and became Japan's third most profitable company. In 1993 its 890 employees made more profit than did the 150,000 people then working for Hitachi, the world's biggest consumer electronics manufacturer. In turn Nintendo was outplayed by Sega's Saturn and then by Sony's PlayStation (PS). PS1 sold 102 million consoles, and many hundreds of millions of games, and had over 70 per cent of the world's games market. By 2000, revenues from PS1 consoles and games brought in 25 per cent of Sony's income and 38 per cent of its profits. Sony launched PlayStation2 in 2000 and sold 100 million units and PS3 in 2006. Currently, the industry is dominated by the continued attractions of Sony and its PS series, the re-emergence of Nintendo with its Wii and Microsoft's marketing efforts behind the Xbox 360. The major games developers continue to be American, Korean and Japanese.

One of the most successful game authors is Shigeru Miyamoto who designed Nintendo's *Super Mario* and *Donkey Kong* (with worldwide revenues in excess of $5.5 billion). The US and UK each design about one third of new games. Video games routinely cost as much to develop and write as a major movie (although production costs average one-tenth as much). A successful game can match revenues with a top-grossing film, especially in Japan where *Final Fantasy VIII* sold 3.2 million copies and grossed about $150 million in its first three weeks.

Video games, like films, generally consist of several copyright works; for example, literary, artistic and dramatic works, as well as works categorized as films. In Europe, the data set may also qualify as a database and be protected by the EU law on copyright in databases. This complexity, and the constantly changing technology, often results in difficult and time-consuming rights negotiation. Games like Nintendo's *Pokémon*, which started as a video game and then extended into TV, merchandise and cards (exploiting Nintendo's origins as a playing-card manufacturer) depend increasingly on trademarks.

Global turnover in video games is about $21 billion, to which consoles add $3 billion (I exclude consoles from the creative economy for the same reason as I exclude TV sets and audio equipment). The major markets are America (35 per cent), Japan (15 per cent and UK (12 per cent). The market for games grew at an average of 11 per cent a year in 2004–5 and is expected to grow at 15 per cent through to 2009. The Japanese are fanatical game players and their country dominates video games as much as America dominates feature films.

The US market for games was worth $7 billion in 2005 (and $3.5 billion for consoles). The new generation of games is not just for children. The Entertainment Software Alliance says 69 per cent of American heads of households play video games and the average age of a game player is 33 years old. Electronic Arts Inc, the world's largest video games publisher, had gross revenues of $3.1 billion in 2005. The main long-term trends are an increase in console games, a decline in PC games and an increase in online gaming. PWC predict wireless games will increase from $646 million in 2006 to $2.3 billion in 2010.

The UK market for games is worth £2 billion, up from £200 million in 1990, representing about 56–58 million games sold each year. Sony says it has sold 15 million PlayStation consoles in the UK, which implies that one on every 2 homes has one (and some probably have two). The British industry often claims to be more successful in video games than in TV or films but they only account for 16 per cent of games worldwide (UKTI) because many designers, like many British film-makers, fail to make enough money to sustain their independence. It is tempting to sell out to America: Richard Branson sold Virgin Interactive to America's Viacom Inc and Bullfrog went to Electronic Arts Inc. The industry employs about 15–20,000 people but is notably fragmented and has few major players.

In China, online games are much more popular than console or PC games, making up 80 per cent of the market. Chinese operators dominate the market, providing games under licence from Korea, America and Japan. The market is dominated by two companies, Shanda (whose founder Chen Tianqiao became one of China's richest men) and 9th City, whose most popular game is the Korean *World of Warcraft* which has an average of 600,000 online players at any one time, paying 45 cents an hour (WOW's global user base totals 8 million). WOW has a total of 6 million regular users and 30 million registered users. 9th City's 2005 revenues were RMB 465 million and are expected to be $900 million in 2006.

SUMMARY

The table below gives the size of the creative economy at the beginning of the twenty-first century.

Table 3: The Creative Economy - Market Size (2005, in $ bn)

Sector	**Global**	**US**	**UK**	**China**
Advertising	55	22	16	1
Architecture	45	25	7	1
Art	11	5	4	. . .
Crafts	30	3	2	1
Design	140	49	23	4
Fashion	16	5	2	0.4
Film	81	28	8	0.3
Music	80	27	10	0.2
Performing Arts	50	13	3	0.5
Publishing	605	126	44	10
R&D	676	330	42	17
Software	600	410	26	3
Toys and Games	59	22	6	3
TV/Radio	237	85	21	5
Video Games	21	7	4	5
Total	2709	1157	218	51

. . .under $0.2 billion

These industries and markets represent the core processing of and sale of creative ideas and works, covering the economic activities of commercial, professional, subsidised and amateur work.

TOWARDS 2020

In 2005 the creative economy was worth about $2.7 trillion, which is 6.1 per cent of the global economy. In the past three years, some industries have had mixed fortunes, such as music and design, while some have grown rapidly, such as architecture, art and R&D. Future growth will depend on the rates of increase in supply (as more people create more works) and in demand (as more people move up the hierarchy of desires). Some industries will grow faster than others, with the fastest growth coming in businesses where more people are creative or where technology enables each product to attract more revenues. The reason the music industry has had a difficult few years is that companies have not yet developed a new business model for the Internet. In other words, then as now, the size of the creative economy depends as much on how products are managed and distributed as on what is produced. This is the subject of the next chapter.

4

MANAGING CREATIVITY

LAW 4: CREATIVITY IS A PROPER JOB

'Everyone must begin to trust their dreams because out of that trust is born the artist, and the artist is the role model for the entrepreneur we now need.'

Ernest Hall, entrepreneur and musician

BOB GELDOF

Bob Geldof, leader of the Boomtown Rats, founder of Live Aid and Internet entrepreneur, may seem a surprising example of a manager, but he epitomizes Ernest Hall's artist-as-entrepreneur in the quotation above. He works alone, armed with a telephone. He told me, 'I have four or five offices that I can use, including my manager's, my record company's, Planet 24's (his TV company, since sold) and deckchair. com's, but I never go to them. I don't have a PA or a secretary. If you have staff, you start to think about them and you get interested in their ideas, and you lose the freedom to think and write.' I have chosen him in preference to someone more conventional because he does, manifestly, succeed in being creative, making creative products and getting things done. He doesn't wait to be told what to do. He takes charge of his own talent.

He is a big, tall, rangy man. When at home, he wanders around with his guitar in his hand, breaking off to make telephone calls. He has the restless energy of someone who gets bored easily. When I wrote asking to meet him I was warned by friends I might hear nothing; and I didn't; until, four months later, he left me a message, simply saying, 'Let's meet.' One of his colleagues, Waheed Alli, now Lord Alli, insisted

Geldof get a fax machine and when he refused Alli slipped into the flat and installed one. Geldof was unimpressed: 'I beat him by letting the paper run out and not replacing it.' He doesn't have an answering machine and he doesn't use e-mail.

I told him I have a feeling that he's a man who is very protective of his own heart and soul. He replied, 'I don't know about that, but I won't do things that are alien to me. It wouldn't wash with me or with other people, especially people who know me.' When I say that he does manage to do a great number of things, much more than almost any other pop star, Geldof says first that, yes, but it is very tiring and then he says, 'If my mind is not irritated and distracted all the time, not active all the time, I get depressed and bored: not acute depression like Winston Churchill's "black dog" when you can't get off the sofa, you can't face the day, but a depression which seems endless and debilitating.'

I ask if he can write songs when he is depressed. 'Perversely, it's the best time. Depression is a state of tiredness where the fore-conscious clashes constantly with the subconscious. It is at this woozy moment, that unconnected or seemingly unconnected moment, when you leap across the synapses.' But sometimes he can't write at all. When I met him he had not been able to write songs for about four years because of being separated from his wife, Paula Yates. He wrote hundreds of poems – 'I literally could not stop' – but no songs. 'Songs are a different process. Songs didn't enter into it at all.' The final 'at all' was spat out, vehemently.

He had the idea for Band Aid when he witnessed the terrible hunger in Africa and saw the need to do something. The first Band Aid record in 1984 raised £8 million, the two Live Aid concerts in 1985 raised £50 million and Sport Aid in 1996 raised another £50 million. At one time Band Aid had 600 trucks and 12 ships. Turning an idea into a business, an operation, requires both the original idea ('something from nothing') and the hard work to make it happen. He says everything boils down to two questions: 'Why?' and 'Why not?'

Boredom and imagination are a strong cocktail. One evening he was in Warsaw with the Boomtown Rats and discovered that the city had no nightlife for young people. He researched the demographics, saw the need for a club, and helped to found the Atomic Club (so called because it rented a disused nuclear bomb shelter). I am reminded of Terence Conran's remarks about knowing history, understanding what is happening and seeing a gap in the market. He invested in deckchair.com, a travel website, when he became frustrated with traditional travel agents. He says his life is a combination of 'impatience and discipline'. Ideas come from irascibility and invention.

'I find business – it's a cliché – absolutely as creative as anything. Business creates ideas. Around something as dry as a boardroom meeting there can be a confluence of ideas that creates and promotes more ideas.' Business is as creative as songwriting but not as personal. The idea for a business might be personal but the business plan is not. When Geldof writes a song, the work and performance always remain his, but his business ideas become impersonal, open to the market.

Geldof gets the greatest satisfaction from a 'song that *works*'. He is an entrepreneur of his own talent. He is not a straightforward entrepreneur, nor a straightforward songwriter-performer. Perhaps 'straightforwardness' is an inappropriate term for either role. He is so obviously not a model in any normal sense. But when it comes to managing himself, his songs, his band, Band Aid, Live Aid and Internet start-ups, he does all right.

THE ECONOMICS OF THE IMAGINATION

This chapter is about how to manage an idea and how to make a profit. There are people on both sides of the creative/management coin who believe 'creativity' and 'management' are incompatible, and creativity and economics mutually destructive. One of the tasks of management is to manage this tension; to make people more creative, not less.

Managing creativity starts with understanding the economics of creativity. It has to deal with two intertwined value systems. One is based on the physical products, the devices, carriers and platforms, that are tangible and behave much like any other physical material. The other is based on intellectual property, which is intangible and has some rather odd characteristics, as we have seen. Mainstream economics is well able to explain the former since they are similar to conventional manufactured goods and services. But it is hard pressed to explain the latter. For example, it can explain the manufacturing of a book in terms of the physical good but it is less adept at explaining the words and pictures inside. It is expert in the process of manufacturing a medical pill but not so good at the patent on which the value of the pill depends.

This is because ideas are 'non-rivalrous' in that I can have an idea and whether one or a million people also have it does not affect my having of it. In contrast, if I own or rent a space, nobody else can own or rent the same space; if I use some equipment, nobody else can use it. Whether an idea's non-rivalrous nature is a good thing or a bad thing, whether it enhances or destroys its economic value, depends on the management.

This non-rivalrous nature encourages 'free-riding', which means benefiting from another person's ideas without paying. People use free-riding to enhance their own knowledge and skills. Patent laws deliberately require 'disclosure' in order to ensure ideas are non-rivalrous and to encourage free-riding. From a supplier's viewpoint, the inevitability of free-riding shortens technological and product life cycles. Being first to market is a major advantage but an innovator has only a short time to establish a new product before others begin to compete. Some companies make a virtue out of necessity and under-price or give away their products, knowing that competitors will be able to move in quickly. Both these attributes apply to ideas in all industries, but their effect is multiplied when the idea is the product.

When an intangible idea is embodied in a tangible product, it becomes highly rivalrous. We can share the same song, but we cannot share the same copy. The whole point of copyright and patents is to restrict access, either absolutely or for a price. In order for some people to benefit, others must go without. Economists fiercely debate the social utility of this exchange. Some say that any constraint on ideas hampers creativity, drags down economic development, and is a misallocation of resources. Others say that some kind of monopoly is necessary to reward innovation and that monopolies are a good means of allocating resources.

Another economic characteristic of ideas is that the cost of copying or replicating an idea is often negligible. Almost all the requisite knowledge, skills, competencies and other intellectual inputs are required at the thinking, research and development stages. Once fixed, or made, the cost of copying the product is insignificant.

Managing creativity involves knowing, first, when to exploit the non-rivalrous nature of ideas and, second, when to assert intellectual property rights and make one's own ideas-as-products rivalrous. These two decision points are the crux of the management process.

The economics of creativity consequently differs from conventional economics in the central role of the individual. From the days of Adam Smith, conventional economics has been centred around the firm, in the belief that firms are more efficient than individuals in identifying and using resources. Smith's 'division of labour' is greatly facilitated if everyone involved is working for the same firm. When economist Ronald Coase showed in the 1930s that firms have lower transactional costs than individuals, the central role of the firm seemed permanently assured. But creative people, as they puzzle over their imaginations, are not dependent upon organizations to the same extent. They do not need large resources of capital and equipment. They often have low transaction costs.

They are also irrational. For a period, notably from the 1940s to the 1980s, economic theorists assumed individuals acted in a rational manner to maximize their personal utility and satisfaction (otherwise they would be acting against their own best interests), and also assumed firms acted rationally in response to market information to maximize their profits (otherwise shareholders become upset, and probably employees too). But the creative individual is not only free to be irrational but may move more swiftly and generate more value (greater novelty, more inventive steps) that way. Richard Thaler of the University of Chicago, who has studied the psychology and economics of decision-making, and brought irrationality back into mainstream economic thinking, has said that it is 'rational to include the irrational'. Perhaps a better word than 'irrational' is 'subjective' or 'imaginative'. *Everyman's Dictionary of Economics* describes a firm as an 'island of conscious power'. It is a powerful image, and applies even more so to an individual and the use of the creative imagination.

The nature of ideas changes the nature of competition. Whereas conventional goods of similar nature compete on cost or price, creative products seldom do so. Peter Drucker, one of the most insightful writers on modern management, has pointed out that if he wants to listen to music, say Tchaikovsky's Violin Concerto in D Major, he has three options: playing a CD, going to a concert or listening to a radio. The three products compete with each other but not in conventional economic terms. The first option requires capital expenditure on a CD player and a small amount of cash expenditure on a CD; the second requires no capital expenditure but a (larger) cash cost; and the third requires capital but no cash. The cost of each experience is not related to the quantity of production and, once produced, the experiences do not compete on price. The price of a ticket seldom reflects the cost of the production (in some industries, like pharmaceuticals and films, prices bear very little resemblance to costs). As Peter Drucker says succinctly, mainstream economics 'cannot handle that'.

It is also worth noting that these three experiences do not fit the conventional categories of goods and services. The CD is a good (the CD itself) based on a recording (a service) of a performance (another service). The live performance is a service. And the broadcast is a service based either on another service (if it is a live broadcast) or a good (if it is a CD). This flagrant disregard for the normal categories is troublesome not only to economists but to government treasuries and trade officials, who apply different tax rules to goods and services; at least, they try to.

It follows that the law of diminishing returns, first formulated by David Ricardo in the 1810s and a bulwark of modern economic theory, hardly applies. This law states that each additional input factor of production (typically, physical resources and labour) becomes harder or more expensive to acquire and that therefore at some point the cost of producing one more unit exceeds the revenue obtained from selling it. The point at which marginal cost meets marginal revenue is called the equilibrium point. This makes sense in a world of limited resources and price competition. But in an economy based on intangible and often unlimited resources the costs of production are less important.

If we combine these characteristics, we can sketch the following picture. Companies in the ordinary economy operate with scarce material resources, over which they assert permanent property rights, and compete primarily on price. In the creative economy, individuals and firms use resources which are infinite, over which they assert intellectual rights, which may be short-run, and which do not compete primarily on price. We have moved from a world of diminishing returns, based on the scarcity of physical objects, to a world of increasing returns based on the infinity of possible ideas and people's genius for using those ideas to generate new products and transactions. A company's control of product and price become less relevant if production resources are freely available, if products are intangible, if price competition is negligible, and if the market is driven by demand not by supply. In the knowledge economy, says Joseph Stiglitz, former chief economist of the World Bank, firms either charge prices well in excess of marginal costs, or they give their products away for free.

It appears as if what Thomas Carlyle called the 'dismal science' (after hearing one of David Ricardo's lectures), while fully capable of explaining our economic behaviour towards physical, material products, is less well able to predict the economics of the business of thinking and of creative products.

Put it this way. The economy of ideas has the same relationship to the ordinary economy, in which companies shuffle around solid goods, as Albert Einstein's Theory of Relativity does to Isaac Newton's Law of Gravity. Today's scientists know that the simpler Newtonian Law explains almost everything; the level of error is infinitesimally small and usually irrelevant. Apples still fall down. But they also know that Newton's Law does not completely describe the way things really are.

CREATIVE MANAGEMENT PRINCIPLES

Given these economics, I will now describe ten management principles or levers that affect the creativity process:

- creative people
- the job of thinker
- the creative entrepreneur
- the post-employment job
- the just-in-time person
- the temporary company
- the network office and the business cluster
- teamwork
- finance
- deals and hits

Creative People

When Igor Stravinsky was writing *The Rite of Spring* in 1911, he was living in a small room in a house in Clarens, Switzerland. Robert Craft has recounted how the landlady received complaints from the other tenants that he was playing the 'wrong' notes. Stravinsky, unamused, later retorted, 'They were the wrong notes for them but they were the right notes for me.' Creative people start from within themselves and must be true to themselves; their chief task is to manage their own intellectual assets. They must be persistent, even when the public (or their fellow-tenants) do not recognize their talent. As a result they often become deeply, passionately involved in their work, whether they are full-time or part-time, paid or unpaid. They transfer life from their minds to their work; their job is to believe and to imagine. They acquire a sixth sense for what 'works' in their medium or field; for what they *want* to work.

For these people, betting their creative imagination against the world may appear a more secure proposition, and certainly more fun, than becoming a little cog in a big organization or another bit in the information society. Their ambition to be singularly successful can make them more interested in their project's mission than in the management structures and finance needed to get them there. As a result, they often prefer to work alone or for a leader who is similarly visionary. This quality of 'mission ruthlessness' can make them difficult partners.

It is often asked whether creative people are born or made. Some say they never considered doing anything else, like Terence Conran, who started making furniture at school and is still making it. Others, like Richard Rogers, do not realize their vocation until quite late. Creative people never seem very interested in the question. In truth, it is the wrong question. The right question is whether the person was born to take charge, to be chairman of their own intellectual assets.

The individual who takes charge is the starting point for the management of creativity. All individuals who want to be creative, whether they work alone or with a large organization, must take control.

The Job of Thinker

At the back of the St James Hotel near Buckingham Palace is a secret courtyard surrounded by glossy apartments. One windy night an Ethiopian businessman called Noah Samara led me and four others up in the lift to the top floor, then up some stairs to the roof, then up to the highest point of the roof where we stood precariously looking at a point in the sky some 22,000 miles away. We were not New Age romantics; next to me stood a man who had commanded British troops in Bosnia. We had come to witness a new kind of radio set which Noah was carrying under his arm like his own baby (which it was). He placed the set on the parapet, twiddled the dial and suddenly the sound of a Johannesburg radio station came clear over the rooftops. Noah is the proud owner of the world's first satellite system for broadcasting digital radio signals. He had the idea for what became WorldSpace Corporation when he read a newspaper report in the *Washington Post* about the difficulty of distributing information about AIDS to rural Africa. Ten years later, we stood and listened to a fully functioning global satellite system representing an investment of over $100 million.

Six months later I sat in a drawing room in Kensington listening to novelist Vikram Seth, the author of *A Suitable Boy*, tell a story about a walk across Hyde Park. He and his companion had noticed a man who was standing near the Serpentine Lake contemplating, as if listening. Seth suddenly had the idea that the man was somehow important for his next as-yet-unthought-of novel. He wondered what his occupation might be. His friend, who is a musician, said, 'Musician.' I wonder what instrument, said Seth. 'Oh, a violin,' came the reply, for that was the musician's own. Seth demurred because he preferred the viola but his friend pointed out that violas were heavier things which might hamper a character's movements and complicate the plot, and so he realized that violinist was correct. A dedication at the front of the book says, 'Had our words turned to other things / In the grey park, the rain abated, / Life would have quickened other strings.' The result is the idea, the sparks-spawn, of the magnificent *An Equal Music*; although the word 'result' does not do justice to the process or the product.

These small stories of how people 'have an idea' show three things.

The two 'commencement' incidents, reading a newspaper and walking in the park, are trivial and ordinary. Millions of us do these things, every day. The nature of the incidents and the outcomes is pure happenstance. If Noah Samara had not read the article about AIDS in one newspaper he might have read about it in another and WorldSpace would still have been born. Or might he have read a newspaper article about something else and now be chairman of something completely different? What would have happened if Vikram Seth had not crossed the park that night? Or if the man had not been there? What 'other things' might have occurred?

Third, and most important, both men used these incidents as the springboard of a new idea and a new work. The incident itself is not the point. The point is what we do with it. A newspaper article is enough. A walk in the park is enough.

The job of thinker involves all the elements within the RIDER process described in Chapter 1. It is not just being a thinker in the sense of pondering. It requires the use, the management, of every kind of thought process.

It isn't easy, and it may look odd. The American essayist and poet Ralph Waldo Emerson wrote in his journal with a certain resignation, 'If a man sits down to think he is immediately asked if he has the headache.' A group of managers was once asked what they would do if they had their feet on the desk and the boss walked by. Everyone said they would take their feet off the desk. The questioner then asked: 'Does your boss like you to think?' to which the answer was, 'Sure.' 'Does he put a high value on you being original and thoughtful?'; 'Sure.' 'Do you sometimes think best by being relaxed – maybe staring into space, maybe staring out the window – maybe putting your feet on the desk?'; 'Sure.' Finally: 'So having your feet on the table may be a sign you are working at thinking?' 'No.'

It does not matter where you are or how you do it. A BT/*Management Today* survey asked managers, 'Where do you have your best ideas?' What it called 'office work' generated a meagre 15 per cent of good ideas. The more productive occasions were 'at home' (17.8 per cent), 'while commuting' (17.1 per cent) and 'during leisure activities' (16.9 per cent). Even 'in the bath/shower' scored 11.7 per cent.

Note the job is 'thinker' not 'thinking'. We all think, from time to time. But the job of thinker is a full-time job, as serious and dedicated as any job can be, and doing it means accepting the responsibility that goes with the job. Jeff Bezos gave himself the job of thinker in the early 1990s when as a computer expert he wanted to exploit the Internet's capacity to sell things, and looked around for the easiest products to sell. He had no experience of the book business but he thought the book industry's large output, so much bigger and more diverse than any other consumer good, made it the ideal candidate, and in 1995 he opened Amazon.com. When, three years later, he set up Amazon.co.uk in Britain he was determined to keep the same attitude and hired a number of young, bright graduates who knew little of bookselling but who knew how to think. The existing booksellers had put thinking too low down their list of priorities. For them, thinking wasn't a proper job. Some other people may have thought as Jeff Bezos did, but idly, which is useless. Thinking is a proper job.

The Creative Entrepreneur

One of the businessmen I most admire is Nolan Bushnell, founder of Atari, which developed the first mass-market video game. Atari was astonishingly successful, producing profits of $300 million within a few years and becoming the fastest growing company in American corporate history, although later it flopped with equally spectacular losses. Bushnell tells how

A guy wakes up in the morning and says, 'I'm going to become an entrepreneur.' So he goes to the best software programmer in the company where he is working and whispers, 'Would you like to join my company? Ten o'clock my place. And bring some doughnuts.' Then he goes to the best finance guy and says, 'Bring some coffee.' And then he goes to the best patent lawyer and the best marketing guy with the same invitation. Ten o'clock Saturday rolls around.

They ask, 'Hey, what is your company going to do?' You say, 'Build a new computer program.'

Another hour, and you've all got an idea and a business plan. The finance guy says he knows where he can get some money [whenever I tell the story the Americans look bored at this point and the British look wistful]. Then they say to their host, so what have you done?

What, indeed? You've not provided the coffee. You've not provided the doughnuts. You've not provided the idea. You've been the entrepreneur. You made it happen.

The French economist and journalist, Jean-Baptiste Say, who lived at the time of the French Revolution, invented the term 'entrepreneur' to describe someone who unlocks capital tied up in land and redirects it to 'change the future'. He was one of the first economists to introduce the idea of change and uncertainty as something normal and even positive. Whereas Adam Smith, David Ricardo and others wanted to improve the efficiency of existing manufacturing processes by identifying the point at which demand, supply and price were in stable equilibrium, Say wanted to start new ventures. He was interested in the moments of disequilibrium and risk. The Austrian economist, Joseph Schumpeter, writing in the first half of the twentieth century, said the entrepreneur exploits innovation to create a monopoly (or tries to), which is then challenged by another entrepreneur, who creates a new monopoly, and so on. In the words of economist Andrew Shonfield, who wrote *Modern Capitalism*, Schumpeter 'believed the nature of traditional capitalism to be violent, to move forward by fits and starts, and that the reason for its uneven progress lies in the discontinuous process of innovation'. Compared with Adam Smith's search for the more efficient use of existing resources, Say wanted to see how an investment in one resource could be taken and reused to exploit a completely different resource. It was an early version of what economists describe as 'unlocking value'.

Entrepreneurs in the creative economy (often called 'creative entrepreneurs') operate like Say's original model entrepreneur but with an important difference that demonstrates how far we have moved in the intervening years. They use creativity to unlock the wealth that lies within themselves. Like true capitalists, they believe that this creative wealth, if managed right, will engender more wealth. Workers in a traditional factory may have better ideas about how to run their factory than do the existing managers, but the workers can never put their ideas into practice. They have no access to financial capital and their own intellectual capital is unlikely to be sufficient. Outside communism, where they have access to state or public resources, the workers in a steel mill have never started their own steel mill. The steel economy does not permit it. But creative workers can start their own business tomorrow. The creative economy *encourages* it.

These entrepreneurs share five characteristics:

• **vision** The entrepreneur has a dream, and wants to bring the dream to life. The beginning is really as simple as that.

• **focus** They are determined, dogged, and fixated. Austrian-born but Cambridge-resident Hermann Hauser, who is one of Britain's most successful venture capitalists, says entrepreneurs must focus on only one thing. He says he distrusts anyone who says their company can do two things or even one-and-a-half things. Jeff Bezos would agree: 'It's very hard to do even one thing in a truly excellent way. Doing two things in a truly excellent way can get very tricky.' World chess champion Gary Kasparov says the difference between a good chess player and a great chess player is not really that the great chess player knows which moves to look at but that he also knows which *not* to look at.

• **financial acumen** Some entrepreneurs are inseparable from their spreadsheets while others make do with any scrap of paper. The means do not matter; what does is the focus on the single objective of building a business. Entrepreneurs need not be financially first-rate so long as they realize that their success will be measured purely in financial terms; the rest is shadows. Financial skills assist one to avoid pitfalls, move faster and sleep at night.

• **pride** Trevor Bayliss, inventor of the clockwork radio, says, 'You need an ego the size of a truck to be an inventor.' Entrepreneurs believe not only that their particular idea will work but that they are the only one who can make it work. They treat their proposal as the centre of the universe; for them, it is. They have pride in themselves and their idea and they are very reluctant to give up. This pride is seldom dented by failure; many serial entrepreneurs regard their start-ups, whether successful or not, as campaign medals.

• **urgency** All the vision, focus and pride comes to nothing if the entrepreneur is not in a hurry. The entrepreneur always wants to 'do it now', partly for competitive reasons and partly because they cannot be bothered to think of anything else. Many start-ups in the creative economy are 'momentum' businesses, gathering attention and assets like a snowball.

Entrepreneur Tony Elliott got together with three friends ('Ten o'clock my place') and £70 to start the London listings magazine *Time Out*. Since then, living off cash flow and refusing successive offers from much bigger companies to give him money in return for some of the equity, he sits atop a company that, measured by conventional methods, is worth about £50 million, but if the value of the company's trademark and copyrights, and the staff's intellectual capital, are taken into account, considerably more than that. Elliott was able to launch *Time Out* in New York because he could use this intellectual capital as leverage. More recently, when Simon Needham and James Somerville started their design company in Somerville's grandmother's attic, they had £300 of their own money and a £1,000 loan from the Prince's Trust. They grew the business entirely from cash and now Attik has offices in London, New York, San Francisco and Sydney, and revenues of £15 million. Again, the company's growth and current value is dependent entirely upon its intellectual assets.

Entrepreneurs mainly work on their own or in small groups. As such they have distinct advantages over large organizations: they have fewer commitments, and the instinct and freedom to respond rapidly to new ideas and changes in the market. The Digital Media Alliance in London describes them as having 'an easy ability to group and regroup talent, fast decision-making and hot-house conditions for distilling creative ideas'. Sometimes their size makes them vulnerable. They live on the edge financially, they lack corporate resources and stability, and they lack strategic negotiating power. And although they can take decisions quickly, equally they can go for months talking and talking and not taking any decisions at all.

Towards the end of his life, in the 1940s, Joseph Schumpeter said that the entrepreneur was becoming just another 'office worker – and one who is not always difficult to replace'. I am not sure entrepreneurs are now so common. But his forecast that the entrepreneurial function might become 'routinized' was far-sighted.

The Post-Employment Job

Not everyone wants to be an entrepreneur, but many people gain pleasure from pursuing their own ideas and being independent, and it is fair to say that creativity flourishes most freely where this is possible. The opportunities for being independent have grown as the nature of the economic process has changed, rewarding different kinds of work and management. Say saw the opportunities for taking capital tied up in land and investing it in commerce. Schumpeter saw the opportunities for technology to give the entrepreneur a competitive advantage in manufacturing industry and commerce. In the early twentieth century Americans identified the organization and general management as the core economic function. Daniel Bell and others saw information as a powerful lever of management change, bringing about a new 'post-industrial' society. Peter Drucker invented the term 'knowledge worker'. These concepts come together in a new triangle of work: the Job of Thinker, the Creative Entrepreneur and the Post-employment Job.

In the late 1700s, when Say was writing, about one third of the workforce in England, Spain, Germany and Italy was unemployed in today's sense of the word (not working for someone else, usually for cash) or employed on a part-time or irregular basis. Most people worked as and when they could, dependent upon land tenure, social obligation, patronage and opportunism. Towards the end of the century, the Industrial Revolution called into being, for the first time, a mass workforce which, although initially hired on grounds of physical strength or agility, was later contracted on other kinds of personal merit and skill. Industrial output and commerce grew. Full employment, by which I mean full-time, permanent employment, became the norm. For 250 years Europe has experienced a unique 'age of employment' in which, with some exceptions, most men and recently a substantial number of women are employed with full-time jobs and if unemployed can confidently expect to find another such job soon.

It is now accepted that this era of full employment is coming to an end. It is still the dominant mode overall but other ways of working, such as permanent freelance work, portfolio part-time work and the one-person company have emerged as viable alternatives. In several creative industries, these alternatives, many quite informal, are how the majority manage their work. Britain's workforce amounted to 71 per cent of the total population in 1975 and has remained around this level ever since. The Employment Unit at Warwick University estimates that in 1999 only 60 per cent of this workforce was in full employment. The remaining 40 per cent were either employed part-time (22 per cent), self-employed (12 per cent) or unemployed (8 per cent). This 60:40 split is expected to become 50:50 by 2015–20. Most new jobs do not offer full employment. According to the Office of National Statistics, of the 750,000 new jobs created between 1992 and 1996 less than one third provided permanent full-time employment. The actual proportion varied each year from a low of 9 per cent to a more common high of 40 per cent. Since the 1970s, most of this full employment has been provided by or within the public sector. A report by Morgan Stanley Dean Witter in 2000 showed that the public sector continues to be the main provider of these full-time jobs. The private sector, wherein lies the bulk of the creative economy, and virtually all its growth, prefers short-term, part-time jobs.

There are interesting differences between Europe and the rest of the industrial world. Europe now suffers from the lowest levels of employment of the three largest global regions, and the trend is downwards. Thirty years ago, the differences were marginal. In 1975, 64 per cent of Europe's working population between the ages of 15 and 64 had jobs, compared to 63 per cent in America and 68 per cent in Japan. By 1998 the figures had become startlingly different. Europe's working population had drifted downwards to 62 per cent while America's had climbed to 75 per cent and Japan's to 74 per cent. Again, the bulk of Europe's new full-time jobs had come from government and the public sector; the private sector saw an overall decline in spite of growth in the service industries. The data on unemployment are complementary: 10 per cent in Europe but only 4 per cent in America and Japan.

Britain's high numbers of self-employed people compared to America and other European countries is often regarded as a welcome indication of the growing number of individuals starting their own business, which it is. But the same figures also reveal how few of these entrepreneurs have moved up the business scale to start a company and employ other people; at which point, the self-employed person becomes an employer. The high level of self-employed people in Britain may be as much a reflection of the tax structure as a desire to start a business. It is notable that America has the highest numbers of new company start-ups in the OECD. It also has the lowest proportion of self-employed people, and the number is falling. We might reasonably expect the opposite to be true; in other words, for America, land of the entrepreneur, to have more self-employed people than anywhere else. But many Americans prefer to start their own company, if they can, than to be the hired hand of someone else or to work on their own.

This decrease in full employment and the matching increases in independent or freelance jobs do not fit easily into most national arrangements for tax and social security. Government tax systems are locked into concepts of jobs-as-employment, not jobs-as-things-to-be-done. Officials often have difficulties in understanding the spirit and circumstances of independent work. The large pool of independent, self-employed and freelance people typically earn income from a range of different sources, some of which relate to the current year and some to jobs done years ago. Many work in a combination of paid or unpaid, full-time or part-time, permanent or temporary jobs. As more people move between a portfolio of projects, as they move from working to not working and back to working again, and from employment to self-employment, the tax and social security rules begin to creak. Government policies that try to create work and wealth solely by creating conventional employment are aiming at too narrow a target.

Unsurprisingly, since it was mass industrialization that stimulated the growth of permanent full-time employment, so its relative decline has caused employment to diminish. The shift has political, social and economic implications on a global scale. Applying the rule of comparative advantage, which suggests countries should specialize in what they are best at, the main OECD countries have concentrated on their service and creative industries and, if manufacturing was necessary, employed low-cost countries in Asia and elsewhere. Throughout the OECD, information technology and the 'knowledge' economy led ineluctably to the emergence of post-industrial work.

The sudden increase in the speed and power of microprocessor calculating power from the 1970s onwards, and the emergence of

Bell's post-industrial society and then the information society, led to claims that machines would replace men and women, and raised the spectre of severe unemployment. The first prediction proved right but the second was wrong. Machines did indeed replace many people for many routine tasks and made a certain kind of job redundant but, far from leading to a net loss of work, generated a whole new range of business opportunities.

The gap was filled by thinkers and creative entrepreneurs who used their own inner talents. Their way of work, often freelance, and independent, proved as capable of generating jobs, sustaining business relationships and creating wealth. The post-industrial society needs the post-employment job.

The Just-In-Time Person

The reliance on individual knowledge and creative talent, and the specific job requirements of many creative industries, result in a high demand for people who are available at a moment's notice. Many copyright industries cannot function without a large pool of people who, according to the conventional model, are unemployed and 'out of work'.

The ordinary economy uses the term 'just-in-time' to describe a logistics system that saves money by maintaining very low levels of stock and obtains an item only if and when a customer wants it; in other words, 'just-in-time'. I use the same term to describe people who are hired only when and where they are wanted. These people have two assets: their specific expertise, and their social ability to slot into a group of people and to be sensitive to its ways of working. They are managers of their own timetable, flexible and able to work late (for these reasons, they are more likely to be men than women).

A just-in-time person may be appointed a manager and given a line responsibility, or used as an adviser. They are not emergency stand-ins, although they are often used as such, nor are they cheap labour. The advantage to employers is less any financial gain and more the benefit of ensuring they have the exact people they want for as long as they want. As work becomes more volatile and specialized, organizations need to change their mix of workers more frequently.

Many trade unions strongly resist what they see as this casualization of labour. They fear their members will be hired and fired arbitrarily, lack employee rights, be paid less and seldom given any training. Their fears are justified. Just-in-time workers have to assert their own job rights by way of personal deals and contracts and have to select and pay for their own training. The trend is unmistakably towards the individual taking charge in this way. The economic conditions (and, in the public sector, the political conditions) for large monopoly organizations are fading fast.

A just-in-time person can work for several companies at the same time, exploiting his talents in a portfolio of projects; and most do so. Portfolio working is highly efficient, in that it allows just-in-time people to concentrate on their own skills and contribution. Whereas Adam Smith's workers and later the workers on industrial production lines worked for a single employer and concentrated on a single function, the modern just-in-time worker contracts with several people and may provide either one function or many. Adam Smith would surely approve. Moreover, since many just-in-time workers sell ideas, not physical labour, they are not limited to contractors in one place but can sell their services anywhere.

The result can put a strain on loyalties. People in a just-in-time operation (or a temporary company; see below) can be torn between centripetal and centrifugal forces. The centripetal forces, drawing them into a new project, may engender a stronger team spirit and loyalty than in an ordinary company. Visit a rehearsal room when the actors are getting to know each other, or the office of a business project team, and the determination to bring everyone together is palpable. Everyone has limited time and works that much harder; tomorrow really doesn't count. Equally, because nobody is giving their undivided loyalty, managers have to work harder to maintain cohesiveness and momentum.

The Temporary Company

Entrepreneurs and just-in-time people congregate naturally in temporary, ad hoc organisms that are set up for the sole purpose of meeting a specific, short-term objective. A temporary company is a 'minimalist' company, focusing on the raw ingredients of work: objective, people, and jobs-as-things-to-be-done. Its lifetime is generally less than a year. It is well suited to the post-industrial, post-employment job, since the workers can more easily retain ownership of their skills and their own intellectual capital.

A temporary company provides the social, intellectual and managerial framework for managing a creative process. It is fit-for-purpose and tightly drawn. Hermann Hauser's plea for entrepreneurs to focus on only one thing at a time applies with even greater force to a temporary company. It has no baggage from the past. It works best if it requires few of the traditional factors of production (the physical assets of land, buildings, equipment) and has access to an indefinitely large amount of intellectual assets. As a result, typically, it will have both its own in-house people and links with outside people, and usually blur the boundaries between them. It may be hard, even for those inside, to tell who is central and who is peripheral, who is being paid a fee and who is earning a share of the revenues, who is likely to be there next month and who is not.

It has the same autonomy as a permanent company, with total authority over the process from beginning to end, and thus differs from a project team, which reports to someone outside the team. The chief executive breaks each task into separate functions, identifies the people best qualified to carry out each function, and brings them together for the specific task over a specific period of time. In this way, costs can be tightly controlled. Ask the managers of a conventional company how much it costs to keep the business going and they may not know; but ask the heads of a temporary company, and they know.

Temporary companies need a positive cash flow (in other words, they need cash in the bank). This is more important than making a profit, let alone distributing profits to shareholders. Their function is more often to generate ideas, patents and other creative outputs that will be handed over to and exploited by another company. Any excess of revenues over costs can be removed by increasing the payments made to the workers in terms of fees and royalties (so the individual makes a profit but not the company). Temporary companies much prefer to increase their costs, and make a loss, than to decrease their costs and make a profit. They do not need profits; the company is a temporary unit which has no need of a track record, and any profits would be taxed.

The Network Office and the Business Cluster

A director of AT&T once invited me to use the company's headquarters boardroom in New York to hold a meeting for about forty people on the future of communications. We spent the two days in splendid isolation in the two top floors of Philip Johnson's striking AT&T building at 550 Madison Avenue in a cocoon of corporate wealth. Chairman John DeButts had asked Johnson to build a 'temple to commerce; make it the front door to our empire'. But while we were ensconced, none of the company's directors were in their top-floor offices. They preferred to be in the 'working' headquarters in Basking Ridge, New Jersey, where they could network with friends and colleagues. The overall impression was of absence and timelessness. I was not surprised when AT&T sold the building to Sony in 1991 (and Sony sold TV sets inside the front door of DeButts' temple).

The BBC manages to be both a global corporation and a vast gathering of noisy individuals. It veers between the two states, causing tensions between 'managers' and 'programme-makers'. In 1982, in a rare jump of corporate inspiration, it commissioned a brand-new headquarters in the centre of London; a building, it said, for the twenty-first century. George Howard, BBC chairman (and the proud owner of England's largest private estate), invited seven architects to propose 'an idea' for the building. Among those chosen was Norman Foster, then building the headquarters of the Shanghai and Hong Kong Bank, who asked me and TV producer Roger Graef to advise him on what the BBC would be like ten or twenty years ahead. We provided a series of images, starting with a photo of the Earth in space, which progressively showed the BBC as a global broadcaster, a great national institution, a London landmark and a neighbourhood message board. We suggested that, sitting at the centre of these networks, the building be open and inclusive, and provide workspaces that were personal, friendly, flexible, territorial, well-lit, not hidden, and comfortable. But George Howard retired, and the BBC lost its nerve and constructed a standard box of a building near its Television Centre in West London.

Creative people, whether thinkers, entrepreneurs, post-industrial workers or just-in-time people, need offices for all the same practical reasons as other people: to go to in the morning, knowing one's colleagues will be going there too; to store papers; to hold meetings;

to do 'office' work. But their particular job ('create or die!') needs special accommodation. Above all, they need quiet spaces and they need network connections; places to think and places to do. For creative people, whose job is to think, thinking and doing may be the same thing.

Harlan Cleveland, whose accomplishments included being American Ambassador to NATO and President of the University of Hawaii, and who was awarded the first Prix de Tailloires for 'accomplished generalists', said the creative office is built 'more around communities of people than communities of place'. Communities of people need internal networks; internal to the community. As well as private spaces for private cogitation, they need network spaces for socializing. Victoria Ward, banker-turned-entrepreneur and one of the founders of Spark Team (helping young Internet companies to get off the ground), says they need areas for 'forced serendipity' ('encouraged' or 'enabling' might be more welcoming), spaces that provide 'knowledge shelters', and spaces where two people can meet on neutral ground ('third spaces'). Everyone who has worked in an office, or been to a conference, will know what she means. People like to congregate in corners and corridors, around the water-cooler or the coffee-machine. Arie de Geus, businessman-turned-writer, says, 'A good decision is like an intelligent conversation'.

Being a community of people, not places, the network office extends outside its physical location. Its workers, or members, behave as if they are members of an extended family or tribe although, as anyone who is a member of a family or tribe knows, this does not imply undiluted happiness. They blur the boundaries between home and work, making personal telephone calls at work and being accustomed to working at home. For many people, especially young people, their work-based network may be a nicer and more convivial place than home; often, they spend more time there and meet more friends there. The St Luke's advertising agency in London encourages people to set up a new working team or 'family' every time the core workforce exceeds thirty people. New York's Eye Image does the same. Gerard Fairtlough, the former chief executive of Celltech, believes the ideal size of a working group is about seventy, which he calls a 'creative compartment'.

Harlan Cleveland's 'community of people' does not rely only on face-to-face meetings; but nor does it rely only on telecom-based electronic meetings. The growth of independent working, the freedom from tangible resources, the growth of the temporary company, and the increasing need for and viability of just-in-time working have given people extraordinary freedom. The Internet and mobile cellular communications have helped. But they have also upped the need for face-to-face meetings. The two reinforce each other. Research into telephone communication, videoconferencing and e-mail shows consistently that outside a few specific circumstances (typically, a group of scientists working on a technical project over a long period of time) the more people communicate by electronic means the more they want to meet each other. The network office therefore works best in a cluster of similar communities.

Theories of economic clusters originated in Cambridge in the late 1890s. Alfred Marshall, sometimes described as the 'father of modern economics', wrote in *The Principles of Economics* that when a number of like-minded companies engaged in similar tasks cluster together 'the mysteries of trade become no mysteries, and are available to all'. They are 'in the air'. The modern theories of networks and communications clusters originated with Everett M. Rogers, whose teenage observations of how farmers choose new hybrid corn seeds led to postgraduate work on Iowa farms and then to a study of networks in South Korea, published in *Communications Networks* (1981). He followed up with *Silicon Valley Fever*, written jointly with Judith K. Larsen in 1984. Rogers showed how networking enhanced the exchange of information, and why few people like to be alone, or work well on their own, for long stretches of time. Creative people need creative people next door to hasten success on their current project and to test ideas for the next one.

There are exceptions. Many creative people, such as writers, artists, and composers, need to work on their own for much of the time. For them, being alone is an absolute, non-negotiable requirement. Some writers work in extreme isolation. Marcel Proust went to bed for years to write *A la recherche du temps perdu*. Famously, Samuel Taylor Coleridge was alone when he wrote 'Kubla Khan' and stopped abruptly in the middle of a line when he was interrupted. All writers need to be alone a lot. Sometimes, the solitude is a performance, a manner of speaking. Coleridge's friend, William Wordsworth, was adept and even ruthless at recreating solitude. One day he and his sister, Dorothy, were walking together when she pointed out some daffodils. Wordsworth returned to the house to write his famous lines, 'I wandered lonely as a cloud / That floats on high o'er vales and hills'. Most of us (in this respect) are like Wordsworth. Our minds are ready to pick up any scrap to make a product, and we therefore need, as well as the mind, the scraps. And then we need to be alone again to write.

Rogers's and other studies of networks, as well as anecdotal evidence, show that managing isolation and managing networks are equally important. Managing isolation allows a creative person to manage their consciousness. Networking allows the exchange of ideas and information. When Wordsworth and Coleridge did come together in a creative community in 1798 they produced one of the most radical and beautiful books of the English language, *Lyrical Ballads*, which sounded the real beginning of the Romantic movement in Britain.

Clusters, 'where the mysteries become no mysteries', provide mutual support psychologically, financially and technically. In industrial terms, they increase the efficiency of the local market, bringing together buyers and sellers. They are centres of excellence, upholding and distributing best practice as a matter of course, and stimulating competition. They also offer high 'multiplier' effects. Any inputs from outside the cluster are quickly disseminated, and internal knowledge and skills do not leak out. Clusters can lead to a high rate of synergy, the positive interchange of complementary resources that creates a result that is more than the sum of its parts.

A cluster's ability to act as a defence against mediocrity can be seen in Britain's collection of racing car companies in southern England, which I call 'Vroom Valley'. These companies are responsible for the research, design and construction of seven out of the world's top ten Formula-1 cars. A study by Birmingham University found a group of companies operating at frantic pace, with employees driven more by enthusiasm than by pay; relentless innovation; imaginative design; and flexible working. Companies are set up and fail at a rate unmatched elsewhere in the country. Vroom Valley has a dynamism that spits out incompetence like a spinning top throws away whatever hits it. In this way, it protects itself from the failures and negativism in the remainder of Britain's declining car industry.

Because clusters have such competitive advantages, the number of world-class clusters in each of the fifteen core creative industries is relatively small; typically under ten and often as few as five. There are only six countries in the world where you are likely to find a world-class architect: America, Britain, Germany, Japan, Spain and Italy. The art market is dominated by New York and London followed, some way behind, by Paris, Frankfurt, Milan, Tokyo and Sydney. London's West End and New York's Broadway dominate world theatre, especially musicals. The same dozen or so cities make multiple appearances. Industrial designers do not cluster physically to the same extent, but they tend to be very aware, like architects, of what is happening in other countries. Scientists not only cluster but also routinely collaborate on international projects and need to stay abreast of international trends in order to justify patent applications. The exceptions are industries that are based on language (publishing, TV and some performing arts – although even here each linguistic group sustains few main centres), and those that are culturally specific and make and sell for a very local market (crafts).

These manifest economic benefits have led some public authorities to attempt to create a cluster by a kind of a reverse engineering, saying, in effect, their city is a suitable place for a cluster and subsidizing companies to set up shop. In New York, which is strong in creative industries but relatively weak in new media, Mayor Giuliani gave tax credits and energy subsidies to companies in that field in return for guaranteed employment; the city also promoted a Plug 'n' Go Program of cheap office space for creative companies. Other less well-known and less favoured places are thinking the same way. Huddersfield, in the north of England, was a declining town with no obvious focus and no special talent until a group of council officials and young media tyros decided to develop it as a 'creative city'. The slogan was persuasive. They won a €3 million grant from the European Commission, which generated matching local support of €7 million, and aim to create 350 new jobs, safeguard 75 existing jobs, refurbish 7,000 sq. m. of buildings and train 6,500 people in media, design and related skills.

The network office is the natural habitat of the thinker, the entrepreneur and the post-industrial, just-in-time worker. It is their means of managing distance and managing time.

Teamwork

The network office thrives on a particular kind of teamwork: 'leaderwork' and 'teamship'. Johan Staël von Holstein, founder of the Icon Medialab in Stockholm, described the four people in one of his project teams as a computer hacker, an artist, an intellectual and a radical. He says, 'We thrive on creative conflict.' It seems to work. Icon has offices in more than fifteen countries and Nicholas Negroponte, Director of the MIT Media Lab and a leading digital guru, has acknowledged that 'Icon is simply superior to our domestic web bureaux.'

John Kao, a Stanford University professor of management and a jazz pianist, made the connection in his book, *Jamming: The Art and Discipline of Business Creativity*, which takes jazz and jamming as a metaphor for the process of creativity. He would appreciate London's Tomato advertising collective (with credits for campaigns for MTV, Nike and IBM) whose Steve Baker says, 'I run the company like I'd manage a band.' Online publisher N2K (named after the military phrase, 'need to know') formed a company band, the N2K All Stars, which plays in-house and professionally. As one of the members admits, 'A lot of us at N2K are musicians first and employees second.'

Benjamin Zander, the conductor and director of the Boston Symphony Orchestra, and an inspirational teacher, credits his success as a musician and his popularity with business corporations to his discovery that 'The conductor is the only musician who doesn't make a sound. His power lies in his ability to make other people powerful. He is a silent releaser of the players' energies.' The dynamic of a successful team encourages different leaders at different moments. As well as the overall leader (maybe someone who doesn't make a sound, like Zander) it needs someone to report on what is happening, someone to ask awkward questions, someone to make proposals, someone to sum up, someone to scout ahead, someone to close the meeting and someone to organize the next one. Keith Johnstone, who taught improvisation at the Royal Court Theatre for many years and wrote the classic *Impro*, says 'People in a group are amazed when I explain that they're supposed to work for the other members, that each individual is to be interested in the progress of other members; yet obviously if a group supports its own members strongly it'll be a better group to work in.' Working together in this way should not be an indulgence for special occasions but recognized in everyday practice.

Finance

It must be stated at the outset that the routine management of money in the creative economy and the conventional economy are not substantially different. Every business, whatever its assets and its products, needs financial systems, budgets and accounts, and an understanding of accountancy and tax rules. The similarities greatly exceed the disparities, especially as the business grows in size. There are, however, some special issues, notably the intangible, one-off nature of intellectual assets, especially when the business is starting or growing.

I am frequently asked three questions by people who want to exploit the financial value of their intellectual assets. The first question is how to start. The second question is whether to set up a company. The third question is how to grow. These questions reflect three different levels of cash but they are not only about cash. The first question is about self-confidence, the second about management and relationships, and the third about risk. There is a fourth question which I am never asked but which is equally important: what happens when it all goes horribly wrong? What happens when the money runs out or, much worse, you run out of ideas? The best guide here is the opening sentence of Tolstoy's *Anna Karenina*: 'Happy families are all alike; but every unhappy family is unhappy in its own way.' Successful businesses may be alike in their successes but each will fail in its own way.

First, starting. It is possible to be creative and make a tradeable product with little direct cash expenditure. Indeed, this openness (what economists call 'low barriers to entry') is one of the creative economy's most distinctive and admirable hallmarks. But that does not mean it is free. Someone once said that thinking is free. I hope they got paid for saying so. Thinking is not free. Likewise, creating is not free. It requires skilful use of intellectual resources. Our brains are a valuable and precious asset in which our parents, and our schools and then, if we wish, we ourselves, invest considerable time and money. As with any other investment, the amounts, strategies and results vary. Creating also has an opportunity cost. The cost of creating something is the cost of not creating something else. Working at creativity, whether thinking (I refuse to say, 'just thinking') or doing (or, indeed, 'just doing'), has unavoidable costs.

The amount of finance required at this early stage is small. A variety of sources can be tapped: savings; borrowings; loans from family and friends; credit card loans; grants; and bank overdrafts. One of the most problematic needs is for seed money at the very early stage when the idea is not much more than an idea and the sums are too low to interest a bank let alone a private investor or a venture capitalist. At this point, a few thousand pounds may make all the difference between going on and giving up, as much as by giving confidence as by paying the rent. But there is a limit to the amounts which savings and friends can supply.

The next question is about starting a legal entity such as an incorporated company or partnership. The legal procedure of registering a company is easy in Britain and America, where it requires only a name, an address and one or two directors. In contrast, almost all other European countries, notably France, require several thousand pounds of capital to be deposited as security (French companies are obliged to state their capital deposit on their corporate letterhead). According to the European Commission, this cash deposit is a disincentive to entrepreneurs. In Britain and America, the governments' rules on legal and financial reporting responsibilities, while bureaucratic, are straightforward. But the heart of the company is not these cash deposits or legal formalities but the arm's-length entity, with limited liability, that can take in other people's money. The question about starting and operating a company is primarily about the management skills of handling other people's money on a large scale.

This money may be divided into debt (i.e., borrowing substantial cash from a private investor or, more likely, a bank) and equity (i.e., selling shares in a company for cash). The choice depends on a number of factors: the existing financial situation, the degree of future risk, and the nature of future rewards. Each has its own advantages and disadvantages. Debt allows the company to keep control but requires some security (assets) as collateral, as well as regular repayments. A creative business, with little past record of earnings and few assets as collateral, often finds it difficult to borrow. Selling equity allows the borrower to get cash at no financial cost but involves relinquishing a degree of control, and the lenders will also want their investment to be backed by some asset as collateral. The choice of debt or equity depends on the risk/reward profile. If something is routine and safe, then the better option is debt. If something is risky, the better option is either a loan from family and friends on a non-commercial and possibly interest-free basis, or equity.

These same issues affect all companies but the tactics depend on the nature of the assets. The success rate of net company formation requires both the company and the lender/investor to be comfortable with the value given to the assets and the risk/reward profile. The cost of operating a business with intellectual assets alone (people and intellectual property) is typically lower than the cost of starting a conventional business which uses both physical and intellectual assets. The former also has the advantage that it can delay paying for the intellectual assets, or pay them with equity, in ways seldom possible with the owner of physical assets. But, conversely, the insubstantial nature of these assets deters many potential investors, and even those who are enthusiastic have problems in valuing the business and therefore their stake in it. These difficulties confront both the person operating the company and the person considering an investment. A report by accountants Arthur Andersen, *The Use of Intellectual Property as Security for Debt Finance*, says that, as a result, patents, copyrights and trademarks, despite their considerable importance to many businesses, have rarely been used as collateral for loans and, when they are, their value is underplayed.

There are reasons on both sides. On the demand side, the company that wants finance may find it hard to offer any collateral. At start-up, which is when it has the greatest need, the value of its intellectual property is usually most negligible. It may prefer equity finance at this stage if it is happy to share risk and wants to benefit from other people's experience. Later on, it may be cash-generative more quickly than an 'ordinary' business and therefore have less need of debt. Finally, at all times, businesses are reluctant to put their intellectual property at risk because it is difficult or even impossible to replace. On the supply side, lenders prefer securities and collateral that can be easily valued and traded; for example, they like offices and factories because there is an established market in commercial property. They prefer assets that can be easily separated from the borrower and used in other circumstances, rather than ideas that are legally and economically tied to an individual.

The banks' attitudes towards intellectual property became more favourable throughout the 1990s. Pharmaceutical companies like Glaxo Wellcome and Pfizer regularly borrow against their patents, although smaller biotechnology companies whose assets consist mainly of research-in-progress and a few patents-under-test often have difficulty for the reasons given above. Entertainment companies borrow against copyrights. Disney issued seven-year loan notes in 1992 worth $400 million, using film copyrights as collateral, and Cecchi Gori, which produced the Oscar-winning *Life is Beautiful*, raised Ł500 billion (£172 million) with a bond that pays 0.5 per cent above equivalent corporate bonds. David Bowie was the first pop artist to turn copyright into a bankable asset, raising $55 million by capitalizing his future song royalties as ten-year bonds at 7.9 per cent. Rod Stewart later issued a $15.4 million securitized loan, and Iron Maiden raised $30 million. In business terms, Bowie and Stewart have a balance sheet where previously, like most artists living off fees, they only had income. In economic terms, Bowie is a 'capitalist' while others remain employees. Many artists are forced to sell their rights at the beginning of their career in order to get much-needed cash. This means giving up their best opportunity to change from being a freelance-for-hire to building up a company with capital assets.

The fourth, often unasked, question is not about growth but about decline, and what to do when in trouble. Many businesses, both large and small, get into financial trouble because they worry about their costs but not (or not sufficiently) about their income. People who are paid a regular wage, especially in the ordinary economy, seldom run into trouble so long as they ensure their income exceeds their costs; and since their wages, which make up the larger part of their income, are known in advance, this is not a demanding task. Their priority is their costs. People living off their wits in the deal economy have the opposite concern: their priority is their income. Many get into financial trouble because they bring the attitudes of the ordinary, job-as-employment economy (and try to reduce their costs) to the business of the creative economy where they should focus on new ideas and new projects (and try to increase their income).

If the ideas do not come, there is no easy solution. In such circumstances, the only way forward is to dig deeper within one's own creative resources and intellectual assets. In a free society, these can never be taken away, although they can dry up. One of the advantages of being a creative is that the essential requirements of the job are built in. And, once begun, the mining is hard to stop. 'Ideas are like rabbits,' said John Steinbeck. 'You get a couple and learn how to handle them, and pretty soon you have a dozen.'

Quality counts, too. When Einstein was asked how many original ideas he had had in his lifetime he replied, 'Only two, but they were good ones.' In all situations, the market rewards a hit.

Deals and Hits

The singular nature of ideas (most are novel, many are unique) results in a high number of deals and contracts. There are more deals done in the creative economy than in the ordinary economy, even if the latter is significantly larger; or, to be more precise, there are more deals done in connection with intangible values than with the tangible.

The thrust of the ordinary economy is to buy as many of the same materials as possible, set up a permanent production line, and turn out as many identical products as possible. As Alvin Toffler points out, 'The one point on which assembly-line capitalist Henry Ford and assembly-line Marxist Joseph Stalin could agree was the virtue of mass production. The larger the quantity, the cheaper the run.' This principle holds true with milk cartons as with blank CDs. In contrast, the thrust of the creative economy, when it deals in intangible ideas and rights, is to produce a new idea and celebrate its uniqueness.

A deal is an attempt to reconcile two people's valuations of these ideas and rights at a specific moment in time. Sellers desire to protect their capital while increasing revenue, and buyers desire, for as low a cost as can be negotiated, to increase opportunities for future revenue. A deal reflects each party's knowledge of present values (likely to differ) and their forecast of future values (almost certain to differ).

The scope for deal-making is enhanced because ideas, properties and rights can be merged, consolidated or divided virtually without limit. Physical matter may be varied only within physical limits and to a small degree. But intangible matter can be manipulated merely by thinking it, or wishing it. The only constraint is the inventiveness of the parties to the deal; in other words, an intellectual constraint on an intellectual thing. Consolidations and splits can be fast and numerous. New technologies are a major factor in stimulating new rights, notably in film, music, software, TV and video games. A second cause is globalization, which has brought into being many new markets, locally and globally, for each of which the rights-holder generates and sells a new right. The rights-holder's objective is to assert as many rights as feasible and then to maximize the income from each right.

The need to optimize value through continuous, multiple deal-making has several far-reaching implications. It emphasizes the role of the individual, since deals are always between people. It puts a premium on managers who are skilled at deal-making rather than operating a routine business. It requires a high level of legal expertise, especially about contracts and intellectual property. It can result in large variations in an asset's value in a relatively short space of time, which complicates the way in which investors can calculate the asset's value. It puts pressure on permanent fixed employment. As old, stable institutions with long-term employees are replaced by smaller and more temporary organizations, with a mix of internal employees and external contractors, an increasing number of workers are negotiating individual one-off job contracts for themselves and their intellectual assets. Companies, whether permanent or temporary, are changing from being a block of workers to being a marketplace of deals.

The same factors (one-off products, high gearing) result in the creative economy being a hits business. The rewards are spread unevenly, with success bringing a higher proportion of a buyer's attention and cash than in the ordinary economy. Having a hit, whether a successful drug or a bestselling book, does not have the brutal mystique of a top athlete or sports player whose successes and failures are publicly displayed on the scoreboard, but it shares some of the same economic qualities.

The instinctive and perfectly logical response is to strive for every idea, every product, to be a hit. However, this strategy gives no help as to how much effort to give to each idea; in essence, how to balance the attempts to achieve quality with the need for quantity. A variation, favoured by many companies, is to set a desired level of output, and within that framework adopt a portfolio approach to investment. This has the side effect of freeing up each production to settle at its own level of content and cost. Instead of producing at an equilibrium price, which is sensible if each product is identical and marginal costs and revenues can be maintained over a long run, these companies produce a bundle of differentiated products. They make the assumption that some products will be hits and some will be misses; and they manage the company on the assumption that the hits will compensate for the misses. Absolute costs and product prices are not so relevant, which is why a marginal change in costs, such as a change in interest rates, that may have a major effect on a conventional company, has less impact on a business that lives off hits.

By selecting the optimum level of output, a company can enhance its chances of success overall. The minimum number varies according to the structure of the industry and the size of the risk. Few industries manage a ratio greater than one in ten, which means they need to produce ten works to be confident of a hit.

ZEST IS BEST

These ten management principles apply to almost every free-market country but are most evident in America. Americans enjoy a zest for novelty, and for turning novelty into a business and wealth. More people in America have an intuitive understanding of turning an idea into a business, of company creation; more people take business or law degrees and are competent, as corporate executives must be, in mixing the two; more know how to prepare a business plan; more can pitch an idea to investors; more know how many shares to issue and at what price; and more feel comfortable in spending the cash raised and reporting back to the investors.

America has exported many of its national characteristics but it has not exported this one, which implies that the reasons for the gap are more cultural than economic, industrial or demographic. Certainly, in the past, Europe has been a good place to start a company. Over the centuries the Italians, Spanish, French, Hungarians, Dutch, English, Scots, Germans, Poles and Czechs have shown as much technological imagination and entrepreneurial flair as Americans do now. But today America has the edge.

Size counts. America has a much bigger domestic market of 250 million people compared to Germany, Europe's biggest market, which has 81 million people. Britain, France and Italy each has between 57 and 58 million people. America also has highly efficient national media, marketing, advertising and distribution systems. It has a national legal system for patents and copyright, whereas Europe, although edging closer, maintains many local irregularities. The European Commission may claim a 'single market' but national cultures dominate in many areas including, naturally enough, in the cultural industries of art, literature, theatre, design, music, TV and film. At a Global Business Network meeting on 'The Future of Europe', analyst Peter Bennett asked this question: 'Why are there fewer big/innovative information technology companies in Europe compared to America and Japan?' He gave six reasons for Europe's paucity: relatively fragmented markets; over-protected industries; lack of venture capital; lack of innovation; a lower level of defence spending; and the 'brain drain'.

Schumpeter's entrepreneurial function is virtually 'routinized' in America where, according to research by the London Business School, 8 per cent of people are engaged in starting a business in any one year. In Britain the figure is 3 per cent and in Germany and France it is 2 per cent. The same research indicated that in an average year 57 per cent of Americans say they see a good opportunity to start a business next year whereas in Britain the figure is only 16 per cent. Many governments regard entrepreneurial activity as a positive contributor to the creation of jobs, to company formation (the net balance of new company start-ups) and to international competitiveness, and therefore try to encourage it. Britain's New Labour government has made several initiatives, including tax breaks, and a scheme for 200,000 school pupils to study entrepreneurialism at school. It has also set up the National Endowment for Science, Technology and the Arts (NESTA), with a capital endowment of £200 million. These schemes are admirable, although the only safe conclusion from looking at entrepreneurs' past histories is that they follow no pattern.

Raising money is easier. The biggest sources of start-up money in America are people who started their own company a generation previously, and expect to invest it back into business. Each generation of American entrepreneurs gives funds to its successors. In Europe, would-be entrepreneurs are obliged to turn supplicant in front of banking officials with little experience of running a business or government officials with no experience at all. The arrival of the Internet and e-commerce businesses may have a major impact not only on those that benefit first time around but also, if they are successful, on the amount of private capital looking for investment in the next generation.

Once started, Americans like to keep their businesses going. Their attitude to a business in trouble is to save the company as a 'going concern' even if the creditors who are owed money are not paid. Britain takes a different approach and tries to protect the company's assets in order to pay off the creditors (usually headed by the Crown and the Inland Revenue, so the money leaves the private sector) even if the company has to stop trading. America tries to protect the company from a creditor who might wish to close it down and sell the assets; while Britain tries to protect the creditors from the company. In a word, America is debtor-friendly and Britain is creditor-friendly. The British approach affects all businesses but is more damaging to companies whose assets are mainly intellectual.

America's skills in originating and developing ideas come both from general economic and demographic factors (such as the size of the market) and from an understanding of the economics of creativity, as expressed in knowing how to turn an idea into a business, when to assert intellectual property ownership, when to pay, and how much to charge. But the main factor is the country's treatment of creativity as always having an economic element.

TOM'S BEAUTIFUL CAREER

Over the last few years I have met numerous people who are managing a creative business. I started to build up a fictional picture of a young man called Tom. Although a fiction, Tom is created from real people. He sums up how the overarching principles of creative management apply to young people. One, start with the individual. Two, facilitate his or her access to other individuals and their intellectual resources. Three, educate their understanding of money. This is Tom's story.

Tom, who was born in Manchester, plays guitar in his bedroom as a teenager and joins a few friends every Friday in a converted garage to practise. They sometimes play in local clubs for free. He writes a few songs. After school he and his friends, with a few changes of line-up, make a bit of money by performing in the local pub. He writes more songs, one of which attracts an A & R scout from a local label. (His mother says, 'Why don't you get a proper job?')

When he leaves school his parents move to London. He starts to work as a DJ earning £50–100 a night. During the day he works in a music shop where his knowledge of new bands and Manchester's club scene impresses the manager and attracts customers. For the first time, he appears as a worker in the government statistics. Then a year later the shop closes down and he is out of a job and spends more time playing in the band. In the eyes of the government and his mother, he is out of work.

A year later a recording of one of his songs becomes a hit and Tom has a chance to become rich. This and other songs provide some income for many years. I said, 'Tom has a chance to become rich.' Tom fails to repeat his one success and turns to scoring and performing audio tracks for advertising commercials as well as continuing to write his own songs. It's good, steady work. He and his partner set up a music production company to design and produce CDs for new bands. He shifts from being a part-time musician and a part-time something else to being a full-time musician. The company has a turnover of £55,000 from which he takes a salary of £18,000, most of which he spends on recording his own work, investing in his own career.

One year Tom discovers that a licensee who acquired some rights to one of his songs about ten years ago did not hand over all the royalties. It is the kind of scenario all too familiar to someone in the creative industries whether you are an aspiring musician/manager like Tom or a top star like Sting. Tom has to spend a lot of time and a bit of cash to get the money.

Here's a trick question that would never appear in a school economics examination paper: when in these years is Tom (a) working and (b) earning? According to British law, someone who is *self*-employed like Tom can be broke, can even be ill and unable to work, but he cannot be *un*employed. So Tom can be working and not earning, and earning but not working. Tom's answer is forthright. He is always working; and he is usually earning a bit of money whether from his current work as a musician, from the results of previous work as a musician or from something else entirely.

Many business executives give a slightly different answer, treating Tom as working only when he had a proper full-time job in the shop. And when he is working he must be earning. 'Ah,' says Tom, 'I wish I was.' The tax authorities give a different answer again. They favour full-time employment over all other kinds of work to the extent that self-employed people and part-time workers are not given the same rights as their full-time colleagues.

Two things are happening here which don't fit the conventional wisdom. First, Tom is part of a real-life business process that clashes with the theories of modern economics. He is neither employer nor employee, owner nor apprentice, trainer nor trainee. In spite of having little cash, he behaves more like an investor. He is investing in his own talent. He has a post-industrial attitude towards work, jobs, employment and wealth. Second, Tom is skipping around the margins of the government's rules on – well, on most things, including education, employment and social security. In his view – in reality – he works and he has a job, in fact many jobs all at the same time.

In the past, people like Tom existed as a small minority on the outskirts of society while economists and politicians concentrated on the majority of people who were employed in manufacturing industries. Today, the music industry is work for more people than are the manufacturing industries. I came close to saying it 'provides' work for Tom. But that is an old-fashioned phrase. Tom provides creativity to the industry just as much as the industry provides him with work.

Economists and politicians do not know much about Tom, let alone how to deal with him. Be certain Tom is not worried about this and certainly is not going to change his behaviour just because some people do not understand him. He is bright enough to know that his own talents could give him as much security as a conventional company or the government's social security. The work of a creative person may be intermittent and volatile, but someone who creates his own intellectual property and manages his own work can be more secure than a salaried employee of a large corporation. To Tom, a 'job as thinker' in the creative economy appears more secure than a career as a manager in the ordinary economy. These people instinctively think for themselves, instinctively network, instinctively keep several balls in the air at once. They are the shock troops not only for new ideas about our culture but for new ideas about working in it.

TEN RULES FOR SUCCESS

I conclude this chapter by giving ten rules for success in the creative economy. These rules have been tested by the progenitors of Tom, who is just starting, and by others who are further along their own paths.

1. Invent yourself. Create a unique cluster of personal talents. Own your image. Manage it. Build momentum. Leave school early, if you want, but never stop learning. Dance as if no one is looking. Break the rules. Be clear about your own assets and talents. They are unique. And they are all you have.

2. Put the priority on ideas, not on data. Create and grow your own creative imagination. Build a personal balance sheet of intellectual capital. Understand patents, copyright, trademarks and other intellectual property laws that protect ideas. Entrepreneurs in the creative economy are more worried if they lose their ability to think than if their company loses money. Think about it.

3. **Be nomadic.** Nomads are at home in every country. You can choose your own path and means of travel, and choose how long you stay. Being nomadic does not mean being alone; most nomads travel in groups, especially at night. Writer Charles Handy says leaders must combine 'a love of people' and a 'capacity for aloofness'. Nomads appreciate both the desert and the oasis; likewise creatives need both solitude and the crowd, thinking alone and working together.

4. **Define yourself by your own (thinking) activities,** not by the (job) title somebody else has given you. If you are working for a company X on project Y, say you are working on project Y at company X. People who are brave call themselves 'thinkers'. Computer companies try to concoct and sell 'business solutions' to their client's problems; in the creative economy, we each can think and exchange creative solutions with each other. Play Charles Hampden-Turner's 'Infinite Game', in which everybody seeks a mutually positive outcome.

5. **Learn endlessly.** Borrow. Innovate. Remember the US Electric Power ad, 'A New Idea is Often Two Old Ideas Meeting for the First Time'. Use retro, reinvention, revival – be a magpie. Creative artists scavenge for new ideas. It does not matter where you get ideas from; what does matter is what you do with them. If you're bored, do something else. Use networks. If you cannot find the right network, start it. Take risks and do unnecessary things. Completely ignore Frederick Winslow Taylor's famous instruction to the Ford Motor Company's workers that they should 'eliminate all false movements, slow movements and useless movements'. Wayward movements can lead to amazing discoveries.

6. **Exploit fame and celebrity.** The production costs are small and relatively fixed. Fame is what economists call a 'sunk cost', which cannot be recovered but which can be freely exploited at no further expense, and both fame and celebrity bring virtually unlimited rewards in terms of the ability to charge more for one's services and to revitalize a life or career that is momentarily stuck. Being well known (even slightly known) is as important in the creative economy of the twenty-first century as good typing speeds were in the clerical economy of the twentieth. The essence of being a star, as shrewdly revealed by David

Bowie, is 'the ability to make yourself as fascinating to others as you are to yourself'. This is not about being famous for fifteen minutes, which is how Andy Warhol characterized the transience of media attention, but being famous for being creative, which was Warhol's own achievement, long after he had stopped painting or indeed working at all.

7. Treat the virtual as real and vice versa. Cyberspace is merely another dimension to everyday life. Do not judge reality by whether it is based on technology but by more important and eternal matters such as humanity and truth. Bandwidth is useless without a message, without communication. At all times, use the RIDER process: review, incubation, dreams, excitement and reality checks. Mix dreams and reality to create your own future.

8. Be kind. Kindness is a mark of success. Data never say 'please'. Humans can and should say 'please', and mean it. People treat each other as they themselves are treated; exactly as a fast computer produces data more quickly, so a kind person will be invited to more networks, receive more knowledge and create more.

9. Admire success, openly. Martina Navratilova, who won Wimbledon nine times and the US Open four times, was right when she said: 'The person who said, "It's not whether you win or lose that counts," probably lost . . .' Equally, do not be fixated on success: be curious about failure. Creative people are the strictest judge of their own successes and failures because they want to learn from them (see rule 5). The worst thing is depression, not recession. You will never win if you cannot lose.

10. Be very ambitious. Boldly Go.

11. Have fun. Film-maker David Puttnam, who starts the next chapter, says, 'The most exciting, creative period of my life was in the early 1960s at the Collett Dickinson Pearce advertising agency when I was a group head working with Charles Saatchi, Alan Parker [who later directed *Midnight Express* and *Evita*] and Ridley Scott [who later directed *Alien*] – a pretty good group, you'll agree. But the only thing I remember doing a lot, a really lot of, was tap dancing. We spent hours practising tap dancing and in between we'd work out an ad. It was a fantastic thing. We'd be screaming with laughter, absolutely falling about and meanwhile creating some very remarkable work.' People who enjoy themselves are not only happier but they achieve more, faster. Above all, do not worry; Tom Wehr of the National Institute of Mental Health, Maryland, says the sleeping brain sorts out the previous day's affairs as 'a creative worry factory'. Feed it.

And when writing the ten rules for success in the creative economy, don't worry if you end up with eleven. You can break your own rules (see rule number 1).

5

THE ENTERTAINMENT GENE

LAW 5: STORIES COME FIRST

'The future is not the result of choices among alternative paths offered in the present – it is a place that is created – created first in the mind and will; created next in the activity.'
Walt Disney

DAVID PUTTNAM

David Puttnam is Britain's best-known film producer, having not only produced more films and won more Oscars than any of his contemporaries (his films include *Midnight Express*, *Chariots of Fire* and *The Killing Fields*) but also led from the front in persuading, cajoling, and sometimes kicking the British government to support the national film industry. He is also the only Briton to head up a Hollywood studio, Columbia Pictures, in recent times. In the early 1990s he decided to reinvent himself and work in education, helping to reform the national school system. It wasn't such a big leap. He is using his experience as an ad-man, a film-maker and a family man. He was created Lord Puttnam by Tony Blair's government in 1997.

He demonstrates three characteristics of a creative person and thus also of the creative economy. First, he has a core creative talent (in his case, telling stories in pictures) which he exercises passionately. Second, he is not only a creator in the sense of someone who has ideas but also a manager in the sense of someone who makes ideas happen. Jim Warner, President of CBS-TV, once told me that he judged people by how they managed their own careers because someone who did that well would be good at managing other people. Third, Puttnam has used these personal skills not only in his own core industries of advertising and film-making but in the ordinary economy, notably education. This restless inter-industry transfer of skills is typical of many creative people.

He is an elegant man, with prodigious passions, and hard-working. In twenty years I have never seen him indecisive. He may say that he doesn't know what to do, but he makes that a firm decision, if an interim one, merely awaiting more facts before the next and final decision is made.

When we met to discuss creativity, he described a creative man as someone who sees the upside in everything. It is a quality of creative people that they want to change things, to make something better. In his current role as a government adviser on education he is often battling with people who think only about the downside. It is a clash of opposites.

Puttnam says there are not many rules for film-making. For him, the most important is the balance between discipline and freedom. Too much discipline hobbles the imagination; too much freedom leads to indulgence. He has a profound admiration for advertising, where he started his career, because of the absolute obligation to promote the product.

When making a film, he says, the first thing is to know what the story is; what it really is. The producer has to know, and the director and writer have to know, and then the audience will know too. The second is to tell the story in a way that hooks the audience's emotions. The third, affecting these, is to make the picture within budget. The fourth is to manage an extremely complicated process involving hundreds of people (a temporary company with lots of just-in-time people). Making a film is like a very expensive and tightly planned military operation.

In 1995 Puttnam had the idea for a World Learning Network that would distribute the best of Britain's and later the world's educational courses. The model was the world's film distribution network, then controlled by four companies, UIP, Warner Bros, Buena Vista and Fox, which had a lock on distributing international films in all countries. The objective was a global network that would promote and deliver academic courses as swiftly and efficiently as these film distributors sell a film.

It is hard to say what Puttnam does now. Like many people who live off their imagination and their wits, he has a portfolio of jobs, relationships and networks, centred on his restless relish for getting things done and a mission for education. He has the American talent for 'get up and go'. His real passion is bringing things to life. When I met him, his priority was the government's education programme and, as founding chairman, the launch of the National Endowment for Science, Technology and the Arts (NESTA). He was also preparing the release of his film, *A Life So Far*. But listing his projects does not capture the essence of one person using his creative imagination at full stretch – and having fun.

THE DREAM FACTORIES

This chapter illustrates the 'management of creativity' in practice. I have chosen film-making as my principle example because I know from personal experience it is the home of the simplest ideas and the most complex and expensive products. It is totally dependent upon technology, and therefore its attitude towards new technology is interesting. It is well documented over a period of time. Finally, I admit, I take a perverse delight in choosing an industry more noted for glamour and excess than management skills.

In the 1940s anthropologist Hortense Powdermaker described Hollywood as a 'Dream Factory'. It is a factory, but the raw materials and the products are ideas and dreams. Producers like David Puttnam have to manage some of the world's most egotistical people and control large, complicated management processes and budgets. It has been said that of the two million people who work in Los Angeles in one way or another (and this figure includes everyone, however tangentially employed), everyone has a script or agent's telephone number in their back pocket. They are dealing, or wanting to deal, in creativity, creative products and transactions at their most vivid. They are dealing almost entirely in intangible values and intangible products. Their work exhibits all the principles of creative management: the importance of people, the job of thinker, the temporary company, the just-in-time person, deals and hits.

I use the term Hollywood to cover all companies based in Los Angeles which produce and distribute films. It is centred around the so-called 'major' studios: Warner Bros (owned by AOL Time Warner), Disney (The Walt Disney Company), Paramount Pictures (Viacom), Universal Pictures (NBC Universal), Columbia Pictures (Sony Pictures Entertainment), Fox (News Corp.) and DreamWorks SKG. I also include the so-called 'independent' production companies, which depend upon these majors for finance and distribution. Hollywood as an industry and as a neighbourhood is quintessentially American, even though Vivendi is French, Sony is Japanese, and News Corp. is run by an Australian who took American citizenship in order to circumvent the rule that a foreigner may not control a TV network. By owning a major Hollywood studio these foreign media conglomerates have bought into the American entertainment industry (which is the point of the deal) and they get a seat at the top table.

These seven companies determine the shape of the global entertainment industry because they own or control the stories, the characters and the stars that the world loves best. Warner and Universal also own almost 40 per cent of the world's music publishing rights, including the world's most popular songs. Their main rivals (apart from each other) are America's telephone, cable and Internet companies, who want to move into the entertainment business. Companies as otherwise different as Microsoft, AT&T and Yahoo! already have significant networks and software packages and a large customer base for their services. They could easily afford to acquire any of the major studios, if they were for sale; subject as always to regulatory approval under anti-trust rules. The merger between Time Warner and AOL marked an ambitious alliance between 'old media' and 'new media'.

Several other companies are present at the top table. They can stand, so to speak, but they cannot sit down. Europe's film companies have declined over the past thirty years, in spite of large public subsidies, and they favour small-scale, low-budget, literary, intricate films rather than the more populist, star-driven movies that mass audiences want. Europe's public broadcasters (BBC, France Télévision, Germany's ARD) are constrained by their public service obligations, and Europe's private broadcasters (ITV, RTL, Sat-1, TF-1, Italy's Mediaset) are too much focused on their national broadcasting markets, especially the move to digital. The British government has said frequently that Britain must be the world's leading creative economy, but its policies on broadcasting, however admirable in protecting the existing services, have a negative impact on national film-making as well as on the new digital media. The national telecommunications networks (British Telecom, France Télécom, Deütsche Telekom) understand the importance of filmed entertainment but prefer to be buyers rather than producers and show little sign of wanting to take the risk of direct involvement.

The Japanese and Korean electronics manufacturers are contenders but, apart from Sony, they have not been in a mood to invest outside their core business for several years. Several large Indian and Malaysian entertainment conglomerates want to boost their output in Asia and a link with Hollywood is one way of doing so, but none of these companies would have any more impact on Hollywood's management style and business processes, or the films, than did their predecessors from Europe, Japan, Australia and Canada.

HOLLYWOOD LESSONS

Looking at the ten management principles for creativity, the first to strike anyone is that the film business is obviously centred around *creative people* both in front of and (even more so) behind the camera. Throughout the industry, from the chairman to the writers, everything revolves around individuals and their powers of persuasion. As an industry that lives off ideas, it knows how elusive and puzzling they can be, and how casual their birth. William Goldman, screenwriter of *Butch Cassidy and the Sundance Kid* and *All the President's Men*, said in *Adventures in the Screen Trade*, his wise book on Hollywood, that 'nobody knows anything'. Which is true, and his colleagues have adopted his remark as a badge of honour. Nobody knows who will have the next idea, or which idea will succeed. The reasons for the success of *Titanic* (another film about the *Titanic*?) and *Toy Story* (a cartoon about toys?) are imponderable. The reason why they got made is that a few people believed in them and managed to make a deal. The art of Hollywood film-making is persuading others to share your vision; persuading actors to perform, directors to direct and, finally, the studio to give you $50 million to play around with.

Hollywood has always been open to anyone who has ideas; who wants to join in; who has a vision. Most of the founding investors were immigrant Europeans. Carl Laemmle, who founded Universal in 1912, was born in Germany. The next four studios were set up in twelve heady months in the early 1920s. The four Warner brothers, whose father was Polish, founded Warner Bros. in April 1923; the Disney brothers founded Disney in October 1923; Harry and Jack Cohn, born of a German father and a Polish mother, founded Columbia in January 1924; and Marcus Loew and Louis B. Mayer, who was Russian, founded MGM in April 1924. Adolph Zukor and William Fox, who jointly founded Fox, were Hungarian. These studio heads attracted people from all over America and Europe and hired (and fired) a succession of directors, technicians and actors.

The second principle of creative management demonstrated by Hollywood is that the business revolves around the *job of thinker*. The thinking in Hollywood is serious and promiscuous. People consider everything from which they can make a film and make money. Hollywood will write its own scripts (*The Matrix*), adapt a novel (*The Talented Mr Ripley*) or remake an existing film (*Three Men and a Baby*, *Psycho*). It has remade *The Four Feathers* four times. It loves sequels and prequels (*Star Wars*). It tells stories about real-life people (*The Insider*) and about aliens (*Alien*). It will even mix the two (*Mars Attacks*). No other medium does this. TV could, but lacks the imagination or the money or the crazy courage. Faced with a quadraplegic actor (Christopher Reeve) it remakes a classic film about a man in a wheelchair (*Rear Window*). It has recently made a film about being inside the head of an actor (*Being John Malkovich*). It will take any idea, however simple or crass it may seem, as the start of its dreams. It is unfazed by normal artistic or literary notions of right and wrong.

Its thinking is simple and focused. Hollywood makes only one product but makes it supremely well. In the 1890s, the first films were performed in funfairs and amusement arcades, and Hollywood has stayed close to these roots. It has given its name to an entertainment medium, and defined the audience, in a way that no other industry has come close to. Its single product is a feature film dealing in universal images and themes, and telling a simple story with sparse dialogue. It is very careful not to offend any religious or ethnic group. Each film has to be understood and liked by many different people: the creative team, the studio, the people who promote it and diverse audiences across the globe. The results can be exhilarating or trite.

The job of thinker is focused on the idea not the technology. Hollywood is suspicious of technologies. This is curious. Film-making is wholly based on the technology of illusion. There is a belief in some circles that 'the camera never lies'. In film-making, the camera always lies, or the cameraman isn't doing his job. The basic technology has changed dramatically but infrequently in a hundred years. Sound was introduced in the late 1920s, colour in the 1940s and live-action animation in the 1990s. Hollywood resisted cable TV, satellite TV and video. Hollywood does not like to innovate. It has not put its own money into animation companies, preferring to subcontract the work. The exception is Disney, but Hollywood only accepted Disney as a major studio when they started to make live-action films in the 1980s. It has resisted the temptation to become involved in video games, except by licensing rights. Hollywood and other film-making companies are driven by content while video game companies are driven by technology. It is a major cultural difference that shows few signs of disappearing; and the game companies are more likely to develop their own content than Hollywood become driven by technology. What Hollywood likes to do, and what it does superbly well, is make a movie on celluloid and release it in a cinema on Friday evening. We like it that way, too. As did our great-grandparents, we go into a big room, sit down in rows (usually on plush red seats), wait a few minutes for the lights to be turned off, and then watch moving pictures on a big white screen. Hollywood may love to make films about technology (preferably technology going badly wrong), but it likes to do so in a traditional way.

It is now facing major technological challenges on several fronts. The new generation of low-cost digital production equipment enables anyone to make a reasonable quality film for a fraction of the conventional cost. This, in turn, allows a new generation of people to become film-makers without needing Hollywood's money (for example, *The*

Blair Witch Project). The cost of cinema distribution is also about to fall. A celluloid print of a 100-minute 35 mm film occupies four or five reels, costs over $1,300, is bulky and heavy, and starts to deteriorate after a few hundred screenings. It costs $400,000 to make enough five-reel prints for a national British release and $3 million for an American release. For a hundred years, there was no alternative. But video distribution, either by DVD or direct-to-cinema by satellite, now delivers sufficiently good quality to wean the companies off celluloid. *Screen Digest* estimates that video distribution could cut worldwide distribution costs from about $5 billion to about $500 million a year, although neither the studios nor the cinemas seem willing to pay for the changeover. Distributors are also worried that using digital will open the door to theft. Third, the growth of the Internet may enable producers to distribute their films worldwide for trivial costs (it is already becoming viable for shorts). I discuss the new technologies more fully in the next chapter. What is not in doubt is that, faced with these challenges, Hollywood will behave as it has always done, and as dominant companies tend to behave in any industry. It will try to continue unchanged for as long as possible.

Hollywood also demonstrates the *creative entrepreneur*, the *post-employment job*, the *just-in-time person*, the *temporary company*, the *network office* and *teamwork*. The entrepreneurs who founded the major studios in the 1920s began by putting everyone (directors, actors, writers) on contracts of employment. They operated their studios like production lines (hence Powdermaker's phrase). Their tight control of resources enabled them to achieve a high and regular output, and they soon dominated film-making in America and then Britain and the rest of the world. In the 1950s, these 'industrial' techniques were challenged by the stars and their agents, who wanted to share in the profits. Over several decades, most people changed from being employees to independent workers. Today, the studios only employ senior management and back-office administrative staff. Everyone else is on short-term contract. A producer or director who takes an idea to the studio will have his own company and, more often than not, will set up a new company to handle each project. Since the 1970s, Hollywood has pioneered the temporary company.

The studio behaves like a lead investor. It provides 'intellectual capital' (see Chapter 7) in terms of benchmark management and accounting and, if required, financial capital as collateral against debt and insurance. The producer operates like a chief executive, putting together a complete team of people from accountants to caterers. They subcontract as much as possible, and most contracts last only a few months. They split the deals into two kinds: the variable or 'above the line' costs payable to the 'talent' and the more routine or 'below the line' costs paid to everyone else. The temporary company uses the local Los Angeles support system, both through the producer's personal contacts and through the studio's formal connections. By the time the film is released, and their names appear on the end credits, most of these just-in-time people will be working with another temporary company on another film.

The temporary company raises finance by licensing various media distribution rights to sales companies. In return, when the producer begins 'principal photography', the buyers of these rights pass over the money to provide cash flow for the production. As the film is given the go-ahead at each stage, it operates more and more as a separate entity. By the time it moves to location it will practically be a closed world. When completed, after an average time of two or three years, it will own two assets: the master negative and the accompanying rights. Each film is a new, single-minded company with its own product that it brings to market.

Hollywood also excels at the *business cluster*. It is home not only to the world's biggest film industry but to the world's biggest TV production companies, which together support a high level of industry skill and experience, supplying everything from animals to lawyers. Whatever people decide to produce, they have access to an efficient manufacturing process with which everyone is familiar. The downside is a me-too quality. Everyone knows what everyone else is doing, and the temptation to follow someone else's success is strong, although this is common in many industries.

Clusters are exclusive. Some newcomers have not realized that, although Hollywood is voraciously open to new talent and money, it likes to use that talent and money in its own special way. Like other clusters, it has an insider mentality. Many investors have been hit. Coca-Cola tried to start a wave of synergy, hoping to cross-promote films and soft drinks, when it bought 49 per cent of Columbia Pictures in 1982, but neither Coca-Cola nor the studio management were happy. In 1989 Sony bought out Coca-Cola for $3.4 billion. In the words of the locals, Sony came to Hollywood and got mugged. As Jack Grubman of the investment bank Salomon Brothers said, 'These guys don't know anything about entertainment.' Sony invested a further $4 billion before showing any profit, and in 1994 wrote off $2.7 billion.

Japan's largest consumer electronics company, Matsushita, followed Sony across the Pacific Ocean in 1990 and bought MCA's Universal Studios for $6.6 billion. But Matsushita was not happy either. In 1995 after five years of corporate discomfort it sold a controlling 80 per cent interest to Canadian Edgar Bronfman Jr, who sold an $8.8 billion stake in giant Du Pont, one of America's oldest companies, to finance the deal. It was a telling demonstration of the trend away from old-style industries (chemicals and materials) into entertainment. In 2000, Vivendi, France's water-turned-media company, moved in the same direction when it acquired Universal and changed its name to Vivendi Universal, only to sell out again in 2004.

The verdict of the *Wall Street Journal* on the first wave of foreign takeovers was damning: 'Even legendary businessmen who are breathtakingly successful everywhere else usually go down in utter miserable defeat in Hollywood. Whatever they tried, most have lost their shirts.' Sony and Matsushita took two opposite strategies: Sony was generous to a fault, Matsushita kept tight control.

One reason for the failures is the newcomers' inability to understand the people. As Barry Diller, a successful entrepreneur who has made serial fortunes in TV, film and home shopping, said when Sony bought Columbia, 'The issue of corporate ownership is irrelevant. What is important is the energy, character and entrepreneurship of the individuals who run the studio. The rest is noise.' After he bought Twentieth-Century Fox, Rupert Murdoch switched his American base from New York to Los Angeles, and liked to drive himself in his Mercedes coupé through the streets to the studio lot, something he seldom does elsewhere. When Edgar Bronfman Jr bought Universal, Murdoch told him, 'You can't own a business like this, with such a unique culture, without being alongside it. Do what I did. Come out here.'

Hollywood has two *financial lessons*. The first is the importance of distribution. The studios not only have good ideas (anyone, as they admit, can have an idea) but they also own the global film distribution network. Each studio operates two separate businesses: production and distribution. It produces about twenty of its own films a year, which have guaranteed distribution worldwide. It also buys the distribution rights to many more. Most so-called British films are financed and distributed by Hollywood, so the profits go to America not Britain. Murdoch's Fox produced *The Full Monty* and Disney's Miramax financed *The English Patient* and *Shakespeare in Love*. Hollywood's control of marketing, distribution and cinemas is even tighter than its control of the directors and stars. It is difficult for any film, American or not, to be distributed worldwide unless Hollywood decides to take it on. This expenditure, and decades of experience, is its best defence against cheap production and foreign competition. Foreign films may, sometime within the next few decades, match Hollywood in production terms, but they are unlikely to match its worldwide marketing skills.

The most revealing fact about Hollywood's finances is that it spends about six times as much on marketing a film ($40 million) as Britain spends on making one ($7 million). Worldwide, Hollywood's average *marketing* budget is twenty times the average *production* budget.

Hollywood's second financial lesson is 'keep it complex'. Its finances are notoriously opaque, delighting insiders and frustrating outsiders. It is virtually impossible for anyone not intimately involved to know the real cost of a film. The only people who know are the people who negotiate each deal (who will know only their deal) and the studio accountants. The local press estimate production costs by taking a consensus of industry views, and can calculate gross box office revenues by what cinemas say; but how much of these revenues is retained by the studio, especially as the years go by, is a profound mystery. Only twice in recent years have the studios' accounting practices been revealed, and only then under court order: once when writer Art Buchwald sought payment for an original story which Paramount Pictures later turned into *Coming to America*, and again when Jeffrey Katzenberg took the Walt Disney Company to court for not paying his profit-related bonus. This secrecy, which is endemic but which is even greater now that each studio is part of a large conglomerate, prevents others from knowing their business, and inhibits competition.

Film-making is an exponent of 'sunk costs', investments that cannot be recovered. Once produced, a film cannot be unproduced, but the cost of copying is low and, if demand is high, the rewards are tremendous. In a rare burst of confidence, *Variety* estimated that Fox spent $96 million to produce *Independence Day*, made up of advance fees to the two producers, Dean Devlin and Roland Emmerich, of $15 million; a production cost of $71 million, including $23 million for special effects; a studio overhead of $5 million; and advance distribution expenses of $5 million. All these costs were incurred before the film was released and before anyone knew if it was a blockbuster or a booby. *Independence Day* was one of the lucky ones. The total box office revenues on the first release exceeded $800 million, excluding income from video and TV, which should bring in as much again.

Hollywood did not invent synergy (Hollywood invents very little) but it has exploited it further than any other industry. It is not surprising that, according to *Billboard*, the three longest-running top ten singles in Britain's pop music chart have been Bryan Adams's 'Everything I Do (I Do For You)', which featured in *Robin Hood: Prince of Thieves*; Whitney Houston's 'I Will Always Love You', featured in *The Bodyguard*; and Wet Wet Wet's version of the Troggs' 'Love is All Around', featured in *Four Weddings and a Funeral*. Warner Bros.' matching of Kevin Costner and Whitney Houston in *The Bodyguard* was a marketing decision to promote Houston, and her CD with 'I Will Always Love You' sold ten times as many copies as her two previous albums combined.

Making a film of a book is commonplace, and making a book of a film is now equally so. The next logical step was initiated by Andrew Vacchs's *Batman* novel, which was based on Warner Bros.' film *Batman*, which was based on the comics. Full circle was reached with Laurie Lawlor's book of *Little Women*, which was based on Robin Swicord's script for Columbia Pictures' *Little Women*, which was based on Louisa May Alcott's original book *Little Women*. When asked what happens when a customer asks for a copy of *Little Women* without specifying an author, Esther Margolis of Newmarket Communications, who set up the film, admitted, 'I'm not sure the public really know the difference between the versions.' Cross-breeding formats is nothing new. What is new is the deliberate exploitation of ideas in different formats at the same time. All the Hollywood studios now have special divisions to create books from films. This diversity is a sign of health, because it continuously revitalizes the creative gene pool; it stimulates hybrids and crossovers in form and content. The result is a high level of volatility, a loss of identity for authors, and a blurring of the boundaries between the original and a copy, and perhaps between a 'true story' and 'just a story'.

The global entertainers want to own as much of this value chain as possible. Each company's dream scenario is to own an idea or a brand that can be sold through its own media into every home in every country. *The X Files* illustrates how this can happen. Fox showed the first series on the Fox Network where, because the new network had small audiences, it attracted little attention. But Fox was able to license the series to its video label and its BSkyB satellite service, which produced enough revenue to justify making the series for four more years, which was sufficient to sell it for local reruns (helped by the fact that Fox owned eighteen US TV stations). Five years later, *The X Files* became a hit and Fox could exploit it through Fox Interactive, HarperCollins publishers, Fox Licensing and its FX cable channel, and Twentieth-Century Fox could make the films. Without that initial synergy, *The X Files* would probably have died after one series.

Hollywood also leads the world in merchandising, a kind of indirect synergy in which a film licenses its brand to other companies for their goods and services. The rewards can be immense. In its first two years, Disney's *The Lion King* earned three times as much through merchandise as the box office. Warner's *Batman*, a classic brand, earned twice as much. In 1987, Disney toys and other merchandise earned $25 billion worldwide, which is more than twice as much as Toys 'R' Us earned that year. Disney is much courted by hamburger chains. McDonald's paid Disney a reported $2 billion to entice it away from rival Burger King, consisting of a $100 million a year retainer for Disney's base 10–15 titles and an additional $30–50 million a year for each new blockbuster. Doug Investor, when chairman of Coca-Cola, said his company lived off such alliances: 'A hundred per cent of our revenues comes from alliances, originally with bottlers and distributors and now with other brands.'

The tenth management principle is *deals and hits*. Hollywood takes a portfolio approach to each step in the value chain: research, development, production and distribution. At any one time a major studio will have thousands of ideas, concepts and treatments under consideration. Most, if not all, will go to script stage, and the scripts will be used to attract directors and actors. On average, each studio will 'green-light' twenty of these productions a year, of which two or three will make large amounts of money (around ten times their production cost), two or three will flop and the remainder will cover their cost. In essence, the studio sustains itself creatively and commercially by sifting through many thousands of ideas to produce two or three hits. The music and book businesses operate in a similar way.

It helps that Hollywood has the only global star system, and its stars are known worldwide to an extent unattainable in other industries. Every national audience looks at their own national stars and at the bright lights of Hollywood, but seldom glances anywhere else. For example, the British know their national film stars and Hollywood's film stars but they are generally ignorant of, and care little for, the film stars of neighbouring France, Germany and Spain. The same bias is true in every country.

Simply by being, stars promote themselves, their latest film and the Hollywood system. They are the raw material for the world's TV, radio, newspapers and magazines, which carry 'exclusive' interviews with stars whose sole purpose is to promote themselves. The deal gets better. The advertising is free. It is Hollywood's final lesson.

'THAT'S NOT ALL, FOLKS!'

It may be thought that Hollywood and the global entertainment industry is a unique business from which others can learn little. It is true that it is uniquely big and dominant, and operates on a grand scale, but that is no disqualification. It is also true that many other countries produce wonderful films. Many European, Russian and Chinese film-makers (to name my own favourites) have a depth and sensibility and thoughtfulness that Hollywood cares little for and, if it tried, could not deliver. But, according to their own producers and directors, these industries cannot operate without large public subsidies. As a process for turning ideas into business, and as sustainable economics, Hollywood can teach some useful lessons. Working with the people who live and work there has persuaded me that its straightforward focus and business processes are useful models for all creative businesses, in every industry, large or small, commercial or public.

In recent years, the ordinary economy has begun to see the benefits of Hollywood's ways of working. It may wince at some of its grosser extravagance (Hollywood itself forgives waste if the result is a hit, although it never forgives failure), but it admires its creative and technical proficiency. It admires its total, single-minded dedication to turning ideas into brands, stories, stars and profit. As more companies become dependent upon the creative, so they look to these 'Hollywood lessons'. They copy Hollywood's 'temporary company' and business cluster, which film-makers have been operating for decades. They copy its simplicity; its promiscuity; its bravado.

6

CLICK-AND-GO

LAW 6: THE NEW ECONOMY IS CREATIVITY PLUS ELECTRONICS

'Whaddya going to do on the planet today?'
Grateful Dead

'Where do you want to go today?'
Microsoft

RICHARD ROGERS

Architects and designers are the most global of all creative people, as we saw in Chapter 3. They are also amongst the most collaborative of workers, cooperating not only amongst themselves but with a diverse bunch of people who otherwise might have little in common: clients, local planning and zoning authorities, structural engineers and interior designers. To introduce this chapter on the Internet, I could have chosen a computer guru. Instead, as I hope will become clear, an architect seems more fitting.

Richard Rogers is one of the world's leading architects. It was not something that he expected to do: 'I had dyslexia and was backward as a child, a slow learner. At one stage, someone advised me to become a policeman!' But family and friends in Florence, where he was born, saw a talent for design and architecture. He trained at London's Architecture Association and Yale University, and has worked in London ever since, though he still looks the cosmopolitan Italian. In 1971 he and Renzo Piano won against 680 competitors the contract to design the Centre Georges Pompidou in Beaubourg, Paris, which became Europe's best-known new building of the decade. He later won competitions to design the headquarters of Lloyd's of London, the European Court of Human Rights in Strasbourg, and the headquarters of Channel 4 in London. He was responsible for the overall design of the Millennium Dome – but not at all for the contents.

Like Norman Foster, with whom he was briefly in partnership, he has pioneered the use of structural technology. He has made a virtue of making such technology open and visible, as in the Pompidou and Lloyd's buildings, which wear their technology on their sleeve, and in the tent-like shape of the Millennium Dome.

Architecture is a very public profession. 'I always have two clients: the user and the passer-by.' He sees the Pompidou as a very honest building: 'It's open to all, it shows itself to the world.' An original, stylish and exciting building enhances the planet. An ugly one insults us.

He is not sure of the meaning of the word 'creativity', saying, 'It's so broad, like the word "design". When Einstein was asked how he made his great discoveries, he said, "by using the imagination" and I suppose creativity means using the imagination to move forward. We all do this, all the time.' Of the two main meanings of creativity ('creating something from nothing' and 'giving a new character to something'), he favours the second. He says 'giving birth' is too violent. He prefers the idea of 'giving life', because the process is incremental: 'It's quite slow work, even though things do sneak up on one. Everything is based on something else. Very little is new. From the moment we are born, we are imbued with experiences.' He says that as he gets older he becomes more canny at spotting the way ahead.

When I asked which of his buildings were the most creative in this sense he said, 'For me the process is always more interesting than the result; and so whichever I'm working on at the time is the most creative, the most exciting.' He did suggest two, however: the house he built for his parents in Wimbledon, because of the congruity of family and profession, and the Pompidou Centre, which is the most successful integration of the inside and outside, the public and private.

He likes working in public spaces like cafés and on trains. He likes the buzz of the street, of people going about their daily business. His home, just off London's King's Road, contains a large open space which seems to follow Camillo Sitte's principles, expressed in his classic 1889 book, *City Planning According to Artistic Principles*, based on certain relationships of size and shape, height and width, and irregular entrances and sightlines. He has reinterpreted an Italian piazza where people sit and gossip; a haven of creative collaboration.

Like others I met, Rogers sees creativity as a universal talent. 'Everyone has creativity. You can't say scientists like Einstein and Darwin were not creative. You cannot make any distinction between Picasso and Einstein in terms of creativity. You can say the scientist is less *artistic*, but that's a different matter. I think someone who works in business is creative in the same way as is the artist and scientist.'

CREATIVITY AND TECHNOLOGY

This chapter examines the relationship between creativity and the digital technologies of information and communications. By 'digital' I mean the digital symbolic language which codes data, whether text, audio or video, into a stream of digital bits. Compared to the atoms which make up the physical world, these digital bits are weightless and intangible. This digital coding is a major technological influence on how we have ideas and how we express, share and communicate them. I want to look at how it affects their content and their economics.

The history of these technologies since the invention of the transistor in 1947 recounts the design and manufacturing of ever more powerful semiconductor microprocessors (chips) to manipulate digital bits. The first integrated silicon chips in 1958 had about 200 transistors. The latest Pentium chips have about 100 million, and by 2003 the labs expect to be producing chips with over a billion. We use these chips to provide more powerful and faster computers, and wider and more flexible networking, of which the supreme example is the Internet.

The Internet does provide excellent one-to-one linkages, as does the telephone network. More importantly, it provides a wide range of multi-directional communications. MIT researcher Michael Schrage, author of *Shared Minds*, devised a theory in 1990 that networks are primarily used to reach other networks. Robert Metcalfe, who invented Ethernet networking and then founded 3Com Inc., the maker of the Palm Pilot, proposed a 'law of networks' which says that 'the community value of a network grows as the square of the number of nodes increases' (i.e., the people or computers attached to it). The smallest possible network consists of two people who can talk only to each other; in this case, Metcalfe's value is 4. If a third person joins, the number of connections rises to three; and Metcalfe's value is 9. If a fourth, it rises to six; and the value is 16. The number of possible connections always increases faster than the number of nodes. With 200 million access points it is possible to connect with 200 million other people; and the network value is 40 million billion; with a billion it is a billion billion or 10^{17}. The number is too big to grasp, but does demonstrate the exponential scale of connectivity.

Although the Internet is a network of computers, neither the computers nor the wires between them are its main essence. The analogy of the information superhighway is exactly wrong. It suggests wide motorways scything across the country from city centre to city centre. The Internet is not a hard-wired network, like the telephone network, but a soft network, consisting of the manners, rules and procedures by which we use the hard network. It is best described as a set of administrative arrangements for connecting users to information via, as Schrage foresaw, other networks. It is air, not tarmac. In part, this chapter is about these administrative arrangements.

At first, the owners of the hard networks (for example, AT&T, BT) hardly noticed the Internet. For many years, it had no impact on their infrastructures, services or prices. In the 1970s, computers were clumsy and slow (the first desktop PC and Apple Mac did not arrive until the late 1970s) and the Internet and its predecessors were limited to a thin-route exchange for data and short sentences. Both computers and networks could only handle ideas that could be easily and quickly expressed in numerical or verbal formats; the style was brief, staccato. In the 1990s, as computers grew in power and the World Wide Web began to spread, they combined to handle a wider range of ideas (longer texts, and simple diagrams and drawings) and they could share them with more people. In the (current) third stage, ordinary PCs and Macs can produce and copy colours, sounds, pictures and even moving images, and the Internet can distribute them worldwide to millions. In the fourth stage, these technologies will be able to replicate most of the quality as well as the quantity of production and distribution of texts, sounds and images that happen in the physical world. They will do so at the same or at a lower cost. They will be able to reach a market counted in millions or even billions; equally, and perhaps more often, they will link special, smaller groups; and always, of course, instantaneously. (I make no comment at this stage about the Internet's long-term effects on other forms of production and distribution; but I fully expect as many people as now will go to cafés and reach for a blank sheet of paper to express an idea.)

The volume of Internet traffic overtook the volume of telephony in America in 1998 and did so in other OECD countries in 2000. Internet traffic reached over three times the level of telephony throughout OECD countries by 2005. These volumes of traffic are being generated by the relatively small proportion of subscribers who are connected to the Internet and, as the number of Internet users grows as high as the number of telephone subscribers, we can expect Internet traffic to become even more substantial until around 2010 over 95 per cent of traffic on the so-called telephone network will be Internet data and only about 5 per cent will be telephone traffic. The number of Internet users at the beginning of 2001, according to the US Department of Commerce, was about 387 million. They were spread as follows: America and Canada had 171 million users (44 per cent of the total), Europe had 113 million (29 per cent), Asia/Pacific 79 million (20 per cent), South America 18 million (5 per cent), Africa just over 3 million (1 per cent) and the Middle East 3 million (1 per cent). Home access varies widely. In America, Canada, Scandinavia, Singapore and Australia over 40 per cent of households have access to the Internet, in Britain over 30 per cent and in France and Germany 25 per cent. Motorola estimated at the beginning of 2000 that the world had about 800 million fixed-line telephone subscribers, 250 million cellular wireless (cell) subscribers and 250 million Internet subscribers. By 2005, it reported, there were 1 billion fixed-line subscribers, 1 billion mobile subscribers and 1 billion Internet users. One billion people (and their family and friends) will have access to a network that is integral to and custom-made for the making of many creative products and highly efficient for their distribution.

The technical principles will remain the same. The system turns ideas into digital code; enables this code to be put up on the Internet under various kinds of administrative arrangement, of which the most common are either privately to named addresses or published for everyone; and, if published, invites anyone to take it off the Internet and use, store, edit and even resell it. But its content, its *usefulness*, is determined by technical and economic factors, and by questions of ownership.

These factors are being driven by the three trends which I discuss in the rest of this chapter. Computers are becoming faster and cheaper; and not only computers but, in theory, the processes (for example, management procedures) that depend on computers. I say 'in theory' because, while the rule holds absolutely for the chips themselves, their applications are affected by exogenous factors. But the trend, and the speed of development, is remarkably consistent. Second, these cost reductions support the construction of a new kind of network that is variously described as 'obedient', 'transparent' and even 'stupid' (the latter epithet being high praise). These two factors, in turn, support a process best described as 'collaborative creativity', with implications for the ownership of, and compensation for, creative products. The discussion of collaborative creativity leads to some comments about computer code as private law. Finally, I look at the impact on the main copyright industries of publishing, TV and film, and music.

MOORE'S LAW MARK II

My first point is about power and cost. The power of digital, as a symbolic language, has no material but only intellectual limits.

Gordon Moore, one of the pioneers of Silicon Valley, who collaborated with Robert Noyce on the invention of the first microprocessor and later founded Intel, said in the 1960s that the number of components on a chip doubles every twenty-four months. The reason is that designers and engineers continually become more skilful and, yes, creative at their tasks. Moore found that this higher productivity could not be explained by conventional reasons, such as economies of scale; he also found that Ricardo's law of diminishing returns, which might have pulled up labour costs, had little impact. Instead, he realized that the designers were becoming better with practice, and that their cleverness could be quantified and measured. He is still being proved right. As a result, either chip speeds double or, if the manufacturer wishes to keep speeds the same, the price is halved, every eighteen to twenty-four months. So a chip does twice as much for the same cost, or the same for half the cost. To predict these changes in the 'power curve' with such accuracy, in such an apparently volatile business as computer R & D, was an astonishing achievement.

Moore was looking at chip speeds. Joe Carter of Accenture, has extended the principle from the chips in computers to everything that depends upon computers, and asked some provoking questions. What happens when these processes halve in time, or costs halve, every few years? Such rapid changes in such a welcome direction would be incredible in the material world but are feasible in the virtual world of the digital economy. For example, says Carter, the cost of buying and managing property, the cost of transport, warehousing and logistics, and the cost of clerical work are close to being minimal or zero. The unit cost of sending information, whether a text, music or full-colour picture, is trivial.

Kevin Kelly, of the San Francisco-based *WIRED* magazine, put a persuasive case in 1997 that this radical reduction in the cost of digital space and networks is causing a 'new economy' which represents a clean break with previous manufacturing and service economies. He says the new economy has three characteristics; it deals in intangible goods and services, it is global and it is 'intensely interlinked'. A 1998 report by the Department of Trade and Industry, *Our Competitive Future: Building the Knowledge-Driven Economy*, says, 'Markets and supply chains may be radically altered by the widespread adoption of electronic commerce . . . Virtual companies of the future may have little in common with today's organization.'

These changes affect all industries to the extent that they depend upon processing power, which means they have a most emphatic effect on the production and distribution of words, music and pictures. The cost of creating, editing, storing, moving and displaying a still or moving picture is halving every few years. Directors, whether of a home movie, an advertising commercial or a feature film, can either have twice the number of shots every eighteen to twenty-four months or have the same number of shots for half the cost.

To a professional accustomed to paying upwards of £125,000 for a 35 mm film camera, a digital video (DV) camera for under £10,000 is irresistibly cheap. DV tape costs £30 an hour; film costs £1,400 an hour for stock and processing. Thomas Vinterberg recorded *Festen* (*Celebration*), which won the 1999 Cannes Palme d'Or, with cameras costing under £2,000 each, making a virtue of their light weight and grainy picture quality. In 2000, the BBC recorded its first DV drama, *Nice Girls*, for a total budget of £190,000, about a quarter of the average, and few viewers could tell the difference. Sony, which owns Columbia Pictures, financed Hollywood's first DV film, *Time Code 2000*, for about $3 million, a fraction of the normal cost. As TV producer David Thomas says, 'For an enterprising programme-maker, a camera he can operate himself, light enough to carry around all day and cheap enough to use like a tape recorder, is better than a new train set.'

Musicians can use a computer's basic cut-and-paste functions not only to write words but to write music, transposing from one key to another as easily as a writer changes a font size. They can use the same program to compose, record and perform. Software applications on a mid-range PC like Musical Instrument Digital Interface (MIDI) and Virtual Studio Technology (VST) make desktop music as easy as desktop writing and publishing. The effect on content and culture has been dramatic. Without it, Britain's rave and club scene with its techno, drum-and-base and hip-hop music, which was the dominant youth culture of the 1990s, could not have happened. It required cheap production and remixes, portable equipment and technical standards shared throughout the entertainment and leisure industries.

MIDI increased the level of production, and also enabled new formats of music to be produced and distributed. It changed the economics of the composing and recording industry, putting more power and more control over revenues in the hands of individual musicians and DJs. It generated a new kind of club, which has affected how people spend their leisure hours.

Any new technology tends to have these layered, iterative effects. First it cuts costs for existing companies; then it allows new companies to come and produce a new kind of product which has a more general impact. The remarkable attributes of digital are its speed and, so far, its predictability.

THE STUPID NETWORK

The second trend is that networks, as they become cheaper, are becoming more obedient. For decades, the telephone companies built hard-wired networks with more capacious pipes, and more complicated software, in the reasonable hope that they would be able to interpret and handle whatever was thrown at them. Their business strategy was to anticipate customer needs, offer special premium services for high-spending business customers, and generally to control and manage the network. They called it the 'intelligent network'.

But however 'intelligent' they tried to make it, people wanted something more or different. A contrary view was articulated in 1996 by David Isenberg, a senior researcher at AT&T, in an internal paper provocatively entitled, 'The Rise of the Stupid Network: Why the Intelligent Network was once a good idea, but isn't anymore'. Isenberg said the classic telephone company was locked into four assumptions: that infrastructure is scarce and can command a high price; that talk generates most traffic; that hard-wired, network circuit-switching is the key technology of the future; and that the telephone company controls the network. He said that all these assumptions are crumbling. Bandwidth is becoming freely available; data is beginning to outpace voice (he meant digital data which carries text, sound or pictures); hard switches are being replaced by more flexible routers; and enforced liberalization and the growth of competition means that no single company owns the network, let alone controls it. Isenberg envisaged a network that functioned as a dumb servant instead of a master controller. He believed networks should do as they are told. The user should be in control: 'Networks should be guided by the needs of the data, not the design assumptions of the owner.' He put the vaunted 'intelligent network' in the same category as the 'paperless office'; a fruitless attempt to organize people's needs which ignored their real instincts and preferences.

Isenberg's radical paper was described by Tom Evslin, president of AT&T WorldNet Service, as 'like a glass of cold water in the face'. *Computer Telephony* magazine described it as 'potentially the most controversial paper to come out of the telephone industry, ever'. At heart, it was a plea to all network operators to rethink their whole approach. Although the companies did not welcome the message, most realized times had changed and began to deconstruct and rebuild their networks as fast as they could. The choice between intelligent and stupid networks surfaced again in a series of arguments between the PC industry and the network industry a few years later. Where do you want intelligence: in the network or in the devices attached to it?

The new architecture is Internet-based. The Internet communication protocols, regulating who talks to who, and how, will shape all communications technologies for the next two decades. I normally shrink from giving technology forecasts, but I am confident of this one. The old telephone companies planned their existing networks to provide two-way telephony that needs a small fixed amount of bandwidth for a long time (typically for several minutes). In contrast, Internet traffic requires a network that can handle separate packets containing varying amounts of data for very brief periods (perhaps many gigabytes for only a millisecond). The Internet protocols are known as IP, which leads to playful confusion when Internet people meet intellectual property people. All major network companies are now building IP networks not only for Internet traffic but as the basic structure for all traffic. Rex Hundt, former chairman of the Federal Communications Commission, puts it well: 'What we have is a copper-based network designed to carry voice which can also carry data and which we are trying to make capable of carrying pictures. What we want is a network which is designed to carry data and is therefore capable of carrying everything else.' BT puts it even more strongly: 'IP has established itself as the key design point or architectural force for a twenty-first century network.' Just as one IP is the financial currency of the information age, so the other IP provides its networks.

David Isenberg had studied human consciousness under Nobel laureate Albert Szent-Györgyi, a researcher into cells and vitamins who was also a vociferous opponent of the US and global military-political establishment. His background made him aware that the idea of an obedient network had implications beyond network engineering and customer service. It changes the extent that users can communicate their own ideas in the way they wish. In Isenberg's phrase, the network's job is to 'Deliver the bits, stupid'. The user is in control. It is a liberating philosophy. It makes the person, the user, responsible for the idea. It seeks to reduce network constraints to zero (as Isenberg says, to the 'insignificantly trivial') so the message, the content, is absolutely robust.

This hardly matters with telephony but is profoundly important with more complicated content, especially formatted text, audio and video. The dangers of bossy networks can be illustrated by two examples, one (relatively) old, one new. Java is a universal programming language that allows users to access a small program embedded in a web page without having the relevant application. It allows users to access a wide variety of material that otherwise would be unobtainable. This is very useful. But it comes at a cost. It strips out the content's format and design, reducing it to the bare minimum. Much better to have a network that simply transmits whatever I give it. The second, newer example is streaming, which is the core element in webcasting or Internet broadcasting. Streaming uses Internet protocols to send video and audio along a telephone line. It can deliver radio programmes, and over 4,000 radio stations now webcast continually. It can also send TV programmes, but with imperfect picture quality as yet. Steven Spielberg says the technique has 'unlimited potential'; he might also have said 'unknown'. What is certain is that its pioneers are making new 'administrative arrangements' just as fast as they reconfigure the technical constraints, and no network operator, however intelligent, can anticipate them. The successful development of streaming wants a passive, obedient network that knows nothing about each arrangement but can cope with them all, as a road knows nothing about the vehicles that pass happily over its surface.

WORKING TOGETHER

One way an obedient network can assist creativity is through faster, more transparent and more intense collaboration. It can facilitate 'collaborative creativity', involving an open and free discussion around a common purpose, without necessarily stopping at fixed points to claim private property rights. This way of working may be more efficient and produce more elegant results than 'single' working in the conventional manner.

In 'collaborative creativity', everyone is given equal, meritocratic access to the same body of knowledge and is able, even encouraged, to contribute to its development in a free, open and collaborative manner. It is easy, in such a fluid environment, to lose control of one's ideas and products, and to have them replaced by others'. Its adherents believe the risk is well worth taking.

This openness was built into the original Internet and remains its motif. The Internet was designed by the US administration and university researchers to provide a scientific and research network for the exchange of text and data files. In order to be flexible and easily accessible by people with minimal computer skills, it used simple, universal protocols which nobody owned and which could be freely adapted. In order to be safe against hostile military action, it used multi-threaded, packet-switched technologies so that if one part of the network was destroyed the remainder could carry on. These two factors explain its character today: a universal, non-proprietary standard with an indefinitely large number of pathways. Individuals own servers and computers, and the links between them, but nobody owns the system.

From the beginning, few people claimed to control the 'administrative arrangements' or to claim copyright or register a patent. Briton Donald Davies and American Paul Baron, who separately invented packet-switching, claimed no copyright. Tim Berners-Lee at CERN (now called the European Organization for Nuclear Research) in Geneva, who initially developed the World Wide Web, did not assert copyright or claim a patent. Nor did the inventors of the Apache software which operates the majority of servers; SendMail, which runs over 80 per cent of e-mail programs; Bind, which turns numerical e-mail addresses into plain English; and Perl, which facilitates hypertext links. None is private property.

The standard-bearer of collaborate creativity on the Internet is GNU/Linux, whose present form is the result of many thousands of people contributing improvements, adjustments and refinements. Linux is a piece of software known as a program kernel, which constitutes the basic building blocks of one or more programs. It was developed while he was at university by Linus Torvalds, a Finnish programmer. GNU is an operating system which uses the Linux kernel. Its name is a recursive acronym, an acronym that includes itself, for 'GNU's Not Unix!' (computer hackers love verbal puns). It refers to AT&T's Unix language, which is disliked by many Internet users for its strict licensing conditions and high costs. The idea was that Linux and then GNU/Linux should be the opposite: no licensing conditions, and cheap.

Linus Torvalds put no proprietary restrictions on the source code which constitutes his program's essential design elements. Nor did the devisers of GNU. They gave away the source code for free on two grounds: first as a moral absolute that nobody should own something so basic as computer code; and second on the intellectual and economic grounds that private ownership inhibits growth. Torvalds says the person who wants to own source code is like a man who, having invented a printing press, also wants to own the letters so that everyone who wants to rearrange letters into words and words into sentences has to seek his permission. Michael Century of McGill University, Montreal, has described the developers of Linux and GNU as having three principles: a specific, but limited, amount of editorial 'steering'; treating users as competent to modify its content and performance; and requiring these users' contributions to be transparent, modular and non-proprietary. Century makes a distinction between 'transformative' collaboration in which users develop and adapt the open source code (like Linux and GNU), and consumerist collaboration, in which they use the code to obtain existing files (like Gnutella, Napster and Freenet).

The proponents of open source have different views about how far this openness should go. They agree that a program's source code should remain for ever in the public domain. They also agree that a program's spin-off code may be sold commercially, and many companies sell Linux packages (for example, Red Hat and VA Linux). Where they disagree is whether these spin-offs may become private property. Torvalds, promoting open source, says people may claim copyright. Richard Stallman, the originator of GNU and leader of the Free Software Foundation (FSF), argues with evangelical fervour that code, in any form, must never be privatized. He has devised a General Public Licence (GPL) which functions as a copyright licence under the Berne convention and puts a program permanently in the public domain. He calls it 'copyleft' because it does the opposite of copyright. Instead of restraining how people use materials, it liberates them. The GPL says, inter alia:

(4) You may not copy, modify, sublicense, or distribute the program except as expressly provided under this licence. Any attempt otherwise to copy, modify, sublicense or distribute the program is void, and will automatically terminate your rights under this licence . . .
(5) You are not required to accept this licence, since you have not signed it. However, nothing else grants you permission to modify or distribute the program or its derivative works. These actions are prohibited by law if you do not accept this licence. Therefore, by modifying or distributing the program (or any work based on the program), you indicate your acceptance of this licence . . .'

Anyone can run, adopt and distribute the program; but in order to adopt it, one has to gain access to the source code and, by so doing, one accepts the licence. Stallman wants to replace copyright, which supports a rights-owner's right to protect, with this system of copyleft, which would protect a user's right to access. He sees the GPL as the flagship of copyleft.

It is often asked, how do people working for free on open source get paid? They receive what they call 'reward and consolation': reward for success and consolation for failure. The reward might be status and prestige; or offers of other (paid) work. The consolation might be peer support and comfort. Torvalds and Stallman have both kinds of reward and consolation in abundance. It is not irrelevant that both men worked in a university environment, where these community-based remuneration systems are well developed. There are parallels with many other cooperative ecologies where people cluster to carry out collaborative work (restaurant kitchens, sports teams), but open code on the Internet has two distinct features. It centres around a product that is normally subject to property laws, and it operates with unique speed and universality.

By the industry's own standards, Linux and GNU are outstanding successes. According to researchers IDC, Linux had 25 per cent of the server market in 2004, second only to Microsoft NT, which had 38 per cent. IBM, Apple, Sun and other corporations have looked to see how they might include Linux in their programs; and IBM has invested heavily to do so. Microsoft is aware of the threat. In 1997 an internal Microsoft report, dubbed the 'Halloween Report', admitted, 'Linux and other OS [open source] advocates are making a progressively more credible argument that OS is at least as reliable, if not more, than commercial alternatives. The ability of the OS process to collect and harness the collective IQ of thousands of individuals across the Internet is simply amazing.' Computer expert Eric Raymond, whose 1997 article, 'The Cathedral and the Bazaar', inspired Netscape to make its Communicator source code freely available, puts the case forcefully: 'The open source world behaves in many respects like a free market or an ecology, a collection of selfish agents attempting to maximize utility which in the process produces a self-correcting spontaneous order more elaborate and efficient than any amount of central planning could have achieved.'

Many people like it this way, and are hostile to law and regulation. Hippy libertarian computer pioneers and banks and business interests both want to keep government out of the Internet, if for quite different reasons. The former want a free market because they are left-wing, upholding the Internet's original 'gift economy' and are instinctively opposed to 'big brother' intervention; and the latter because they are right-wing and resent government's attempts to regulate content and tax e-commerce. When Peter Martin, deputy editor of the *Financial Times*, set out to describe the Internet's impact on business in 1998 he caught this spirit, which goes far beyond open source and free software, and even beyond the Internet.

> The Internet's ad hoc, flexible, consensual structure offers powerful lessons to everyone in business. It is, in some ways, a prototype of the way companies will have to operate in future. The consensus stems from a shared purpose: the creation of a network that allows easy communication. This is in part a technical vision, and it requires deep knowledge of computer science. But it is also an ideological one, requiring a humanistic commitment to freedom of expression and to a medium of communication that rises above the interests of government and commerce . . . An ethic of collaboration and open discussion around a common purpose is an extraordinarily powerful and creative force.

This collaborative ethic is responsible for most of the Internet's more imaginative and innovative content. It was not the existing music industry, least of all one of the major five companies, that led the development of the Internet for music creation and distribution. The variety of ways in which it is now possible to make, perform, record, publish and send one's own music, and the intricate ways it is possible to identify, capture, retrieve and play someone else's, owe very little to the music industry and almost everything to the Internet pioneers and their computer companies. Interestingly, the traditional companies are based in New York and London (except for BMG in Gütersloh, Germany) while the latter are clustered in northern California.

This ethic is also responsible for most of the Internet's innovative legal relationships. The Internet's 'administrative arrangements', even when they have legal force, which is seldom, are rarely picked up by the official legal system's radar screens. They are developing outside society's consensus on how property should be defined; how contracts are drawn up; how tax is levied; and how the law of tort and misdemeanours is applied. The extent of this vacuum has been vividly described by Lawrence Lessig, Berkman Professor of Constitutional Law at Harvard University, who came to public prominence, and won liberal credentials, when he was appointed 'Special Master' (or friend of the court) to Judge Penfield Jackson in the US government's 1998 anti-trust case against Microsoft. Lessig wrote in *Atlantic Monthly* in the same year, 'Life on the Internet is regulated; its regulation, however, is not primarily through law. Its primary regulation is the code of cyberspace itself – the software and hardware that together set the terms, or the rules, or the law of how behaviour will be. This code allows some people to protect their work and others to copy it.' He concluded, 'Code is private law.' His book, *Code and Other Laws of Cyberspace*, published in 1999, was pessimistic about the likelihood that governments would grasp the issue before it was too late; before code had become so embedded in the workings of the Internet, and everything dependent upon the Internet, that it could not be unscrambled.

Open source code challenges the concepts of individual rights and responsibilities. These concepts are one of the cornerstones of the legal system and underpin the notion of the single author and inventor that lies at the heart of copyright and patent law. As we have seen, the idea of the 'author' and author's rights emerged in Europe around the 1400s and first flowered in the 1700s. Martha Woodmansee, author of 'On the Author Effect: Recovering Collectivity', has shown how we may be moving (or returning) to collective forms of authorship. James Boyle, author of *Shamans, Software and Spleens*, says the concept of an author is a romantic notion ill-suited to an information society.

The literary, artistic and musical works that constitute what is regarded as Western culture are primarily single works (for example, novels, plays, concertos, paintings). Contemporary forms are more likely to be multiple works (for example, illustrated books, films, TV programmes, video games, CD-ROMs, computer programs). At the risk of over-simplification, forms that flourished before 1900 were primarily single works; works that evolved during the twentieth century were a mix of both; and works that grow from, or depend on, digital code have a tendency to multiple authorship.

The chief reason, I believe, is the technologies of reproduction which allow us to mix formats. They also allow us to bring in authors (and to wave goodbye to them, too) at all stages of the creative process, from the thinking of the original idea to its design and marketing. In turn, this has led us to act like editors and impresarios of other people's work; to be tenants, rather than owners, of property rights.

The authorship of inventions is moving in parallel with that of copyright works, from the named individual to the group. From their beginnings, patents were awarded to individuals. When a company applies for a patent it still does so in the name of the employee who did the work. This principle made moral, legal and economic sense when the majority of inventors worked privately and on their own, but today the private inventor is a rarity. The majority of applications are actually made by corporations, even if they are nominally made by individuals; and they typically list not one but three or more names. And it is the corporation, consisting of all shareholders, who own the patent, not the individual inventor.

Open and free collaboration, restrained and discreet editorial steering, ideas held in the public domain, a refusal to rush into property rights, a constant revision leading to more elegant solutions, peer group rewards and consolation, even a moral sense of equity and integrity; these phrases evoke many communal forms of creativity from the historical beginnings of science to the modern idea of the university and the network office. It also characterizes the public Human Genome Mapping Project. Tim Hubbard, director of the Sanger Centre for genome research in Cambridge, says the Project's Ensembl software, which investigates and compares strings of genes, will work like Linux. The Internet vision adds its own qualities of accessibility, immediacy and universality, and on a scale that can vary from the intimate to the massive.

THE ELECTRIC MARKET

Creativity exploits, if in a hesitant and half-formed manner, each of these three trends: it can draw on exponential cost reductions; obedient networks; and collaboration. It can use them to produce more, or more quickly, or differently. It becomes easier to put an idea to work; to turn it into a product. The cost of failure is lower.

These opportunities were first comprehended industry-by-industry, with the copyright industries in the lead. The greatest change came in those ideas and formats where we were already accustomed to intangible products, such as sounds and images. Broadcasters began to take advantage of cheap production and transmission and launch new cable channels. Musicians, instead of contracting with one of the major companies, began to set up their own record labels or to promote themselves by uploading material directly into cyberspace for free downloads.

In the next stage, companies based entirely on digital processing provided cross-industry forms of 'new media'. The producers of the video game Doom, which has sold over 20 million copies, initially manufactured extra copies simply by inserting a floppy disk in their computer and clicking on 'Copy'. Ten years later, producers could distribute games by DVD or the Internet. Companies could put a film on their website as entertainment, news, documentary or advertising. An advertiser could produce a one-minute melodrama, like a TV soap, that people downloaded every morning as they check the sports results and weather. A newspaper could produce a one-minute news bulletin.

A company could webcast its annual meeting to all shareholders. Retailers could produce a continuous video of their showroom, with staff giving asides to the camera every few minutes about new offers, celebrity shoppers and backstore gossip.

Publishers of written texts might seem to have no problems. Publishing a text on the Internet is virtually free, and the number of texts so published is already immeasurable. The publisher has no need for printing and binding; nor for warehouses, trucks or bookshops; and the text arrives in seconds.

Five years ago, TV producer Iain Bruce proposed a national network of on-demand music publishing. He had made too many trips to the local music store to buy scores for his daughter's piano lessons only to be told that they were out of print or unavailable. He realized that all music is printed in simple black-and-white, that many pieces are very short, and that copyright in most classical music, which lasts seventy years from the death of the composer, has lapsed. Several companies now offer the service, including Sunhawk.com, which plays extracts from the music as it is downloaded. Internet publishing also is a boon to poetry, which is similarly printed in a minimal black-and-white style. E-poetry could reverse the decline in printed poetry, because a publisher could discover the most popular poets from the number of hits and be more confident of selling a printed version. The availability of programs like Adobe's Acrobat enables a page to be as highly designed as any book (writers and publishers who want to encode a text must buy the full program but readers can download Acrobat Reader for free). Some publishers are converting texts to electronic data files that can be easily edited, updated (useful for textbooks) and downloaded (Versaware Technologies Inc. has over 700 employees in Poona, India, converting around 20,000 books a month, plus a sales office in New York and a research lab in Jerusalem).

But these are texts, not books. They lack a book's physical appeal. No technology is yet close to delivering a book, as opposed to a text, to the home. Current home downloads are typically printed in black-and-white on A4 or legal-size paper (formats avoided by traditional publishers). However, shop downloads are beginning to be economic. The printer or bookshop downloads a text and provides a professional printing-and-binding service. It's called digital printing or print-on-demand. TV companies use a similar phrase, video-on-demand, to describe an extreme form of personal pay-per-view when each subscriber orders their own films.

Some publishers put texts on the Internet for direct delivery. Stephen King's short story 'Riding the Bullet' was published exclusively online. Over 400,000 people paid $2.50 in the first six days after publication. Britain's Online Originals has commissioned Frederick Forsyth to write five short stories for publication exclusively on the Internet.

Hackers broke the code for 'Riding the Bullet' within six days and sales fell off sharply. King tried a different tactic for his next text, 'The Plant'. He distributed it unencrypted but asked readers to send in $1 if they liked it, saying he would post later chapters if 75 per cent of users paid up. These experiments, like the music industry's battles with Napster, are testing how we receive all media.

Other systems exploit the computer's ability to store and display texts on screen. Electronic book-sized, hand-held systems like the Rocket eBook and the Softbook (both acquired in 2000 by Gemstar TV International) hold the texts of up to ten average-length books, which can be downloaded from the Internet. Titles include the bestselling *Memoirs of a Geisha* at the same price or less than the printed paperback. The eBooks are technically sophisticated, if expensive. But they remain texts, not books, emphasizing how neat, useful and cheap is the traditional book made of paper and ink.

There is a trend to media; even a 'rush to media'. Almost every organization has a website and every website is a media channel. Its design, look and welcome has to compete with other sites. To an extent, the local newspaper's website finds itself competing with CNN's website; the local boutique with Gap. They compete in the way they use text and pictures. They all have to work within the same format; to understand design; to attract viewers; to keep them. A website is a completely new kind of design with a completely new kind of message (it is an example of 'intellectual capital', discussed in the next chapter).

There are few technical limits on how intellectual property rights may be transacted over the Internet. Although natural rights are one of the four principles of intellectual property law, there is nothing 'natural' about the way rights are defined or applied. It is more a question of the rights-holders' ingenuity when faced with a specific technology. A music retailer could set up a catalogue containing every CD ever recorded, including rare, archive and supposedly unobtainable material and allow consumers to choose whatever they like, when and where they like. Would they like a one-day licence? When the time is up, the music becomes unplayable. Or they could pay extra to keep it for ever. They can order a hard-copy CD that includes a 'free' licence to download the same music on to their hard disk for immediate playback while the CD is being mailed. Would they like music that is 'open source' and can be edited and sent on? Would they like a personalized cover? Would they like advance notice of what's on at the local concert hall, plus free access to a sample hour of the performer's previous music? When they book a holiday, would they like a free CD of the local music?

A book publisher could allow me to download one chapter for free as a promotion. Or I could pay for the download and then, if I decide I want a hardback version, offset the price of the download as a discount against the price of the printed book. Booksellers might reward loyal customers with one free download for every ten books bought. Publishers and booksellers have to balance the marvellous opportunities for distributing their material in whatever manner the market wishes against the perceived danger of devaluing the written text. Some people hope that print's physical format and exclusivity (design, cover, boards, binding, paper, typography and print quality) can retain a dominant position. It is more likely that the two markets of print and download will flourish in parallel, as do the markets for hardbacks and paperbacks.

Search engines, free to wander at will along obedient networks, will assist buyers and (therefore) sellers. Centralized file-sharing programs like Napster track exactly who uses its system, and how often. These systems can count users in their hundreds of millions, far outreaching traditional bricks and mortar retailers. Combine an efficient search engine like Yahoo!, a 'smart agent' like Butler, a 'mining' investigator and copier like Napster and a payment system like Visa. A user could type in 'British patents in human genetics' and '£10' and the software would scan the entire Internet for references, paying, if there were a charge, up to £10 for access. It would look not only at websites and web categories (Yahoo!'s speciality) but also at users' hard disks (Napster's). As well as data gathering or 'mining', it could provide combinatorial processing of audio and video; for example someone could ask for a five-minute video of a holiday resort with some open source local music to go with it.

What effect will this have on the companies that now act as intermediaries and agents? There are two conflicting views. The first is that the Internet removes the need for intermediaries. Musicians can put music on their website and artists can scan in their own work. Who needs an agent or a publisher? The second view is that cyberspace is more crowded than real space and people who may be good at creativity may not be good at, or interested in, the rest of the business. My own feeling is that the latter view is surely right. The doors to cyberspace are wide open, and everyone should be encouraged to walk in and wander around. But open access to any area can lead to confusion and noise. Real freedom is the freedom to choose when to wander and when to use an agent, whether of the human or computer sort. It is no surprise that the Internet's most popular sites are portals and search engines.

CREATIVITY PLUS CREATIVITY

We have looked at cost reductions, obedient networks and ways of working together. The effect on content will be quantitative: more people having more ideas, either alone or collaboratively; and more, I believe, of the latter, in the manner prefigured by architects and designers. The modalities of speed and convenience with which texts (not books) were produced, edited, duplicated and distributed in the latter half of the twentieth century will increasingly apply to moving pictures in the first half of the twenty-first century.

The proportion of ideas and products that are sheltered as intellectual property will probably decline, partly because of the increase in collaborative work and partly because at the lower cost levels the effort involved in maintaining protection may not justify the revenues.

New media seldom replace old media. Downloaded texts will not necessarily hurt bound books, and the blooming of a new market for cheap movies, like *The Blair Witch Project* and *Running Time*, will not necessarily dampen enthusiasm for expensive movies like *The Phantom Menace* and *Toy Story*. Each has its own particular aesthetic appeal. But the greatest economic growth will be in the former.

New business models imply new revenue streams. In my experience, these new cross-industry production hybrids are being matched by cross-industry hybrids in terms of revenues. In many cases, the production hybrid is created mainly in order to exploit new sources of revenue. In other cases, it happens because the technology allows it, or because someone has fun in doing it; but in both these cases it will not be sustained unless the revenues follow. Some of these hybrids exploit synergies between discrete kinds of creative products, as in merchandising, but other, more provocative linkages may lead to more novel forms altogether.

At the start of the twentieth century, Lenin said, 'Communism is soviet organization plus electricity.' At the start of the twenty-first, I suggest, 'The new economy is creativity plus electronics.'

7

CAPITAL OF MY MIND

LAW 7: CREATIVE CAPITAL ARISES WHENEVER SOMEONE HOLDS BACK AN IDEA, OR PART OF AN IDEA, FOR THE FUTURE

'Ideas are a capital that bears interest only in the hands of talent.'
Antoine de Rivarol

ANITA RODDICK

I wanted to meet Anita Roddick when I read her comment in *Resurgence*, a magazine about alternative living: 'I've never painted, never written, never taken photos, but I've always thought of myself as a creative person. Business is my canvas.' I admire the co-chair of a £300 million company (the other co-chair being Gordon, her husband) who takes the time to write articles in radical magazines, and I like her sentiment that an ordinary business, with no connections to the arts, can be truly creative.

Anita Roddick's upbringing and education made her a feisty, opinionated, irreverent outsider. She grew up as an Italian in Littlehampton, a small seaside English town in the 1950s; next door is Bognor Regis, a by-word for English gentility. I have a picture of her: this young, talkative, exuberant, questioning foreigner. 'Being outsiders we were not frightened of sacred cows.' She knew she was different ('We *smelled* different'). She escaped to the movies every Friday and Saturday evening and she had a lucky break: her teachers encouraged her to read William Faulkner, John Steinbeck and other American novelists. She nearly went to drama school, winning a scholarship at London's Central School of Music and Drama, but became a teacher instead.

Then came the leap into the dark. She needed an income while her husband was horse riding in the Americas. She decided to create – there is no other word for it – a new concept of skin and hair care. It was not a new chemical formula, as conventional cosmetic companies use the term, but new in the way it treated women. Her shop would be run by a woman for women, selling practical benefits and not promising miracles. Everything would be environmentally friendly.

She told me that she had turned to the two things she knew and cared about: the stories and myths of the body, and the way in which she and other women cared for their bodies. So whereas the global cosmetic industry tells a story about rake-thin girls who are never fat or pregnant or old, the Body Shop tells a story about women as people who grow up, have babies, get wrinkles, get old. She needed to borrow £4,000 to finance the first shop (including £25 for the now-famous logo) but the bank manager, unimpressed with her T-shirt and two kids, turned her down. Chastened, she returned in a suit, and accompanied by her husband, and got the money. Nearly twenty-five years later there are 1,700 shops in forty-seven countries.

Her business really is her canvas. The headquarters of the Body Shop is unlike any building I have ever seen. The building is Asian-style. In front of the entrance are two men wheeling the Body Shop logo into place: I had to look close to check they were models. Around a small lake sit more life-like figures from Georges Seurat's *Bathing at Asnières* and Eduard Manet's *Déjeuner sur l'herbe*. Inside, there is a large American diner, an echo of those sixties films. It catches the spirit of Akio Morita's prospectus when he launched Sony:

> The purpose is to create an ideal workplace, free, dynamic and joyous, where dedicated engineers will be able to realise their craft and skills at the highest possible level. We shall eliminate any untoward profit-seeking and shall constantly emphasize activities of real substance.

Anita Roddick says she does not really know what creativity means: 'I just live it. It is probably the most over-used word in my vocabulary though it's a complete mystery to me.' But, 'Everyone enjoys and glories in the breakthroughs of creativity in their lives.' She says, 'A creative place should not be a comfortable place. Gordon and I call ourselves anarchists.' Although the Body Shop has grown vastly she has been less interested in making profits (sometimes to the shareholders' frustration) than in 'improving the productivity of the human spirit'.

I wrote my ten rules for success before I met Roddick but soon realized that her opportunistic, dogged, clever focus on the 'creative idea' of the Body Shop, rather than its physical size or achievements, epitomizes most of them. She had an idea and created a whole company where it could flourish. Many people have ideas but few turn them into products. Her idea has two different economic values. She could have sold it, realizing what economists call its 'exchange value', but unprotected ideas go cheap, if a buyer can be found at all. Instead, she decided to invest it, as creative capital, and make it work.

THE FOURTH CAPITAL?

This talent of creativity: is it capital? Does it have the same attributes, play the same role, as other capital assets like land, money and equipment? If it does, what are the implications?

Economists define 'capital' as something which is not, or not only, valued for current use but is an investment for the future. The concept of capital therefore developed in tandem with the concept of interest. Capital is stock; it is stable; it has longevity. Historically, the two main types have been money (usually called financial capital) and buildings, equipment, etc. (physical capital). In all cases, capital is something that results from past investment and whose value lies in future uses. The investment, and indeed the production, need not be close in time, or undertaken by the same person. Inherited money is capital, as is a factory constructed by a previous generation. Capital is a major factor of production, part of a historical trinity with land and labour.

Capital is an inevitable element of any society that, in the words of historian Fernand Braudel, has to 'grapple with the necessities and disputes of exchange, production and consumption'. The word first appeared in the thirteenth century in the same great trading cities in northern Italy which later invented double-entry bookkeeping and issued the first patents. Since it was based on the Latin for head, 'caput', it very probably has some atavistic links with phrases like 'capital city' and 'capital letter', but the connections are unclear. It soon began to be used almost interchangeably with other words denoting wealth, assets, funds and principal, as well as property and goods which could be traded. In *Das Kapital* (1867), Karl Marx said, 'The modern history of capital dates from the creation in the sixteenth century of a world-embracing commerce and a world-embracing market.'

Braudel has shown that the word 'capitalist' came later, in the seventeenth century, and that 'capitalism' did not appear with any regularity until the late nineteenth century. Each word has its own semantic personality. 'Capital' is the most neutral and universal, a concomitant of any trading economy. 'Capitalist' originally referred to those individuals who exploited capital on a regular basis. John Stuart Mill said the capitalist's function was to keep back some or all of this year's profits to enhance next year's output instead, he remarked, of spending it on pyramids and cathedrals. But the word evolved into a description, increasingly pejorative, of a special class of person who puts financial profit above all other considerations. 'Capitalism', from the beginning, was given an even more ideological cloak in opposition to Marxism and socialism, and now implies capital's larger-scale and more adversarial manifestations. But the idea of capital predates these words and continues to describe any asset that enables or enhances future economic activity.

The nature of these assets, and their relative value, is continually changing to reflect social and economic development. The change from hunting to farming, the expansion of rural, agricultural societies, the growth of trade, manufacturing and services and the emergence of an 'information society'; each has required a new kind of capital. Hunters need weapons and short-term access to prey. Farmers need their own land. To the thirteenth-century Italians, the most valuable physical capital was their ships and warehouses. Adam Smith encouraged eighteenth-century Scottish farmers to treat their harvests as capital, either replanting the grain and producing more corn the following year, or exchanging it for machinery and producing the same amount more efficiently. Manufacturing industry, especially on a large scale, required access to money and to raw materials, such as water and coal. Its growing capital requirements saw the emergence of full-time, dedicated capitalists who refined these ideas of financial and physical capital as a factor of production. According to Alfred Marshall, John

Maynard Keynes and others, economic growth came predominantly through the accumulation of these two kinds of financial and physical capital. For them, competition was based on capital accumulation, which resulted in economies of scale, which decreased the costs of producing each unit as volume grew; and on greater specialization.

Since the 1950s, the growth of the service industries, notably R & D, design, financial services, data processing, advertising and marketing, required yet another set of assets. For them, competition did not depend upon finding new markets, or reducing the costs of raw materials, but on innovation and diversification, and on creating intangible value. When Moore hit upon his law about the speed of chip development, he was thinking not about economies of scale (although they were present, too) but about how people learnt how to perform their tasks more skilfully, and more quickly. These industries' most highly valued investments, and their main source of competitive advantage, is people.

HUMAN CAPITAL

The monumental research by Fritz Machlup, published in *The Production and Distribution of Knowledge in the US* in 1962, collected evidence that the production and transfer of information was beginning to match manufacturing in terms of its contribution to the national GDP. Machlup coined the phrase 'intellectual investment' to describe investments in those capital assets that supported this growth. Research by E. F. Denison and J. W. Kendrick showed that investments in education and training increased the value of the workforce; that the result was increased output and productivity; and that both the investment and the output could be quantified. In sum, the workforce could be treated as capital. Investments in skill and know-how produced a 'learning curve', as we saw with Moore's Law, that could be just as advantageous as economies of scale. Educationalists used these calculations to press government for more expenditure on education, arguing that it would lead to a more productive and therefore more competitive economy. This argument, being helpful to an education system short of funds, was widely adopted. By the 1970s, many countries, and not only the rich Western ones, were justifying their expenditure on education by saying it would help their industries become more competitive in the global economy.

The macro-economists, educationalists and industrialists who championed human capital trod warily, because it is a common condition of most forms of capital that they are owned (and, owned, indeed, by unpopular capitalists), and they did not want to imply that a worker could become a possession. Indeed, the reverse. They were driven by the meritocratic impulse that skilled 'labour' as a factor of production should be treated with more respect, not less.

The original component of human capital was school education as measured by attendance rolls and examination results; other kinds of education and training, and then scientific research and development, were slowly added. The growth in post-industrial workers selling their own personal bundle of knowledge and skills led to the inclusion of a more eclectic range of attributes. People have a trunk-load of human capital that they pick up throughout their lives, ranging from school qualifications to intuition and slippery bits of half-remembered knowledge to perhaps judgement and wisdom, if they are lucky.

Human capital is a strikingly unusual kind of capital. It was the first to be recognized as something personal and 'within us', whereas financial and physical capital are impersonal and 'out there'.

The task facing the individual is to accumulate and maximize the quality, scope and utility of this inner capital. The task facing an organization is to negotiate its use on fair and reasonable terms; and then to use it, to the hilt. When Jerry Hirshberg was a senior design executive at stuffy Detroit-based General Motors, the design process was traditional and formal and designers like Hirshberg were not permitted to touch the models of their new cars; touching was against union rules. When he was recruited by Nissan to head up its first American venture, Nissan Design International, he was determined to create an organization where designers could flourish. He based the new company in San Diego, California, which is as far away from Detroit as possible, and encouraged everyone to touch whatever they wanted; to work together; to play around. The people were the same; the human capital was the same. What Hirshberg added was 'structural' capital.

STRUCTURAL CAPITAL

I define 'structural capital' (sometimes known as infrastructure capital) as the means by which an organization acquires and organizes human capital. In the advertising and design industries, where the phrase originated, it is sometimes described as 'everything that remains behind when the staff goes home'. Infrastructure capital covers an organization's policies on recruitment, remuneration and training; its management information system and knowledge management system; the way in which people in the organization work together and their attitude to working hard and to working late. It also covers the management of intellectual property, including domain names, trademark protection, patent mining and licensing and copyright protection. Its purpose is to constitute an organization, a community of relationships, where people can turn ideas into property and products.

Given the nature of information, these structures should be open, comprehensive and inclusive. Numerous studies have shown that most R & D processes and innovations are continuous, incremental and cumulative by nature, springing from local, informal, tacit and intuitive exchanges and movements. Eureka moments seldom happen in isolation. An organization learns not through sudden or dramatic discontinuities but through a gradual, mutual process, rather as a sponge absorbs water.

If individuals believe the transfer process is fair, they will happily contribute. If they think it is unfair, they will jealously protect their capital and keep it to themselves. Organizations have the same choice. If they trust people and treat them fairly, they will be rewarded. If they ignore them or keep them in the dark, they will become sterile and static. If the latter happens, creativity suffers. Individuals feel their ideas are not welcome, and organizations shut the door to their own prime source of new ideas. According to two separate research studies by Birkbeck College, London University, into 1,000 people working in the media and pharmaceutical industries, an increasing number of workers are 'very reluctant' to divulge their knowledge to their employer. The researchers described one in five people as 'knowledge parasites' who suck up information from an organization and use it to enhance their own personal careers.

INTELLECTUAL CAPITAL

These ideas about human capital and infrastructure capital were brought together into the single concept of 'intellectual capital' in 1990 by Leif Edvinsson of Skandia, a Swedish finance company. His phrase hit a chord around the world. Amongst his many honours I like the one awarded by the BBC Brains Trust, who chose him as Brain of the Year in 1998 ahead of runners-up Bill Gates and Paul McCartney, each of whom has his own private vault-full of intellectual capital.

At the time, Skandia and many other financial services companies were looking to expand through mergers with and acquisitions of other companies. While analysing potential targets, Edvinsson discovered that investors usually gave a higher value to a certain kind of company than was merited by its annual accounts, known as its 'book' value. He calculated that many companies on the European stock exchanges were valued at three to eight times their book value, and for many companies in Frankfurt, London and New York this multiple was ten or twenty times, or more (Internet companies often reached multiples many times higher). He knew that conventional accounting methods state only a company's financial and physical assets, and ignore its staff's intellectual resources. They measure what the company 'has' and fail to take account of what it 'knows'. He began to refer to the latter as the company's 'hidden assets'. He believed, correctly, that most companies decided their future on the basis of their hidden assets rather than their physical assets.

Edvinsson put it neatly: conventional accounts recognize the value of a company car sitting in the car park but do not recognize the owner's knowledge of where to go. They recognize the equipment in the research laboratory but not the know-how of the researchers. Many people outside the business world are surprised that companies behave in this way, and many creative people who regard their knowledge and their ideas as their most important assets are quick to distrust accountants who give them no value. The Intellectual Capital

Management Group defines intellectual capital as 'knowledge that can be converted into profit'. As Edvinsson says, 'Most of this is common sense. The challenge is to turn it into common practice.'

It is likely the value of the world's intellectual capital exceeds the value of its financial and physical capital. In other words, the value of what we know, the intangible value of what we have created, may exceed the value of the physical material that surrounds us. We do not know, for sure, because even the most sophisticated accounting systems have problems in counting financial and physical capital stock, and can hardly define, let alone count, the intellectual kind; but I suspect it is a fairly matched contest. It is clear that intellectual capital plays a major role in all industries that depend upon patents and copyrights (including Western biotechnology, pharmaceuticals, chemicals, electronics, entertainment and publishing) and all that depend upon brands (most Western manufacturing goods, most consumer goods, retailing, food and financial services). If drugs were unpatented and unbranded, consumers, after a moment of delight at the cheap prices, would become deeply confused and also, if the drug companies are to be believed, frustrated at the slowness of new drugs coming to the market. If tomorrow's newspapers were undesigned, readers would find it difficult to choose between them, and be overwhelmed by a morass of words.

What we know, as distinct from what we have, is equally important in the public sector, notably education and health-care. A school's main asset is the teachers' 'knowledge about' their subject (such as how to teach it), rather than the subjects' content. Health-care depends on the staff's 'knowledge about' medical and nursing matters; not only their accredited professional skills but everything that they 'know about' their job, including how to comfort visiting relatives. These human and infrastructure assets are often tagged by words like 'reputation' and 'goodwill' but they are more central than those words indicate. They are not a description of something else but the thing itself.

But they remain hidden. Writing in the London Business School's *Business Strategy Review* in 1999, Bill Gates of Microsoft said, 'Our primary assets, which are our software and our software development skills, do not show up on the balance sheet at all. This is probably not very enlightening from a pure accounting point of view.' The chairman of Coca-Cola has acknowledged that its intellectual assets have a higher capital value than all its land, offices, factories, vehicles and bottling plants. But, like Microsoft, it is legally obliged, in its annual accounts, to give a higher value to the latter. British companies' accounts also leave out most of their capital value. One might think that Britain's national research councils would be sensitive to the value of their own intellectual worth. But they state their primary 'assets' as land and buildings (£490 million), plant and machinery (£186 million), ships, aircraft and vehicles (£95 million), equipment, fixtures and fittings (£33 million) and assets under construction (£30 million). Some list patents (£19 million). No mention here of the professional qualifications, skills and common sense that enable them to make the right decisions, or indeed any decision at all.

The difference between book values and market values produces some impressive estimates of the size of intellectual capital. Wolff Olins, a London-based design and strategy consultancy, estimates that in 1989 the financial and physical capital assets of the top 350 companies listed on the London Stock Exchange made up 60 per cent of their total market value. Ten years later, the share had fallen to 28 per cent. If these figures are accurate, British investors believed that over 70 per cent of these companies' true value was not being represented in their annual accounts. Kiln & Co., a managing agent at Lloyd's insurance market, reckons that intellectual value now accounts for over 75 per cent of the total value of all Fortune 500 companies. A study by PricewaterhouseCoopers estimates that two thirds of the stock market capitalization of American companies at the end of 1999 was attributable to their intellectual assets and therefore did not appear on the balance sheet. Given that the American stock market was worth about $7 trillion, about $4.5 trillion was unaccounted for.

A large part of this hidden capital is accounted for by brand names. Many early brands, which were based on the trader's own name or personal circumstances and cost nothing, are now worth billions. Brand specialist Interbrand has calculated the Disney name, originally free, is now worth $32 billion which, given Disney's market capitalization of $52 billion, is 61 per cent of the company's total market capitalization. Interbrand has estimated that 59 per cent of Coca-

Cola's 2004 market capitalization of $120 billion was attributable to its brand name. The Nike brand rated over 77 per cent.

The Price of Value

Companies do not downplay their intellectual assets in their accounts because they are perverse but because nobody has yet found a way to give them a financial value; or, at least, not in a way that accountants accept. Accountants only accept assets (and liabilities) that can be given a financial value. Money obviously has a financial value. But, far from setting an example, it may be unusual in this respect. Physical capital is usually valued according to its original purchase cost or the cost of replacing it, and national regulations dictate how a company should state its physical assets in its accounts. But many forms of physical capital are not easily costed according to their original price, or replaceable (think of those ships, and granaries full of corn). These kinds of assets are tradeable only if a market exists and there are sufficient quantities of what economists call 'willing sellers and buyers'. The means by which they set prices may be hard to discern.

Intellectual capital is even harder to pin down. Valuations based on Edvinsson's empirical gap between book and market values are unduly sensitive to stock market fluctuations and investor fashions, some of which may be unconnected to the company's business. Sony has notably suffered in this way. Having invented the Walkman and developed the industry standard for digital video, it decided to move from the patent industries into copyright, and acquired CBS Records and Columbia Pictures. Yet, as chairman and chief executive Norio Ohga remarked, 'We continue to be rated in Japan as an electronics company rather than a content company. All our entertainment businesses, our music and our picture operations, are undervalued. The share price should be higher. I want to make our hidden assets more visible.' Some economists have used the theories of Nobel laureate James Tobin who, wanting a measure of a company's value relative to its stock market valuation, took the company's market value and divided it with the replacement cost of all its assets; the result is known as Tobin's *q*. Tobin said the value of *q* ought to be 1, because shareholders should not rationally pay more for their shares than is needed to run the company. But his purpose was to show that *q* is seldom 1. It is usually higher, sometimes lower. If it is higher, the company is doing nicely, although Tobin pointed out that the rational investor should respond to a high *q* by selling his shares, which would pull down the share price. If *q* exceeds 1 by a wide measure then the company may be able to charge monopoly rents. In the mid 1990s a few theorists of intellectual capital began to use Tobin's *q* as a substitute measure of hidden value. But Leif Edvinsson, Thomas A. Stewart and other analysts are reluctant to use these methods because they are too sensitive to stock market vagaries.

They have another drawback. They are silent about companies that are not listed on any stock market; as well as companies that have no shares at all. They therefore exclude many of the world's largest and most prestigious cultural and scientific organizations as well as all universities and public R & D laboratories. For example, the BBC's hefty intellectual capital includes Europe's largest group of creative programme-makers and the management structures to turn their ideas into programmes, but neither the people nor the structures appear on the BBC balance sheet. Finally, these methods ignore the many people who work on their own, including the vast majority of artists who, in the public's mind, probably sum up the creative spirit more than anybody else.

A few elements of intellectual capital can be measured on their own, regardless of stock market valuations. There are several accepted methods for valuing intellectual property rights, although they normally measure only 'known' or 'certain' revenues within the current licence period and ignore the longer term. But only a few. Most valuations of infrastructure, such as management information systems and their new cousins, 'knowledge management', while competent at measuring the replacement cost of the hardware, cannot value the contents or their benefits to the organization. We are back in Edvinsson's car park, counting the cars but not the knowledge of where to go.

Most methods deny one of the principles of intellectual capital, which is that its ownership brings extra benefits beyond the direct financial return. For example, if a theatre producer spends £6,000 on producing a play, and sells £6,000 worth of tickets, the financial accounts will show nil assets and nil liabilities. Yet the producer has accumulated valuable know-how (skills, competencies and contacts) that will improve his chances of success, both intellectual and financial, next time.

Thomas A. Stewart believes intellectual capital is inherently irreducible to financial quantities or financial value, and opposes most attempts to include it in financial accounts. He says such attempts muddy the financial waters. More important, he says, is to acknowledge its general financial importance – to identify, track and manage it – without wondering at every stage what its exact financial value might be.

THE ITALIAN JOB

We have financial, physical, human and structural capital at our disposal. To see them in action, let us go back to Italy, where capital started, but to look at a typical creative industry in modern times. In the 1980s Italy's Radio-Televisione Italiana (RAI) was being challenged by Silvio Berlusconi's new upstart TV networks. RAI's three channels, fully financed, fully equipped and fully staffed, had dominated Italian TV for decades. But Berlusconi was a brilliant businessman and a skilful politician who was later to become the country's prime minister. The president of RAI decided to put his top executives through a crash course in competitive broadcasting and asked me, as a consultant, to help.

We decided the first step was to bring people together; to create some temporary infrastructure capital. Over six months the company invited a wide range of executives, from every department, to weekend meetings. I remember one day in Perugia we asked everyone to propose a TV series that would exploit all of RAI's resources. The response was unexpected. The board directors and programme-makers were flummoxed. The best ideas came from the engineers and accountants, who generated a prolific stream of ideas about programmes, spin-off books, international sales, new channels, videos, magazines and merchandise, followed by the people in sales and public relations. At first sight, it seemed as if people's ability to be creative was in inverse proportion to their knowledge of the particular topic. Far from encouraging creativity, the company structure inhibited it. We can speak of 'negative structure', when a company is so managed as to prevent or discourage human capital from expressing itself.

We can assess RAI in terms of the varieties of capital. It had sufficient financial capital; although it had lost its monopoly of TV advertising it still earned healthy revenues; it was not short of cash. It had huge amounts of physical capital in terms of studios, offices, equipment and transmitters, most of which was amortized and written off. No problems there. It was also technically advanced and Europe's most active producer of high-definition TV programmes. It had large quantities of human capital, consisting of the country's major clusters of TV and radio expertise: managers, programme-makers, entertainers, newscasters, engineers, accountants, sales and publicity experts, and strategists. But it had virtually no structural capital. Here the problems began. It was a vast, sclerotic bureaucracy, insensitive to creative people inside and out. As a result, most of the human capital was frustrated and unused. It had storehouses full of intellectual property, both in its own programmes and in American programmes, which as Italy's only buyer it had acquired cheaply, but it had few ideas about how to maximize their value. It also had substantial quantities of what economist and banker Hubert Saint-Onge calls 'customer capital', which is the amount of attention, time, loyalty, etc., that customers give to their favoured suppliers. Being the national broadcaster, it was watched almost every night by almost every household in the country. But this capital too was lying fallow. RAI was not much loved.

Our solution was principally to continue the spirit of the weekend meetings into RAI's daily operations. We set up small, multi-skilled 'creative groups' in each major department and at each regional centre; about thirty-seven in all. We called them 'guerrillas'. They were deliberately informal and outside the main management functions and lines of decision-making. We suggested each group met over lunch on a Friday and invite a speaker, who might come from inside or outside the company, to talk about any subject. We invited the groups' own members to speak about their own work, and ideas (which might be related to RAI, or something completely different). We encouraged them to be impulsive, inquisitive, radical and argumentative. There was no agenda and no minutes, but groups could write letters (not memos) to anyone in the company, however senior. If they wanted to, they could send a copy to the president (when the president was sent his first copy, I made sure he knew). The groups soon took on a life of their own. Some were a great success; most lasted years; others faded after a few months. The groups demonstrated that RAI was interested in its management's views; the result was conviviality, trust and more openness; and a certain confidence, even bravery, about saying what should be done. We had also set financial targets, and reviewed programme copyrights, but most people felt that the groups had the greatest effect. Over the next twelve months we monitored the process very closely. Overall, RAI did begin to realize its vast assets, both inside the organization and with outsiders; and the ratings went up. The thing I particularly liked about the guerrillas was their simplicity. They just met for lunch; but from that flowed a stream of ideas about how to be more creative and more effective.

We can learn three lessons. First, RAI's massive financial and physical capital, which gave an appearance of solidity and supremacy, was alarmingly insufficient to fuel its purpose: the provision of programmes that interested the audience. Second, many people have well-thought-out ideas, based on their personal and unique knowledge and their appreciation of what is happening around them. These ideas may be obvious to themselves but hidden to others and unexploited. Third, if people are to contribute to an organization, they need structural capital in order to give their ideas purpose and shape, and to exercise their creativity.

CREATIVE CAPITAL

It seems reasonable to treat creativity as a capital asset. It has the essential qualities. It results from investment, which the owner may increase or vary; and it is a significant input to future creativity and creative products. It is a substantial component of human capital. According to George Bernard Shaw, the only sensible definition of capital was Stanley Jevons's casual remark that it was 'spare money'. We could call intellectual capital 'spare ideas', and creative capital 'spare creativity'. Creative capital may have been implicit in the earlier ideas about human capital, but those concentrated on education and training, and only recently included such fuzzy talents as creativity. It may have been included in some varieties of intellectual capital, but only on the edge. It needs to be fully recognized.

Treating it as capital helps us to understand the nature of the creative marketplace. In bookkeeping terms, it is as much a capital market as a current account market. Capital markets are spheres of speculation, in both senses of the word, a shadowy world of one-off deals rather than the open arena of mass production. Capital lacks the basic characteristics of classical economics: it is seldom a unified good or a commodity; demand and supply are fluid; information is not shared, let alone 'perfect'; people often work alone, trusting to their subjective and often apparently irrational impulses. It is a world of personalities and promises, incidents and accidents. Creativity happens when we take intellectual capital, our own or someone else's, add our own personal value to it, and make something new and original. There is no gold standard, no official rate of exchange. One person's idea may be uninteresting or useless to another. Money is money, but an idea can be good, bad or indifferent; or good one day, bad the next.

Investment strategies vary. We can put cash under the mattress and see its value wither away; spend it; or by investing hope to increase it. Likewise, we can let creative capital lie dormant; spend it; or invest it. The biblical parable of the talents favours investment. God is not afraid of risk.

Creative capital gains most when it is managed and made *purposive*. It flourishes best in small, flexible structures, which allow for the prevalence of full-time thinkers, the network office and the just-in-time worker. It needs rights management: to know when ideas can or should be turned into property; the most cost-effective means of doing so; and the best way to exploit those rights. The creative manager uncovers the intellectual assets that lie hidden in companies and, ultimately, in our minds.

Even a consumer product bought over the counter (or downloaded) may become capital. It may seem, as a consumer, that I have no opportunity for further exploitation; indeed, the terms of sale normally forbid it. But the forces of the creative economy do not give up so easily. Using my new product can inspire me to be creative; and so the cycle of creativity begins again.

This sums up the creative economy. The raw material is human talent: the talent to have new and original ideas and to turn those ideas into economic capital and saleable products. The production resources that are so critical in the conventional economy are less important, although they remain unavoidably essential in some sectors (and always will be), and in all industries become more important as creative products pass along the value chain. The most valuable currency is not money but ideas and intellectual property, which are intangible and highly mobile. The management of creativity puts a premium on entrepreneurial, just-in-time, temporary, ad hoc working. It is driven more by education than by technology. Investments in education, research and *thinking* increase creativity's value and effectiveness as surely as do investments in other capital assets increase theirs.

The growth of this creative economy is likely to outgrow all other economic arenas. The US Patent Office says, 'Trade in creative content will provide the economic basis to grow the global information infrastructure.' The European Commission says, 'Content will drive the new technologies.' These statements are too modest. Creative products are the basis not only of information and new technologies but of the entire modern economy, from software to shoes.

Throughout this book, I have kept strictly to the term 'creative economy' because isolating the economics helps us to understand the business and management issues. But its impact is wider. The way we treat the economics of ideas and inventions obviously affects all social, cultural, ideological and political issues. How we decide, and *who decides*, whether the ownership of ideas and inventions should be private or public has a powerful impact on the kind of society we build for ourselves.

A society that stifles or misuses its creative resources, and signs up to the wrong property contract, cannot prosper. But if we understand and manage this new creative economy, individuals will profit and society will be rewarded.

ACKNOWLEDGEMENTS

Many people have contributed, in various ways, to the thinking and writing of this book. I would especially like to thank Naïma Azgui, Keith Beresford, Jonathan Davis, Janine Edge, Bronač Ferran, Michael Flint, Barbara J. Heinzen, Sophie Johnstone, Deborah Lincoln, Fiona McKenzie and John Newbigin; the staff at the British and American Patent Offices; and Terence Conran, Bob Geldof, Harry Kroto, David Puttnam, Anita Roddick, Richard Rogers, Andrew Wylie and the other people who agreed to be interviewed. A special mention is due to Eddi Ploman who first explained to me why copyright is important. Schuckri Bundakji and Xu Chen, my researcher, were invaluable in the preparation of the 2007 edition. Many thanks to Michael Sissons and James Gill, Peters Fraser and Dunlop, and Stuart Proffitt at Penguin. And special thanks to Ariane Bankes.

NOTES

INTRODUCTION: THE ART OF THE PATENT

vii. Full information on **copyright output** is given in Chapter 3; a useful source for American copyright products is the Washington-based International Intellectual Property Alliance (IIPA).

vii. *Fortune* analysed **Michael Jordan's** earnings in its issue of 22 June 1998, pp. 60–68. Naomi Klein has calculated that in 1992 Nike paid Jordan more than it paid its 30,000-strong Indonesian workforce; see Klein, *No Logo* (HarperCollins, London, 2000).

vii. The data on **theatre costs** is taken from *The Wyndham Report* (London School of Economics and Society of London Theatre, London, 1998) and company reports; the data on **music employment** is taken from *The Value of Music* (National Music Council and University of Westminster, London, 1996), especially Appendix H; and Britain's National Statistics (www.statistics.gov.uk).

vii. **Telecom 1999** was organized by the International Telecommunication Union (ITU), which supplied the data on visitors. The nuclear hospitality was organized by the Geneva Tourist Office; their leaflet says the price is '*service compris*'.

vii. The **US Patent and Trademark Office** data comes from its website, www.uspto.gov. The **UK Patent Office** data comes from its *Annual Report & Accounts 1999–2000* and its website, www.patent.gov.uk.

viii. For example, the European Patent Convention states 'The European patent application must disclose the invention in a manner sufficiently clear and complete for it to be carried out by a person **skilled in the art**' (Article 83).

viii. The case of the **Norfolk housewife** was reported in the *Eastern Daily Press*, 16 July 1999, p. 7.

viii. The phrase **intellectual property** has to be stretched a bit to cover both copyright and the 'industrial property' of patents, trademarks and designs. The traditional view is that an author's rights are natural rights, inalienable and untradeable, and therefore not property; and that trademarks, designs and trade secrets are not very intellectual. However, the term indisputably fills a need and has passed into common usage, and so I continue to use it.

viii. The **Arthur Andersen report** is *The Use of Intellectual Property as Security for Debt Finance* (Intellectual Property Institute and Arthur Andersen, London, 1998); see p. 1.

viii. For **President Washington**, see 'Address to Congress 8 January 1790', in *Copyright in Congress, 1789–1904*, at 115 (Government Printing Office, 1905).

xi. **Colin Ronan's** remark is the second sentence of *The Cambridge History of the World's Science* (Cambridge University Press, 1983); the first is 'Science has proved a vast intellectual adventure.'

xi. **Edward O. Wilson's** comments appear in *Consilience: The Unity of Knowledge* (Little, Brown, New York, 1998), p. 126; the whole book is a comprehensive survey of the making of knowledge. Wilson also quotes Nobel laureate Herbert Simon: 'What chiefly characterizes creative thinking from more mundane forms are (i) willingness to accept vaguely defined problem statements and gradually structure them, (ii) continuing preoccupation with problems over a considerable period of time and (iii) extensive background knowledge in relevant and potentially relevant areas.' Which Wilson summarizes as 'knowledge, obsession, daring' (p. 69).

xiii. The British idea of **creative industries** is expressed in Chris Smith, *Creative Britain* (Faber & Faber, London, 1998) – as the Secretary of State for Culture, Media and Sport, Smith established the Creative Industries Task Force; the Australian approach can be found in *Creative Nation* (Commonwealth of Australia, Australian Government Printing Service, Canberra, 1994).

xiv. **Abraham Maslow** (1908–1970) described his ideas of a hierarchy of needs and motives in *Motivation and Personality* (Collins, London, 1954).

xv. **Jacob Bronowski's** *The Ascent of Man* was a TV series (BBC-TV/PBS, 1973) and a book (BBC, London, 1973).

xv. See **Andrew Curry**, *The Services Boom* (The Henley Centre, 2000); '**Paul** Saffo Predicts' in *Upside*, VIII: 2 (February 1996), pp. 26–39.

xv. The statistics on **British and American household expenditure** are taken, respectively, from *Family Spending* (Central Statistics Office, 1999) and the *Consumer Expenditure Survey, 1984–98* (Bureau of Statistics).

xvi. The **OECD data** is taken from its *Main Economic Indicators*, published annually.

xvi. The data on patents is taken from the World Intellectual Property Organization (WIPO) and the relevant patent offices' annual reports.

xvii. The conundrum of America, is why, after three decades of sluggish growth, it suddenly doubled its annual growth rate in the mid 1990s. There is much anecdotal evidence that investments in computers and networks increased productivity, but data is scarce. Alan Binder, Professor of Economics at Princeton University and former vice-chairman of the Federal Reserve Bank, says there is no evidence that information technology has increased productivity. Paul Krugman, Professor of Economics at MIT, says there is some evidence from 1998 onwards, but only to support an increase of 1 per cent in the technology sectors. Only in 1999 did the data start to support the theory that information technology enhances general productivity; even so, the average increase in working hours was possibly more significant.

xvii. Peter Schwartz's *The Long Boom*, co-written with Peter Leyden and Joel Hyatt (Perseus, 1997), predicted a twenty-year boom in America and most other related economies. Although reflecting substantial optimism, the case is far from proven.

xvii. C. P. Snow, physicist and writer, expressed his idea of two cultures in *The Two Cultures and the Scientific Revolution* (London, 1959).

CHAPTER 1: THE FIRST TALENT

1. For John Keats, see Hyder Edward Rollins (ed.), *The Letters of John Keats*, letter to James Hessey, 9 October 1818.

1. Claude Bernard (1813–78), French physiologist, was quoted in the *Bulletin of the New York Academy of Medicine*, IV (1928).

1. Professor Sir Harry Kroto is Royal Society Research Professor at the University of Sussex. The story of C_{60} is told by Kroto in *C_{60} Buckminsterfullerene: The Celestial Sphere that Fell to Earth* (Royal Institution Discourse, Vega Science Films, VHS, 60 minutes); and in Hugh Aldersey-Williams, *The Most Beautiful Molecule* (John Wiley & Sons, London, 1995).

3. Fred Hoyle made his comment about Einstein in *The Universe: Past and Present Reflections* (University College, Cardiff, 1981), p. 2; in the same paper he quotes Ebenezer Cunningham, who was 'the nearest of all British scientists to discovering the special theory of relativity' before Einstein, as saying: 'I had not been ruthless enough' (p. 3).

4. Most psychological analyses of creativity deal with geniuses; only a few with ordinary people. The former include *Genius and the Mind*, ed. Andrew Steptoe (Oxford University Press, 1998); the latter include Anthony Storr,

The Dynamics of Creation (Secker & Warburg, London, 1972) and D. N. Perkins, *The Mind's Best Work* (Harvard University Press, Cambridge, 1981).

5. See **C. J. Jung,** 'The Development of the Personality', in *The Collected Works* (Routledge & Kegan Paul, London, 1954), especially pp. 106–7, 115–16 and 178.

5. See **Antonio Damasio,** *The Feeling of What Happens* (Heinemann, London, 2000), pp. 315–16. Damasio made the remark about the circle of 'existence, consciousness and creativity' in a lecture at the London School of Economics on 24 January 2000. See also William James, *Principles of Psychology* (Macmillan, London, 1890), especially vol. I, pp. 300ff. James discusses how consciousness is always personal in vol. I, p. 225.

5. For the **enchanted loom,** see Charles Sherrington, *Man and His Nature* (London, 1941).

5. See **Mihaly Csikszentmihalyi,** *Creativity: Flow and the Psychology of Discovery and Invention* (HarperCollins, New York, 1996).

6. **Brainwaves** in the SMR (sensorimotor rhythm) and beta1 range have frequencies of 12–15 and 15–18 hertz and those in the theta and alpha range have frequencies of 4–8 and 8–12 hertz. The characteristics of the two groups in terms of creativity and performance are explored in Siegfried Othmer, Susan Othmer and David Kaiser, 'EEG Feedback: An Emerging Model for its Global Efficacy', in James R. Evans and Andrew Arbabanel (eds.), *Introduction to Quantitative EEG and Neurofeedback* (Academic Press, San Diego, 1999). The link between alpha and theta brainwaves and creativity is explored extensively in Andreas Mavromatis, *Hypnagogia: The Unique State of Consciousness Between Wakefulness and Sleep* (Routledge & Kegan Paul, London, 1987). Mavromatis describes the alpha/theta state as a 'lifting of all the mental faculties'.

6. **Guy Claxton** is Visiting Professor of Learning Science at Bristol University. See *Hare Brain, Tortoise Mind: How Intelligence Increases When You Think Less* (Ecco Press, New York, 1999).

6. **Sam Mendes** made this remark in an interview in *The Sunday Times*, 23 January 2000.

6. See **Charles Jonscher,** *Wired Life* (Bantam, London, 1999), pp. 23 and 32.

7. **Trevor Nunn** made this remark in an interview with the author in 1999.

7. For **Logan Pearsall Smith,** see *Logan Pearsall Smith: An Anthology*, ed. Edward Burman (Constable, London, 1989). Pearsall Smith's essay, 'Worlds and Idioms', is my source for the remarks by John Donne and the usage of '*originalité*' and 'original'; see pp. 93–148.

8. See **Samuel Johnson,** *Dictionary of the English Language* (Strahan, London,

1775); Johnson gives five definitions of 'to create': '(1) to form out of nothing; to cause to exist; (2) to produce; to cause; to be the occasion; (3) to beget; (4) to invest with any new character; (5) to give any new qualities; to put any thing in a new state.'

8. See **Margaret Boden,** 'Computer Models of Creativity', *The Psychologist*, February 2000.

10. See **Teresa M. Amabile,** 'How to Kill Creativity', *Harvard Business Review*, Sept–Oct 1998. See also Amabile, *The Social Psychology of Creativity* (Springer-Verlag, New York, 1983).

10. For **creativity as a basic talent,** see Socrates, quoted by Plato in his *Apology*, 38a; Shakespeare, *King Lear*, I.i.92; Bob Dylan, 'It's Alright, Ma (I'm Only Bleeding)' on *Bringing It All Back Home* (Columbia, 1965); and Kamil Idris, Introduction, *WIPO Annual Report* (Geneva, 1999).

10. **Henry Margenau,** *Scientific Indeterminism and Human Freedom* (Archabbey, Latrobe, 1968). See also Lawrence Leshan and Henry Margenau, *Einstein's Space and Van Gogh's Sky* (Harvester Press, Brighton, 1983), p. 155; and Norbert Wiener, *The Human Use of Human Beings* (Doubleday Anchor, New York, 1954), p. 116.

11. See **Allan Snyder and John Mitchell,** 'Is Integer Arithmetic Fundamental to Mental Processing? The Mind's Secret Arithmetic', *Proceedings of the Royal Society*, B266 (1999), pp. 287–92. See also Rita Carter, 'Tune In, Tune Off', *New Scientist*, 9 October 1999, and Keith Johnstone, *IMPRO: Improvisation and the Theatre* (Methuen, London, 1981), p. 21.

11. See **Michael J. A. Howe,** *Genius Explained* (Cambridge University Press, 1999).

12. See **Johan Huizinga,** *Homo Ludens* (Routledge & Kegan Paul, London, 1949).

12. On **work being fun,** see also Alfred Einstein in the *Observer*, 15 January 1950: 'If *A* is success in life, then *A* equals *x* plus *y* plus *z*. Work is *x*; *y* is play; and *z* is keeping your mouth shut.'

12. **Richard Feynman's** discovery is recounted in *All Our Futures: Creativity, Culture and Education* (Department for Education and Employment, London, 1999); a report on how creativity may be taught to young people.

13. See **Erving Goffman,** *Where the Action Is* (Allen Lane, London, 1969).

13. The purchaser of each **Dyson cleaner** is given a leaflet describing James Dyson's intensive prototype development and complaining of 'outrageous patent fees'.

13. See **Anthony Storr,** *The Dynamics of Creation* (Secker & Warburg, London, 1972).

13. See **F. Scott Fitzgerald,** *The Crack-up* (New York, 1936).

14. Goethe said, 'First and last, what is demanded of genius is love of truth'; see Goethe, *Proverbs in Prose*.
14. See **Peter Bazalgette**, 'How to Spot (and Manage) the Creatives', in *Broadcast*, 20 November 1998.
14. See **Peter Ackroyd**, *T. S. Eliot* (Hamish Hamilton, London, 1984).
14. Belgian scientist **Ilya Prigogine** won the Nobel Prize for Chemistry in 1977, and has written widely on instability and complexity.
14. The story about **Lord Olivier** is recounted in Richard Findlater, *The Player Kings* (Weidenfeld & Nicolson, London, 1971).
15. Rev. **Jim Jones** led a mass suicide of 913 people in Guyana in 1978, and was also responsible for several other deaths.
15. For the story about **Steven Spielberg**, see *Variety*, 25 May 1994.
16. For **Fiona Patterson** and the Innovation Potential Indicator, see www.opp.co.uk.
16. For **dreams**, see the reference to Francis Bacon in *Blains Fine Art*, summer 1999, and Somerset Maugham, *The Summing-Up* (1938) p. 23.
17. **Trevor Nunn's** comment (about managing the pace of rehearsals) was made in an interview with the author.

CHAPTER 2: THE BOOM IN INTELLECTUAL PROPERTY

19. For this chapter I am indebted to W. R. Cornish, *Intellectual Property* (4th edn, Sweet & Maxwell, London, 1999); Michael F. Flint, *A User's Guide to Copyright* (5th edn, Butterworths, London, 2000); and Keith Beresford, *European Patents for Software, E-commerce and Business Methods* (Beresford, London, 2000).
19. See **Charles Handy**, *The Empty Raincoat* (Arrow Business Books, London, 1995), pp. 201–3.
21. See **Hugh Laddie**, *Copyright: Over Strength, Over Regulated, Over Rated?* (Intellectual Property Institute, London, 1995).
21. For comments on the **subtleties of intellectual property law**, see *Intellectual Property and the National Information Infrastructure* (Information Infrastructure Task Force, Washington DC, 1994), p. 5; *Folsom v. Marsh*, 9 F cas. 342, 344 (Mass. 1841); Mark Twain's *Notebook, 1902–1903*; and Kim Howells, Department of Trade and Industry press release, 25 May 1999.
23. See **Thomas Raleigh**, *An Outline of the Law of Property* (Clarendon Press, Oxford, 1890), p. 1.
24. **Thomas Jefferson's** letter to Isaac McPherson, written on 13 August 1813,

can be found in Merrill D. Peterson (ed.), *Thomas Jefferson: Writings* (Library of America, New York, 1984).

25. The **British legislation** is available from HMSO. The **American legislation** is available on-line at www.uspto.gov.

26. For the **Patent Cooperation Treaty** (PCT), see www.wipo.int/.

27. Against **intellectual property as incentive**, John Perry Barlow has written: 'Sophocles, Dante, da Vinci, Botticelli, Michelangelo, Shakespeare, Newton, Cervantes, Bach – all found reasons to get out of bed in the morning without expecting to own the works they created.' ('The Next Economy of Ideas', *WIRED*, October 2000.)

28. See **Paul Goldstein,** *Copyright's Highway* (Hill & Wang, New York, 1996), p. 15.

29. See **Peter Hayward and Christine Greenhalgh,** *Intellectual Property Research* (Economic and Social Research Council, London, 1994), a useful survey of the economic study of intellectual property.

29. See **Immanuel Kant,** *The Critique of Judgement,* trans. J. C. Meredith (Oxford University Press, 1997).

33. The story of **Japan's intellectual property laws,** including Japan's claim for the efficacy of patents, is told in Hisamitsu Arai, *The Japanese Experience in Wealth Creation* (World International Property Organization, Geneva, 1999). Arai is one of Japan's leading negotiators on intellectual property.

34. The story of **John of Speyer** (and much else of the history of copyright) is told in Ronald Bettig, *Copyrighting Culture: The Political Economy of Intellectual Property* (Westview Press, Boulder, 1996).

34. See **W. R. Cornish,** *Intellectual Property,* p. 114.

35. See **US Constitution,** Article 1, Section 8: 'to promote the progress of science and the useful arts by securing for limited times to authors and inventors the exclusive right to their respective writings and discoveries'.

35. The story about **Korekiyo Takahashi** is told in Hisamitsu Arai's *The Japanese Experience in Wealth Creation,* p. 86.

38. The cases of the **patenting of computer programs** mentioned are *Diamond v. Diehr*, 450 US 175 (1981), SC; and *State Street Bank & Trust Co. v. Signature Financial Group Inc.* (149 F 3d 1368; Fed Cir 23 July 1998). See also *Merrill Lynch's Application* (1989) RPC 561 (CA); *AT&T Corp. v. Excel Communications Inc.* (172 F 3d 1352; Fed Cir 14 April 1999); and the European Patent Office's Computer-related invention/VICOM (T 208/84 OJ EPO 1987, 14). All American patents are listed on www.uspto.gov.

41. Soon after the award, **Jeff Bezos** made a proposal that software patents last only three to five years (though he believes his own patent merits twenty years). James Watson, co-discoverer of the structure of DNA, has proposed

that genetic patents should be scrapped in favour of a compulsory licence, as with music broadcast on the radio, in which every broadcaster can use the property but is obliged to pay a royalty for doing so. 'Anyone who discovered the breast cancer gene would get a royalty licence, but not a monopoly on the right to develop a breast cancer test.' (Round table on 'The Meaning of the Genome', *Prospect*, October 2000.)

41. See **James Gleick**, 'Patently Absurd' in the *New York Times*, 12 March 2000. Gleick is the author of *Faster: The Acceleration of Just About Everything* (Pantheon, New York, 1999).

42. **The patent for an apparatus that lowers prices** (US patent no. 6076070) was awarded on 13 June 2000.

42. **Lawrence Lessig** makes a convincing connection between code as the language of computer programs and code that controls, openly or implicitly, social relationships. See his book, *Code and Other Laws of Cyberspace* (Basic Books, New York, 1999). See also www.fsf.org/copyleft/copyleft.html.

42. See **White Paper** on *Automated Financial or Management Data Processing Transactions (Business Methods)* (US Patent and Trademark Office, July 2000).

43. See **Johannes Lang**, 'Europe Grants E-commerce Patents, Too', *Managing Intellectual Property*, March 2000.

43. **The European Commission research report**, by Robert Hart, Peter Holmes and John Reid (ETD/99/B5-3000/E/106), is published by the Intellectual Property Institute, London, 2000.

44. **The European Patent Convention** excludes 'mathematical methods . . . schemes, rules and methods for doing business, and programs for computers . . . as such' (Article 52). The British 1977 Patents Act has the same exclusions (Section 1(2)).

44. **The EPO vote was controversial**. The minority of nine members included Britain, France and Germany; the majority of ten members included Liechtenstein and Monaco. The Internet Patent News Service (IPNS), which provides topical, critical coverage of patent decisions, reported a German delegate as saying, 'We would have problems with the US tendency to patent everything that can be patented. That would stifle innovation and cause a glut of litigation.' See www.std.com and www.bustpatents.com.

44. See **W. R. Cornish**, *Intellectual Property*, p. 212.

45. The declaration, '**Anything under the sun** that is made by man is patentable', was made by the US Congress in 1952; see S Rep No. 1979, 82nd Cong, 2nd Session, 5(1952).

45. See ***Diamond v. Chakrabarty*** 65, Law Ed., (2nd) 144 (1980) SC. See also Genentech Inc.'s patent (1987, RPC 553).

45. America's **division between patentable and non-patentable organisms** is described in Peter Groves, *Sourcebook on Intellectual Property Law* (Cavendish, London, 1997), p. 192.
46. See Harvard University's **Oncomouse** application (1990) OJ EPO 476.
46. See *Moore v. University of California*, 793 P 2nd 479 (1991). See also James Boyle, *Shamans, Software and Spleens* (Harvard University Press, Cambridge, 1996). Boyle is professor of law at Duke Law School.
47. **Thomas Kuhn** conceived *The Structure of Scientific Revolutions* in the late 1940s when he was a graduate student; when published by the University of Chicago Press in 1962, it soon became a classic twentieth-century paradigm of how science evolves.
49. The text of the **Blair–Clinton** policy statement on human genetic research is available at www.number-10.gov.uk/news.asp?Newsld=684; the background lobby briefing is at www.number-10.gov.uk/default.asp?Pageld=1271.
49. The **European Union Directive** on the Legal Protection of Biotechnological Inventions, 98/44, OJ L213/13, is available from the EU website, http://europa.eu.int/eur-lex/en/lif/dat/1998/en_398L0044.html. The British Patent Office has commented, 'This Directive will not lead to anything becoming patentable in the UK which is not already patentable under the present Patents Act 1977 which states that patents can only be obtained for advances which meet the basic requirements for patentability; that is, they must be new, not obvious and have an industrial application' (Patent Office, *Current Issues*, October 1999). The Office is applying the 'as such' rule; biological matter as such is not patentable, but a process involving it may be if it satisfies the three criteria.
50. The **objective of the British Patent Office** is taken from its government remit; the US Patent Office's from its annual report. Their financial data comes from their annual reports.
50. The **British parliament** has recently become very reluctant to discuss intellectual property, having had only two series of debates between 1981 and 2000. Meanwhile, the public has become much more concerned.
51. See **Kevin Rivette** and David Kline, *Rembrandts in the Attic: Unlocking the Hidden Value of Patents* (Harvard Business School Press, Cambridge, 2000), which describes the Aurigin system of identifying patent values.
51. For **Ben du Pont**, see Tyler Maroney, 'The New Online Marketplace of Ideas', *Fortune*, 141/8, 17 April 2000.
52. As an example of **'sloppy' patenting** the Internet Patent News Service cites a recent patent (no. 5,806,048) for managing a portfolio of investment funds whose 'prior art' did not include a single reference from the *Journal of Portfolio Management*, a leading journal in the field. It says, 'An application

[for a patent for portfolio management] which does not quote a single article from over twenty years in the field should be presumed to be invalid.'

52. The US Patent Office's position as the **central bank** of worldwide patenting is demonstrated in Hisamitsu Arai's *The Japanese Experience in Wealth Creation*, which shows the preference of Japanese companies to apply for patents first in Washington (partly because the American office takes an average of three years to make a decision against Europe's five years and Japan's seven years, and partly because it awards more patents per application). The Japanese also prefer to appeal adverse decisions under American rather than Japanese law, and to defend their patents in America rather than Japan.

53. The phrase about **Mother Nature** echoes Peter Drahos' comment, 'Mother Nature's handiwork is never too far away in the case of biotechnological inventions', in his article, 'Biotechnology Patents, Markets and Morality', *European Intellectual Property Review*, 21:9 (September 1999).

55. According to *Copinger and Skone James on Copyright* (Sweet & Maxwell, London, 13th ed., 1991) a standard British textbook: 'Copyright law is concerned, in essence, with the **negative right** of preventing the copying of physical material.'

55. **Martha Woodmansee** is author of *The Author, Art and the Market* (Columbia University Press, 1996); with Peter Jaszi (ed.), *The Construction of Authorship* (Duke University Press, 1994); and 'On the Author Effect: Recovering Collectivity', *Cardozo Arts and Entertainment Law Review*, 10:2 (1992).

55. The **history of copyright** (and much else) can be found in Edward W. Ploman and L. Clark Hamilton, *Copyright* (Routledge & Kegan Paul, London, 1980).

56. For **John Milton**, see Ronald Bettig, *Copyrighting Culture*, p. 18.

56 The remark by **Daniel Defoe** is quoted in Raymond Williams, *The Long Revolution* (London, 1961).

57. See **Ronald Bettig**, *Copyrighting Culture*, p. 25.

57. For **Macaulay** see House of Commons, *Hansard*, lvi, 347, 5 February 1841.

58. **Digital** means a symbol that is discrete and measurable compared to analogue, which means approximate, with no determinate edges. Most symbolic systems and codes are digital, including numerals, alphabets and musical notation. Here, I am concerned only with modern binary digital code in electronic form.

59. See *The Digital Dilemma: Intellectual Property in the Information Age* (National Research Council, National Academy Press, Washington DC, 2000).

59. For John Perry Barlow, see Peter Groves, *Sourcebook on Intellectual Property Law* (Cavendish, London, 1997), pp. 22–40. Barlow's manifesto includes the phrase: 'Information wants to be free'.
60. See Jeremy Rifkin, *The Age of Access* (Penguin, London, 2000), p. 4. See also B. Joseph Pine II and James H. Gilmore, *The Experience Economy* (Harvard Business School Press, Cambridge, 1999).
60. See Esther Dyson, 'Intellectual Property on the Net', *Release 1.0*, December 1994; and 'The Open Source Revolution', *Release 1.0*, November 1998.
61. ***Books Do Furnish a Room*** is the title of a novel by Anthony Powell in his sequence, *A Dance to the Music of Time*.
61. Ben Keen made his remark at a British Screen Advisory Council seminar on the Internet on 25 May 1999.
63. For Forrester Research see www.forrester.com/ER/products/O, 3629.
63. The IFPI made its estimate in April 2000; see www.ifpi.com.
63. The legal arguments between the RIAA and Napster over file sharing can be found at www.riaa.com/napster_legal.cfm. and www.napster.com.
64. For the print-shop case, see *Basic Books, Inc. v. Kinko's Graphics Corp.*, 758 F. Supp. 1522 (S.D.N.Y. 1991). See also L. Ray Patterson, 'Copyright and the "Exclusive Right" of Authors', available at www.lawsch.uga.edu/~jipl/vol1/patterson.html. Patterson is Pope Brock Professor of Law at the University of Georgia.
64. The evidence for Napster's effects on CD sales is mixed. The RIAA believes Napster users buy fewer CDs; but Jupiter Media Metrix, a leading Internet research company, found in July 2000 that users of Napster and other similar systems are 45 per cent more likely to increase music spending (www.jup.com).
66. The WIPO conference results are available at www.wipo.com; for a libertarian, 'Internet' view, see *WIRED*, March 1997.
68. In Britain, it is possible to trademark a face. America has a separate 'right of publicity' to protect faces and personalities, including people's catchphrases.
70. America uses state, not federal, law to protect secrets.
71. The data for Kodak's losses are based on Kevin Rivette and David Kline, *Rembrandts in the Attic*. See also www.bustpatents.com/awards.
73. The data on theft are taken from the US Trade Representative, Washington DC, and trade associations.
74. The economic analysis of trade in intellectual property is a new, sparse activity; data is patchy; most governments and academia give it a low priority. See Keith Maskus, 'Trade-Related Intellectual Property Rights', *European Economy*, 52 (1993), pp. 157–84, and John Revesz, *Trade-related Aspects of Intellectual Property Rights* (Australian Productivity Commission, 1999).

74. See *Task Force on National Information Policy* (National Commission on Libraries and Information Science, White House, 1976), p. 61; and 'The Role and Control of International Communications and Information', Committee on Foreign Relations, US Senate, 95th Congress, 93–147, 1977.
76. See Jeffrey Sachs, 'By Invitation: Helping the World's Poorest', *The Economist*, 14 August 1999, pp. 16–22.
77. For cultural and information imperialism, see Herb Schiller, *Mass Communication and the American Empire* (A. M. Kelley, New York, 1969), Jeremy Tunstall, *The Media Are American* (Constable, London, 1977), and Peter Drahos, 'Intellectual Property and Human Rights', *Intellectual Property Quarterly*, 3 (Sweet & Maxwell, London, 1999). See also 'Intellectual Property and Ethics' in *Perspectives on Intellectual Property*, 4 (Sweet & Maxwell, London, 1998).
77. Gandhi is quoted in D. R. Mankekar, *Media and the Third World* (Indian Institute of Mass Communication, New Delhi, 1979).
77. The history of gentian and dogbane is taken from *Plants of India* (National Book Trust, New Delhi, 1992).
78. Pennapa Subcharoen, Director of the National Institute for Thai Traditional Medicine, was quoted in the *Financial Times*, 9 January 1998.
78. For Rio, see Michael Blakeney, 'The International Framework of Access to Plant Genetic Resources' in *Perspectives on Intellectual Property*, 6 (Sweet & Maxwell, London, 1999), pp. 1–22; and other articles in the same issue.
78. See John Vidal, the *Guardian*, 25 November 1999.
79. See 'Is Free Trade Fair Trade?', *Pfizer Forum*, January 2000. See also 'Intellectual Property: The Patent on Prosperity', *Pfizer Forum*, November 1998.
80. The UN research is quoted in Robin Mansell and Uta Wehn, *Knowledge Societies* (Oxford University Press, 1998); see especially pp. 204–14.
80. The World Bank's remark is taken from its Annual Report, 1999.
81. Juvenal's *'Quis custodiet . . .'* is translated, 'Who is to guard the guardians?'

CHAPTER 3: THE CORE INDUSTRIES

82. The main general source for figures on the 15 core creative industries are Creative Industries Unit, Department for Culture, Media and Sport, London; Bundesanstalt für Arbeit, Nüremburg; Bureau of Labor Statistics, Washington, DC; European Commission, Brussels; Institut National de la Statistique et des Etudes Economiques (INSEE) Paris; Ministry of Culture, Beijing;

National Bureau of Statistics of China, Beijing; Beijing Research Centre of Science, Beijing ('The Blue Book'); National Statistics, London; Patent and Trademark Office, Washington DC; Patent Office (renamed Intellectual Property Office in 2007), London; United Nations, New York; Veronis, Suhler & Associates, New York; Frontier Economics, London; World Intellectual Property Organisation (WIPO), Geneva; World Trade Organization, Geneva; HM Revenue and Customs, London; UK Trade & Investment, London; Department of Trade & Industry (DTI), London; National Endowment for Science, Technology and the Arts, London; Wikipedia; and company annual reports. Each of these organizations has provided data for more than one of the 15 categories listed below.

83. The proportion of US GDP attributable to intellectual property is taken from '*The Economic Value of Intellectual Property*', **Robert J. Shapiro** and **Kevin A. Hassett**, *USA for Innovation*, October 2005.

83. The data on EU creative industries is taken from a European Union report, '*The Economy of Culture in Europe*', *KEA European Affairs*, Brussels.

85. The data on China's service sector is based on a news release from the Shanghai International Creative Industry Forum, November, 2006. See *People's Daily*, 24 November 2006.

87. The main sources for the **advertising sector** are **A. C. Nielsen**, London; *Advertising Age*, New York; Advertising Association (AA), London; American Advertising Association (AAA), New York; Institute of Practitioners in Advertising (IPA), London; World Advertising Research Center (WARC), Henley on Thames, and Zenith Media, London.

90. The main sources for the **architecture sector** are the American Institute of Architects (AIA), Washington DC; the Bundesarchitektenkammar, Berlin; Archiworld, Rome; Construction Industry Council, London; F. W. Dodge Inc., New York; the Royal Institute of British Architects (RIBA); Mirza & Nacey Research, London; Union of International Architects, Geneva; UNESCO; *Building Design*, London, Ministry of Constrction, Beijing; Claydon Gescher Associates, and *World Architecture*.

92. The main sources for the **art sector** are the *Art Newspaper*, London; the Art Dealers' Association of America, New York; the Arts Council of England, London (and the Arts Councils of Scotland, Wales and Northern Ireland); the British Art Market Federation, London; Christie's International, New York; artprice, Paris; the German Art and Antiques Association, Cologne; the National Endowment for the Arts, Washington DC; and Sotheby's Inc., New York. See also *Museums and Galleries in Britain*, London School of Economics, 2006).

95. The main sources for the **crafts sector** are the Bundesverband Kunst-

handwerk, Frankfurt; the Crafts Council, London; and the Hobby Industry Association (HIA), Elmwood Park, New Jersey.

95. The remarks about **woodturning** are taken from *Resurgence*, 194 (May/June 1999). **Herbert Read's** comment is taken from *The Meaning of Art*, (Faber & Faber, London, 1936).

96. The main sources for the **design sector** are the American Institute of Graphic Arts, New York; British Design Innovation, London; Design Council, London; International Council of Societies of Industrial Designers, Helsinki; and Industrial Designers Society of America (IDSA), Virginia.

96. The **London Business School** research was published in 'Research and Development: technology foresight', *Business Strategy Review*, February 1997, pp. 55–6.

97. **Tony Blair** made his comment about politicians and design in his article 'Britain Can Remake It' in the *Guardian*, 22 July 1997.

98. The main sources for the **fashion sector** are the British Fashion Council, London; Council of Fashion, Washington DC; Designers of America, New York; *Women's Wear Daily*, New York; and *International Herald Tribune*, 'Style & Design' section, New York.

100. The main sources for the **film sector** are A. C. Nielsen EDI, Los Angeles; American Film Institute, New York; British Screen Advisory Council, London; British Academy of Film and Television Arts (BAFTA), London; UK Film Council, London; Motion Picture Association of America, Los Angeles; *Screen Digest*; *Variety*; European Audiovisual Observatory, Strasbourg; The Internet Movie Database (IMDb); *Hollywood Reporters*, Los Angeles; and the State Administration of Radio, Film, and Television (SARFT), Beijing.

102. The main sources for the **music sector** are *Billboard*, New York; the British Phonographic Industry (BPI), London; Market Tracking International (MTI), London; International Federation of the Phonographic Industry (IFPI), London; Jupiter Communications, New York; and Recording Industry Association of America (RIAA). See also *Globalisation, Technology and the Music Industry* (City University Business School, London, 2000).

104. **George Geis** made his remarks at a music conference at the University of California, Los Angeles; they were reported in the *Los Angeles Times*, 25 June 1998.

104. Useful information on the **British music industry** is contained in *A Sound Performance* (KPMG and National Music Council, 1999); and *The Value of Music* (National Music Council and University of Westminster, London, 1996).

105. The main sources for the **performing arts sector** are Americans for the Arts, Washington DC; League of American Theatres and Producers, New

York; National Endowment for the Arts, Washington DC; Opera America, Washington DC; Society of London Theatres (SOLT), London; *Variety*; *Stage*, London; and Arts Council England, London.

107. The main sources for the **publishing sector** are the International Federation of Periodical Publishers (FIPP), London; International Publishers Association, (IPA), Geneva; Magazine Publishers' Association (MPA), New York; the National Union of Journalists, London; Periodical Publishers' Association (PPA), London; Publishers' Association (PA), London; Booksellers' Association, London; Newspaper Society (NS), London; Newspaper Publishers' Association (NPA), London; UK Publishing Media Alliance; Newspaper Association of America (NAA); Association of American Publishers (AAP); *Publisher's Weekly*; UNESCO; European Publishers' Council; and the World Association of Newspapers, Paris.

107. The **history of printing** in Europe is given in Lucien Febvre's *The Coming of the Book* (Verso, London, 1984) and of printing in America in Joseph Blumentahl's *The Printed Book in America* (David Godine, Boston, 1977).

110. The main sources for the **research and development (R&D) sector** are the Department of Commerce, Washington DC; Office of Science and Innovation, DTI, London; Patent Office, London; Patent and Trademark Office, Washington DC; European Patent Office, Munich; Japanese Patent Office, Tokyo; World Intellectual Property Organization (WIPO), Geneva; OECD, Paris; World Bank, Washington DC; National Copyright Administration of China, Beijing; and company reports. See also *The Science, Technology and Industry Scoreboard – Towards a Knowledge-based Economy* (OECD, Paris, 2005); and *Engines of Growth – Economic Contributions of the US. Intellectual Property Industries*, (Economists Incorporated, 2005).

113. The British **R&D Scorecard** is published annually by the Department of Trade and Industry, London. In the 2006 edition, the DTI says (1) British R&D is 'skewed' towards chemistry-based (including biology) industries rather than physics. In Britain, the ratio is 60–40 whereas elsewhere, it is 30–70; (2) 39 per cent of British R&D is contributed by one sector – pharmaceuticals – whereas in other countries the top sectors are IT hardware and automotive; (3) 'Britain has a much higher proportion of total company sales in low R&D intensive sectors such as oils and construction; nearly 50 per cent compared with only 12 per cent elsewhere and 22 per cent for America.'

113. For the research on **the effect of R&D on company sales**, see 'Research and Development: Technology Foresight', *Business Strategy Review*, 97/2, pp. 55–6. For the effects on business performance see *The R&D Scoreboard*, pp. 35–43 and 75–83.

114. The main sources for the **software sector** are the Alliance for Digital Media, London; Business Software Alliance, Washington DC; *Computer Weekly*, London; Software Publishers' Association, Washington DC; Software and Information Industry Association (SIIA), Washington DC; and company reports.
114. **The wages of American software workers** were reported in an economic impact study submitted to the Business Software Alliance on 5 June 1997.
115. The main sources for the **toys and games sector** are the British Toy and Hobby Association, London; International Council of Toy Industries; Toy Industries of Europe (TIE), Brussels; and the Toy Manufacturers of America, New York.
116. The main sources for the **TV and radio sector** are the European Audio-visual Observatory, Strasbourg; Federal Communications Commission (FCC), Washington DC; ITR, London; BBC, London; Motion Picture Association of America, Los Angeles; Ofcom, London; *Screen Digest*; *Television Business International*; UNESCO; and *Variety*.
118. The main sources for the **video games sector** are the Entertainment & Leisure Software Publishers Association (ELSPA); E3, New York; *PC Data*; *Screen Digest*; Entertainment Software Association (ESA), Washington DC; and company reports.
121. For **World Bank statistics,** see its annual report.

CHAPTER 4: MANAGING CREATIVITY

125. See **Ernest Hall,** *In Defence of Genius* (Arts Council of England, London, 1996). Hall is a pianist and composer; textile manufacturer; and property developer. He is chairman of the Dean Clough Business, Arts and Education Centre.
128. The idea of **non-rivalrous** goods and services is based on the idea of 'public goods', which if consumed by one person remain equally available to others. The economists' favourite example is a lighthouse; another is broadcasting financed by licence fees and advertising.
129. See **Adam Smith,** *Wealth of Nations* (1776).
129. See **Ronald Coase,** *The Nature of the Firm* (1937).
129. **Richard H. Thaler** is Robert P. Gwinn Professor of Behavioral Science and Economics at the University of Chicago Graduate School of Business. See Richard Thaler, *The Winner's Curse* (Princeton University Press, 1994) and *Quasi Rational Economics* (Russell Sage Foundation, 1994).
129. For **'an island of conscious power'** see Arthur Seldon and F. G. Pennance,

Everyman's Dictionary of Economics (Dent, London, 1965), p. 173; they also describe the firm as a unit of 'control and decision'.

130. See **David Ricardo,** especially *The Principles of Political Economy and Taxation* (London, 1817).

131. See **Joseph Stiglitz,** 'Public Policy for a Knowledge Economy', a speech delivered at the Centre for Economic Policy Research in London, 27 January 1999. Stiglitz is a former chief economist at the White House and chief economist at the World Bank.

132. For **Stravinsky,** see Robert Craft, *Stravinsky: Chronicle of a Friendship* (Vanderbilt University Press, Nashville, 1994).

133. The two events described here took place in 1998; with thanks to my hosts, **Noah Samara** and Yan-Kit So; and to **Vikram Seth.** See Vikram Seth, *An Equal Music* (Phoenix House, London, 1999), preliminary pages.

134. For the remark by **Emerson,** see Bliss Perry, *The Heart of Emerson's Journals* (Dover, 1995).

134. The **BT/*Management Today* survey** was published in 'Information Strategy', *The Economist,* March 1997.

136. See **Jean-Baptiste Say,** *Traité d'économique politique* (1803); Joseph Schumpeter, *Capitalism, Socialism and Democracy* (Allen & Unwin, London, 1943), especially p. 131; and Andrew Shonfield, *Modern Capitalism: The Changing Balance of Public and Private Power* (Oxford University Press, 1965).

137. **Hermann Hauser,** co-founder of Acorn and chairman of Amadeus Capital Partners, made this remark at a meeting at CREATEC (a digital video R & D lab) at Ealing Studios in 1998.

137. **Jeff Bezos** was quoted in *Upside,* October 1996.

137. **Gary Kasparov** said this before his match with Deep Blue 3 in 1997.

137. See **Trevor Bayliss,** *The Times,* 14 March 2000.

138. The information about ***Time Out*** and **Attik** is based on interviews with their respective owners. David Landau used the same intangible value of copyright in the arrangement of data to build up his *Loot* magazine company, which he sold in 2000 for £180 million.

138. See *Recommendations for Growth: UK Digital Media* (**Digital Media Alliance,** London, 1998).

139. See **Daniel Bell,** *The Coming of Post-Industrial Society* (Basic Books, New York, 1974) and *The Matching of Scales* (IIC, London, 1979).

139. See **Peter Drucker,** *The Age of Discontinuity* (Harper & Row, New York, 1968).

139. Data on **jobs and employment** can be found in *Employment in Europe* (European Commission, Brussels; annual) and *European Economic Themes* (Union Bank of Switzerland, 1997).

140. See *Review of the Economy and Employment 1998–99* (Institute for Employment Research, University of Warwick).
140. See *Employment in Europe* (Employment and European Social Fund, European Commission, Brussels, 1999).
145. See Norman Foster, *A Response to the British Broadcasting Corporation* (Foster Associates, London, 1982). In 2000, the BBC revived the idea.
146. See Harlan Cleveland, *The Knowledge Executive* (Dutton, New York, 1985).
146. See Victoria Ward, *Pool*, 8, at www.poolonline.com.
146. Arie de Geus is the former head of group planning at Royal Dutch Shell and author of *The Living Company* (Harvard Business School Press, 1977). He made this comment at a Global Business Network meeting in London in 1998.
146. See Gerard Fairtlough, *Creative Compartments* (Adamantine Press, London, 1994).
147. See Alfred Marshall, *The Principles of Economics* (1890).
147. For Everett Rogers' work on clusters, see Everett M. Rogers and D. Lawrence Kincaid, *Communications Networks: Towards a New Paradigm for Research* (Free Press, New York, 1981); and Everett Rogers and Judith K. Larsen, *Silicon Valley Fever* (Basic Books, New York, 1984).
148. Dorothy Wordsworth describes how she told William, her brother, about the daffodils in her diaries.
148. The British motor sport cluster is described in Nick Henry and Steven Pinch, *A Regional Formula for Success* (Birmingham University, 1997).
149. The data on New York was supplied by Charles Millard, New York City Development Corporation, in 1999.
149. The data on Huddersfield was supplied by Matt Locke, director of the Media Centre there, in 1999. More information is available from www.creativetown.com.
150. The account of Icon Medialab, a leading Internet consultancy, is taken from the *Financial Times*, 23 June 1997. See also Melina Muth, 'Stewardship Theory and Board Structure', *Australian Graduate School of Management: Corporate Governance*, 6:1 (January 1998), which supports these ideas.
150. See John Kao, *Jamming: The Art and Discipline of Business Creativity* (HarperBusiness, New York, 1997), especially Chapter 3. See also B. Joseph Pine II, and James Gilmore, *The Experience Economy* (Harvard Business School Press, Cambridge, 1999).
150. See Rosamund Stone Zander and Benjamin Zander, *The Art of Possibility* (Harvard Business School Press, Cambridge, 2000).
150. See Keith Johnstone, *IMPRO: Improvisation and the Theatre* (Methuen, London, 1981), p. 29; see also the chapter on status.

151. The taxation of creative companies is analysed in *Reform of the Taxation of Intellectual Property* (Inland Revenue, London, 1999).
153. See **Arthur Andersen,** *The Use of Intellectual Property as Security for Debt Finance* (Intellectual Property Institute and Arthur Andersen, London, 1998).
158. The **Global Business Network meeting** was held in Windsor, near London, on 11–13 October 1998.
158. For the **London Business School research** on starting a company, see Hermann Hauser, 'Entrepreneurship in Europe', *Business Strategy Review*, 11/1, January 2000.
162. The motto, **'Dance as if no one is looking'** is a precept of Andy Allan, former chief executive of Central Television.
163. The idea of intangible **nomadism** is the theme of Jacques Attali's *Lignes d'horizon* (Fayard, Paris, 1990).
163. See **Charles Handy,** *The New Alchemists: How Visionary People Make Something Out of Nothing* (Trafalgar Square, New York, 2001).
163. **Charles Hampden-Turner** described Asian ideas of win-win playing in *Mastering the Infinite Game* (Fons Trompenaars, Amsterdam, 1997). See also his *The Intelligent Economy* (Scottish Council Foundation, Edinburgh, 1998), and (with Fons Trompenaars) *Building Cross-cultural Competence: How to Create Wealth from Conflicting Values* (Yale University Press, 2000).
163. The **famous instruction to the Ford Motor Company** was made by Frederick Winslow Taylor, inventor of time-and-motion studies and sometimes named as the world's first management consultant.
163. The comment by **David Bowie** appeared on his website in 1998. See www.bowie.com.
164. See **David Puttnam,** *Behind and Beyond the Screen* (The Utopian Papers, Newell & Sorrell, London, 1996), p. 16.
165. Dr **Tom Wehr** is the head of the Clinical Psychobiology Branch at the National Institute of Mental Health, Maryland.

CHAPTER 5: THE ENTERTAINMENT GENE

166. The life of **Walt Disney** is told in Bob Thomas, *Walt Disney: An American Original* (Simon & Schuster, New York, 1976) and John Taylor, *Storming the Magic Kingdom* (Alfred A. Knopf, New York, 1987).
168. See **Hortense Powdermaker,** *Hollywood: The Dream Factory; An Anthropologist Looks at the Movie-Makers* (Secker & Warburg, London, 1951).

170. See William Goldman, *Adventures in the Screen Trade* (Futura, New York, 1990).
171. The history and practice of Hollywood is told in Kevin Brownlow and John Kobal, *Hollywood: The Pioneers* (Collins, London, 1979); James Monaco, *American Film Now* (New American Library, New York, 1983); Nicolas Kent, *Naked Hollywood* (documentary and book, BBC, 1991); David Puttnam with Neil Watson, *The Undeclared War* (HarperCollins, London, 1997); and Peter Bart, *The Gross* (St Martin's Lane, London, 1999).
172. For digital cinema, see Patrick von Sychowski, *Electronic Cinema: The Big Screen Goes Digital* (*Screen Digest* special report, London, 2000).
175. Jack Grubman was quoted in the *Financial Times*, 6 September 1994.
175. The *Wall Street Journal* gave its verdict on 10 April 1994.
175. Barry Diller was quoted in the *Financial Times*, 10 March 1990, and Rupert Murdoch in the *Wall Street Journal*, 10 April 1994.
177. For the finances of *Independence Day*, see *Variety*, 25 February 1998.
177. The pop music sales figures are based on *Billboard* data.
177. The remark by Esther Margolis was quoted in *Variety*, 31 March 1999.
178. The relative sales of Disney and Toys 'R' Us were given in *The Economist*, 23 June 1998.
178. Doug Investor was quoted in *The Economist*, 4 April 1998 and in *Variety*.

CHAPTER 6: CLICK-AND-GO

181. The quotes are from a Grateful Dead poster, 1970, and a Microsoft advertising campaign for Microsoft Office, 1998.
182. See Camillo Sitte, *City Planning According to Artistic Principles* (Phaidon Press, London, 1965).
183. The history of electronics and the Internet is recounted in 'Solid State Century', *Scientific American* special issue, 8:1 (1997); Charles Jonscher, *Wired Life* (Bantam, London, 1999); and John Naughton, *A Brief History of the Future: The Origins of the Internet* (Weidenfeld & Nicolson, London, 1999). The remark about the Internet's 'administrative arrangements' is taken from Jonscher, p. 163.
183. See Michael Schrage, 'Multi-Media: The Business Issues', presentation at a *Financial Times* Conference on Cable, Satellite and New Media, London, February, 1995 (proceedings published by the *Financial Times*). His book, *Shared Minds: The New Technology of Collaboration* (Random House, New York, 1990) shows how people can use networks to work together.

183. For the 'law of networks', see Robert Metcalfe, *Packet Communications* (Thomson Computer Press, New York, 1996).
185. The main sources for **Internet data** are *Digital Economy 2000* (Department of Commerce, Washington DC, 2000) and *Information Technology Outlook 2000* (Organization for Economic Cooperation and Development, Paris, 2000).
185. See **Motorola** press release, 17 January 2000.
186. **Gordon Moore** first presented his law in *Electronics*, 35th anniversary edition, April 1965.
187. See **Kevin Kelly**, *New Rules for the New Economy* (Fourth Estate, London, 1998); originally published in *WIRED*, September 1997. See also writings by Danny Quah, Professor of Economics at the London School of Economics, listed at www.lse.ac.uk/~dquah.
187. See ***Our Competitive Future: Building the Knowledge-driven Economy*** (Department of Trade and Industry, London, 1998).
189. **David Isenberg**'s paper, 'The Rise of the Stupid Network', is available at www.isen.com. The quotes by Tom Evslin and 'Computer Telephony' were supplied by Isenberg.
190. **Rex Hundt** made his comments at the Telecom 95 exhibition in Geneva, 1995.
190. See **BT's** Annual Report 1998.
191. **Steven Spielberg** was quoted in the *New York Times*, 14 July 1999.
192. Information on **GNU, Linux, open source and free software** can be found on the Free Software Foundation website, www.fsf.com; and in Eric Raymond's 'The Cathedral and the Bazaar', available at www.tuxedo.org/~esr, or published in print form by O'Reilly, Cambridge, Massachusetts, 1999.
193. See **Richard Stallman**, 'The GNU Operating System' in *Open Sources* (O'Reilly Publishing, Sebastopol, 1999) (and www.fsf.com). Another variant of copyright, with some similarities to **copyleft**, is an 'accessright' proposed by Simon Olswang in *European Intellectual Property Review*, 1995, pp. 215–18.
194. The phrase **'reward and consolation'** comes from Alan Blackwell, joint director of the Crucible Centre at Cambridge University.
194. The **IDC** report was quoted in *The Economist*, 17 June 2000. The main commercial suppliers of Linux software are VA Linux and Red Hat.
195. See **Peter Martin**, *Financial Times*, 20 October 1998.
196. See **Lawrence Lessig**, *Atlantic Monthly*, 10 September 1998, and *Code and Other Laws of Cyberspace* (Basic Books, New York, 1999).
197. See **Martha Woodmansee**, 'On the Author Effect: Recovering Collectiv-

ity', *Cardozo Arts and Entertainment Law Review* 10:2 (1992). Woodmansee is executive director of the US Society for Critical Exchange, an academic forum for literary theory and criticism.
197. See **James Boyle,** *Shamans, Software and Spleens* (Harvard University Press, Cambridge, 1996).
198. Tim Hubbard's remark about **Ensembl** was reported in the *Guardian*'s G2 section, 22 June 2000, pp. 2–3. See also www.ensembl.org.uk.
198. The story of the four people who developed and sold **Doom** was told by Bruce Bond in the 1996 Fleming Lecture, published in *Television*, April/May 1996, pp. 6–10.
200. Information about **Stephen King** and his online publications can be found at www.stephenking.com. See also www.barnesandnoble.com.
200. For **Online Originals,** see www.onlineoriginals.com.
200. For the **Rocket eBook,** see www.ebook-gemstar.com.
201. **Yahoo!** regularly appears in lists of the world's most-used Internet sites. Napster say 28 million people have downloaded its software, although it refuses to divulge how often they use it. Visa is the world's biggest bank in terms of the number of customers.
203. See **V. I. Lenin,** *The New External and Internal Position and the Problems of the Party* (Moscow, 1920).

CHAPTER 7: CAPITAL OF MY MIND

204. See **Antoine de Rivarol** (1753–1801), *Discours sur l'universalité de la langue française* (Paris, 1784). He was a journalist and publicist.
204. See *Resurgence*, 194, May/June 1999.
205. The story of **Akio Morita** is told in John Nathan, *Sony: The Private Life* (HarperCollins, London 1999).
206. Accounts of **capital** can be found in Fernand Braudel's *Civilization and Capitalism: 15th–18th Century*, especially vol. 3, *The Perspective of the World* (Collins, London, 1984). See also works by Adam Smith, John Stuart Mill, Karl Marx, Joseph Schumpeter and John Maynard Keynes. For capitalism since the 1930s, see Andrew Shonfield, *Modern Capitalism: The Changing Balance of Public and Private Power* (Oxford University Press, 1965).
208. See **Fritz Machlup,** *The Production and Distribution of Knowledge in the US* (Princeton University Press, 1962). See also Marc Porat, *The Information Economy: Definition and Measurement* (Department of Commerce, Washington DC, 1977). Porat was one of Machlup's students.

208. See J. W. Kendrick, *The Formation and Stock of Total Capital* (Columbia University Press, 1976) and E. F. Denison *Why Growth Rates Differ* (Brookings Institute, Washington DC, 1967). See also Louis-Marc Ducharme, *Measuring Intangible Investment* (Organization for Economic Cooperation and Development, Paris, 1998); T. W. Schultz, *Investment in Human Capital* (Free Press, New York, 1971); and G. S. Becker, *Human Capital* (Chicago University Press, 1975).

209. See Jerry Hirshberg, *The Creative Priority* (Penguin, London, 1998), especially, pp. 40–42.

210. For incremental, not sudden, R & D see G. Dosi, *Technical Change and Industrial Performance* (Macmillan, London, 1984); and R. R. Nelson and S. G. Winter, *An Evolutionary Theory of Social Change* (Harvard University Press, Cambridge, 1982).

210. The research by Birkbeck College, University of London, was presented by Adrian Patch at the British Psychological Association Conference, Brighton, on 7 January 2000.

211. For intellectual capital, see the survey 'The Management of Intellectual Capital', which includes an article by Edvinsson, in *International Journal of Strategic Management*, 30:3 (June 1997); and Thomas A. Stewart, *Intellectual Capital* (Nicholas Brealey, London, 1998).

212. See Bill Gates, 'Business @ the Speed of Light', *Business Strategy Review*, February 1999, pp. 11–18.

213. For UK national research councils, see the councils' reports to Parliament for 1999. Only one council mentions intellectual property.

213. The Interbrand survey of the 'World's Most Valuable Brands' is available at www.interbrand.com.

214. Norio Ohga made his comments while presenting Sony's 1998 Report and Accounts.

214. For James Tobin's theories, see *Asset Accumulation and Economic Activity* (University of Chicago Press, 1982).

217. See Hubert Saint-Onge, 'Tacit Knowledge: The Key to the Strategic Alignment of Intellectual Capital', *Strategy & Leadership*, 24:2 (March/April 1996), pp. 10–14. Hubert Saint-Onge is senior vice-president of strategic capabilities at Mutual Group; he was formerly at the Canadian Imperial Bank of Commerce (CIBC), where he developed the idea of customer capital.

218. See George Bernard Shaw, *The Intelligent Woman's Guide to Socialism* (Constable, London, 1929), p. 465.

220. The American comment about the future of trade in creative products comes from the Commissioner's Report, Annual Report, 1998, US Patent and Trademark Office; the European comment from President Santer's address at

the European Audiovisual Conference in Birmingham, 1998. See also *Content as a New Growth Industry* (Organization for Economic Cooperation and Development, Paris, 1997).

SELECT BIBLIOGRAPHY

Ackroyd, Peter, *T. S. Eliot* (Hamish Hamilton, London, 1984).

Amabile, Teresa, *The Social Psychology of Creativity* (Springer-Verlag, New York, 1983).

Amabile, Teresa, 'How to Kill Creativity', *Harvard Business Review* (September 1998).

Arai, Hisamitsu, *The Japanese Experience in Wealth Creation* (World International Proprety Organization, Geneva, 1999).

Aranguen, J. L., *Human Communication* (Weidenfeld & Nicolson, London, 1967).

Attali, Jacques, *Noise: The Political Economy of Music* (University of Minnesota Press, Minneapolis, 1985).

Attali, Jacques, *Lignes d'horizon* (Fayard, Paris, 1990).

Bart, Peter, *The Gross* (St Martin's Lane, London, 1999).

Benthall, Jonathan, *Science and Technology in Art Today* (Thames and Hudson, London, 1972).

Beresford, Keith, *Patenting Software under the European Patent Convention* (Sweet & Maxwell, London, 2000).

Berger, John, *Another Way of Telling* (Writers and Readers Publishing Cooperative, London, 1982).

Berrely, Peter, 'The Hunter-Gatherers of the Knowledge Economy', *Strategy and Business* (March 1999).

Bettig, Ronald V., *Copyrighting Culture: The Political Economy of Intellectual Property* (Westview Press, Boulder, 1996).

Boyd, Frank, and others, *New Media Culture in Europe* (Uitgeverij de Balie, Amsterdam, 1999).

Boyle, James, *Shamans, Software and Spleens* (Harvard University Press, Cambridge, 1996).

Brand, Stuart, *The Media Lab* (Viking, New York, 1987).

Branscomb, Anne Wells, *Who Owns Information?* (Basic Books, New York, 1995).

Brewer, John, and Roy Porter (eds.), *Consumption and the World of Goods* (Routledge, London, 1993).

Burke, James, *Connections* (Little, Brown, London, 1995).

Burke, Sean, *Authorship* (Edinburgh University Press, 1995).

Castells, Manuel, *The Information Age* (3 vols., Blackwell, Oxford, 1996–8).

Choo, Chun Wei, *The Knowing Organization* (Oxford University Press, 1997).

Claxton, Guy, *Hare Brain, Tortoise Mind: How Intelligence Increases When You Think Less* (Ecco Press, New York, 1999).

Cleveland, Harlan, *The Knowledge Executive* (Dutton, New York, 1985).

Coombe, Rosemary, *The Cultural Life of Intellectual Properties: Authorship, Appropriation and the Law* (Duke University Press, Durham, 1998).

Cornish, W. R., *Intellectual Property* (4th edn, Sweet & Maxwell, London, 1999).

Creative Industries Mapping Document 2001 (Department for Culture, Media and Sport, 2001).

Creative Nation (Commonwealth of Australia, Australian Government Printing Service, Canberra, 1994).

Csikszentmihalyi, Mihaly, *Creativity: Flow and the Psychology of Discovery and Invention* (HarperCollins, New York, 1996).

Cultural Trends (Policy Studies Institute, London, annual).

Dewulf, Simon, and Caroline Baillie, *How to Foster Creativity* (Department for Education and Employment, London, 1999).

The Digital Dilemma: Intellectual Property in the Information Age (National Research Council, National Academy Press, Washington DC, 2000).

Drahos, Peter, 'Intellectual Property and Human Rights', *Intellectual Property Quarterly* 3 (Sweet & Maxwell, London, 1999).

Ducharme, Louis-Marc, *Measuring Intangible Investment* (Organization for Economic Cooperation and Development, Paris, 1998).

Eisner, Michael, and Tony Schwartz, *Work in Progress* (Random House, New York, 1998).

Fairtlough, Gerard, *Creative Compartments* (Adamantine Press, London, 1994).

Febvre, Lucien, *The Coming of the Book* (Verso, London, 1984).

Findlater, Richard, *The Player Kings* (Weidenfeld & Nicolson, London, 1971).

Fisher, Desmond, *The Right to Communicate* (Boole Press, Dublin, 1983).

Flint, Michael, *A User's Guide to Copyright* (5th edn, Butterworths, London, 2000).

Fromm, Erich, *Fear of Freedom* (Routledge & Kegan Paul, London, 1960).

Frye, Northrop, *Creation and Research* (University of Toronto Press, Toronto, 1980).

Gates, Bill, 'Business @ the Speed of Light', *Business Strategy Review*, February 1999.

Gleick, James, 'Patently Absurd', *New York Times* (12 March 2000).

Goldstein, Paul, *Copyright's Highway* (Hill & Wang, New York, 1996).

Hardwick, Philip, Bahadur Khan and John Langmead, *An Introduction to Modern Economics* (4th edn, Longman, London, 1994).

Hayward, P. A., and C. A. Greenhalgh, *Intellectual Property Research* (Economic and Social Research Council, London 1994).

Hirshberg, Jerry, *The Creative Priority* (Penguin, London, 1998).

Howe, Michael J. A., *Genius Explained* (Cambridge University Press, 1999).

Huizinga, Johan, *Homo Ludens* (Routledge & Kegan Paul, London, 1949).

Human Development Report (United Nations Development Fund, New York, 1999).

International Financial Statistics (International Monetary Fund, Washington DC, 1999).

James, E. P., and others, *Copinger and Skone James on Copyright* (Sweet & Maxwell, London, 1991).

Jardine, Lisa, *Ingenious Pursuits* (Little, Brown, London, 1999).

Johnstone, Keith, *IMPRO: Improvisation and the Theatre* (Methuen, London, 1981).

Jonscher, Charles, *Wired Life* (Bantam, London, 1999).

Jussawalla, Meheroo, *The Passing of Remoteness* (Institute of Southeast Asian Studies, Singapore, 1986).

Jussawalla, Meheroo, and others, *The Cost of Thinking* (Ablex, New Jersey, 1988).

Kao, John, *Jamming: The Art and Discipline of Business Creativity* (HarperBusiness, New York, 1997).

Kelly, Kevin, *New Rules for the New Economy* (Fourth Estate, London, 1998).

Kirova, Milka S., and Robert S. Lipsey, 'Measuring Real Investment' (Working Paper no. 6404, US National Bureau of Economic Research, Washington DC, 1998).

Koestler, Arthur, *The Act of Creation* (Hutchinson, London, 1964).

Kruege, Alan B., and Jorn-Steffen Pischke, 'Observations and Conjectures on the US Employment Miracle' (Working Paper no. 6146, US National Bureau of Economic Research, Washington DC, 1997).

Kuhn, Thomas, *The Structure of Scientific Revolutions* (University of Chicago Press, 3rd edn, 1996).

Lessig, Lawrence, *Code and Other Laws of Cyberspace* (Basic Books, New York, 1999).

Mann, Peter H., *Books, Buyers and Borrowers* (André Deutsch, London, 1971).

May, Christopher, *A Global Political Economy of Intellectual Property Rights: The New Enclosures?* (Routledge, London, 2000).

McLuhan, Marshall, *The Gutenberg Galaxy* (University of Toronto Press, 1962).

Mellor, David, *How to Set Up a Home Recording Studio* (PC Publishing, London, 1996).

Menon, Narayana, *The Communications Revolution* (National Book Trust, New Delhi, 1976).

Naughton, John, *A Brief History of the Future: The Origins of the Internet* (Weidenfeld & Nicolson, London, 1999).

Negroponte, Nicholas, *Being Digital* (Hodder & Stoughton, London, 1995).

Nordström, Kjell, and Jonas Ridderstråle, *Funky Business: Talent Makes Capital Dance* (Financial Times/Prentice Hall, London, 2000).

Petty, Geoffrey, *How to Be Better at Creativity* (Kogan Page, London, 1997).

Pine, B. Joseph, II, and James Gilmore, *The Experience Economy* (Harvard Business School Press, Cambridge, 1999).

Ploman, Edward W., and L. Clark Hamilton, *Copyright* (Routledge & Kegan Paul, London, 1980).

Powdermaker, Hortense, *Hollywood: The Dream Factory; An Anthropologist Looks at the Movie-Makers* (Secker & Warburg, London, 1951).

Provenzo, Eugene, *Video Kids: Making Sense of Nintendo* (Harvard University Press, Cambridge, 1991).

Puttnam, David, with Neil Watson, *The Undeclared War* (HarperCollins, London, 1997).

Raleigh, Thomas, *An Outline of the Law of Property* (Clarendon Press, Oxford, 1890).

Revesz, John, *Trade-Related Aspects of Intellectual Property Rights* (Productivity Commission, Canberra, Australian Government Printing Service, 1999).

Rifkin, Jeremy, *The Age of Access* (Penguin, London, 2000).

Rivette, Kevin G., and David Kline, *Rembrandts in the Attic: Unlocking the Hidden Value of Patents* (Harvard Business School Press, Cambridge, 2000).

Rogers, Everett M., and D. Lawrence Kincaid, *Communication Networks: Towards a New Paradigm for Research* (Free Press, New York, 1981).

Rogers, Everett, and Judith K. Larsen, *Silicon Valley Fever* (Basic Books, New York, 1984).

Ronan, Colin, *The Cambridge History of the World's Science* (Cambridge University Press, 1983).

Roszak, Theodore, *Where the Wasteland Ends* (Faber & Faber, London, 1972).

Ruskin, John, *Unto This Last* (Waverley, London, 1862).

Sachs, Jeffrey, 'By Invitation', *The Economist* (14 August 1999).

Schumpeter, Joseph, *Capitalism, Socialism and Democracy* (Allen & Unwin, London, 1943).

Securing Innovation and Creativity in Design Education (Training Organization for Professionals in Construction, Department for Education and Employment, London, 1999).

Seldon, Arthur, and F. G. Pennance, *Dictionary of Economics* (Dent, London, 1965).

Smith, Chris, *Creative Britain* (Faber & Faber, London, 1998).

Smith, Logan Pearsall, *Logan Pearsall Smith: An Anthology*, ed. Edward Burman (Constable, London, 1989).

Stiglitz, Joseph E., 'Public Policy for a Knowledge Economy' (speech at the Centre for Economic Policy Research, London, 27 January 1999).

Storr, Anthony, *The Dynamics of Creation* (Secker & Warburg, London, 1972).

Strathern, Marylin, *Property, Substance and Effect: Anthropological Essays on Persons and Things* (Athlone Press, London, 1999).

Tapscott, Don, *The Digital Economy* (McGraw-Hill, New York, 1995).

Tunstall, Jeremy, *The Media Are American* (Constable, London, 1977).

United Nations Convention on Biological Diversity [the Rio Convention] (United Nations, New York, 1992).

Von Krogh, Georg, Kazuo Ichijo and Ikujiro Nonaka, *Enabling Knowledge Creation* (Oxford University Press, 2000).

Walker, David, *Understanding Pictures* (University of Massachusetts, Amherst, 1979).

Wiener, Norbert, *The Human Use of Human Beings* (Doubleday Anchor, New York, 1954).

Wilde, Oscar, 'The Decay of Lying' in *Complete Works of Oscar Wilde* (Collins, London, 1966).

Williams, Raymond, *Culture and Society 1780–1950* (Penguin, London, 1961).

Wilmut, I., K. Campbell and C. Tudge, *The Second Creation: The Age of Biological Control by the Scientists who Cloned Dolly* (Headline, London, 2000).

Wilson, Edward O., *Consilience: The Unity of Knowledge* (Abacus, London, 1998).

Winston, Brian, *Dangling Conversations* (Davis-Poynter, London, 1973).

Wolf, Michael, *The Entertainment Economy* (Penguin, London, 1999).

Woods, Gerald, and others, *Art Without Boundaries 1950–70* (Thames and Hudson, London, 1972).

Zohar, Danah, *Rewiring the Corporate Brain* (Berrett-Koehler, San Francisco 1997).

INDEX

AAT 48
Accenture 187
Ackroyd, Peter 14
Adams, Bryan 177
Adobe 67, 199
advertising 90–92, 123, 167
Aharonian, Greg 52
Amabile, Teresa 10
Amazon.com vii–viii, 40, 41
American Beauty 6, 7
American institute of Architects 93
Americans for the Arts 108
Anne, Queen 56–7
AOL Time Warner 169
  Warner Bros 167, 169, 171, 178
  Warner Music 61–3, 105
Apache software 192
Apple 31, 39, 184, 195
Archimedes 13, 15
architecture xii–xiii, 92–4, 123, 149, 181–83
ARD 169
art 94–6, 123, 149
  artists' websites 202
  and copyright xii–xiii, 54, 57
  illegal trade in 94
  unit cost of the physical object xiv
Arthur Andersen viii, 153
Artprice.com 95
arts
  and creativity x, xi
  and sciences xiii–xiv
Arts Council of England 109
'AskJeeves' website 20
AT&T 145, 169, 184, 189, 193
Atari 121, 135
Atlantic Monthly 196
Atomic Club, Warsaw 126–7
Attik 138
Aurigin 51
authors
  concepts of authorship 55
  and copyright 20–21
  rights 55–62, 75

Bacon, Francis 16
Baker, Steve 150
Band Aid 126, 127
bandwidth 189, 190
Barlow, John Perry 59–60, 62
Barnes & Noble 41
Baron, Paul 192
Basic Books 64
Batman 178
Bayliss, Trevor 137
Bazalgette, Peter 14
BBC 104, 107, 119, 145, 169, 188, 211, 215
Beastie Boys 62
Beatles 31
Bell, Daniel 139, 141–2
Bennett, Peter 158
Beresford, Keith 43
Berlusconi, Silvio 216
Bernard, Claude 1
Berne convention on copyright 26, 76, 194
Berners-Lee, Tim 192

Bertelsmann 61
  BMG 62, 196
Bettig, Ronald 57
Bezos, Jeff 40, 41, 135, 137
Big Brother 119
Bind 192
biotechnology
  human genome 46–8
  patenting of viii, 44–50, 77–8
Biotechnology and Biological Research Council 49
Birkbeck College 210–11
Birmingham University 148
Blair, Tony 49, 99, 166
The Blair Witch Project 172–173, 202
blogs 88, 117
BMG. *see* Bertelsmann
Boden, Margaret 8
Body Shop 205–16
The Bodyguard 177
Bohr, Nils 13
books 109–11, 199
  and copyright 31
  most given creative works 110
  powerful symbols of learning and knowledge 61
  spending on 111–112
  theft statistics 73
booksellers 19
Boomtown Rats 125, 126
Borland 39
Bowie, David 62, 154, 163–4
Boyle, James 197
brain
  cognitive processes 11
  electronic scans 11
  an 'enchanted loom' 5
  and sleeping 165
brainwaves 6
brands 20, 68, 69, 73, 79, 85, 90, 213–14
Branson, Sir Richard 122
Braudel, Fernand 206, 207
Brazil
  advertising market 92
  art market 97
  and copyright theft 73
  music market 89
  size of economy 87
  spending 87
Breakthrough 1
Britain *see* United Kingdom
British Museum 96
British Patent Office 38
  and European Directive on biotechnology patents no.98/44 49
  examiners 52
  filing charges 36
  first objective of 50
  number of patents issued 114–15
  patent for the technique of cloning a sheep viii
  and R & D 112–13
  registration 69, 99
  revenues 50
  trademark applications 69
broadcasting 54, 169–71, 198
Broadway, New York vii, 108, 149
Bronfman, Edgar, Jr 175
Bronowski, Jacob xv
Bruce, Iain 199
BSkyB 178
BT 51–2, 105, 110, 170, 184, 190
BT/*Management Today* survey 134
BTG 51, 52
Buchwald, Art 176
Buckminster, Fuller 1, 3
buckminsterfullerene 1–3
Buena Vista *see* Disney
Bullfrog 122
Bureau of Labor Statistics 86
Burger King 178
Bushnell, Nolan 135–6
business
  dependence on creativity xvii
  ideas in 10
  as pleasure 12
business methods, patents for vii, 38–44
business models, new 65, 81, 203
Business Software Alliance 73
Butler 201

C_{60} carbon molecule 1–3, 7, 112
California Supreme Court 46
Canon 114
capital
  creative 218–20
  defined 206
  and economic growth 207–8
  history of 206–7
  human 212–16, 218
  the price of value 214–16
  structural 209, 209–10
  The Italian Job 216–18
  Structural 209, 209–10
capitalism 136, 207
Capitol 62
car industry 148–9
Carlton 169
Carlyle, Thomas 131
Carroll, Lewis 20
Carter, Joe 187
cash deposits 152
Casino Royale 104
Cats 108
Caxton, William 34
CBS Records 214
CDNow.com 42, 63
CDs 61–3, 65, 110, 130
  video games 120
Cecchi Gori 154
Celera 47, 48
cell technology 47, 48
Celltech 146
Centre Georges Pompidou, Beauborg
    93, 181, 182
Century, Michael 193
CERN 192
Channel 4 182
Chariots of Fire 166
China
  advertising market 91, 92
  architecture market 94
  art market 97
  and copyright theft 73, 74
  crafts market 98
  design market 100
  desire to join WTO 78
  fashion market 102
  film production 102, 104–105
  growth of creative industries 87
  music market 107
  performing arts market 109
  publishing market 110, 112
  R & D market 116
  size of economy 87
  software market 117
  toys and games market 118
  TV market 118, 119
chip speeds 186–7, 208
Chow, Lee 90
Christianity, and creativity 7–8
Christie, Agatha 108
Christie's 96
Church of England 8
Claxton, Guy 6
Cleveland, Harlan 146, 147
Clinton, Bill 49
cloning viii, 32, 48–9
CNN 200
Coase, Ronald 129
Coca-Cola 71, 99, 174–5, 178–9,
    213–4
Cohn, Harry 171
Cohn, Jack 171
Coleridge, Samuel Taylor 147, 148
collaborative creativity 186, 191–2
Collett Dickinson Pearce 164
Columbia Pictures 166, 169, 171,
    175, 177, 188, 214
Coming to America 176
common law 25, 29, 36, 69
Community Plant Varieties
    Convention (UPOV) 27
Community Trademark Office 27
competition
  and creative intangible value 208
  and creativity 13
  and diversification 208
  increasing xi
  and innovation 208
  in the marketplace 33, 68
  and monopoly rights 80
  and property rights 27
competitiveness, demonstrated by
    patents 33

computer software 38–40, 116–17, 123, 192–96
  copyright in xii
  patentabilty xii, 38–44
  and a products economic value x
  theft 72–4
Computer Telephony 189–91
computer-aided design (CAD) 116
computers
  becoming faster and cheaper 186
  and creativity 6
confidentiality xii, 70
Conran, Sir Terence 82–4, 127, 132
consciousness
  dreamlike state 5, 6
  heightened 5, 6
consilience xi
Content Scrambler System (CSS) 65
'copyleft' 194
copyright 54–67, 75, 85, 196–7
  acrues automatically xii
  borrowing against copyright 154
  computer programs and 39
  defined 54
  difference between ideas and expressions 9
  digital information 58–61
  five-stage logic of 58, 59
  literary and artistic works as belonging to society 55–6
  moral and economic rights 29–32
  and patents 36
  private copying 64–5, 66, 81
  protection of material 67, 210
  qualifying works xii, 54, 57
  films and TV programmes 54
  literary, dramatic and artistic works 54
  performances and broadcasts 54
  typographical settings 54, 58
  'subtle and esoteric' 21
  'technical' copying 66
  term xii, 25, 54, 58
  theft 71–4
Copyright Act (1710) [UK] 56
Copyright Act (1842) [UK] 57
Copyright Act (1976) [US] 25, 38
Copyright, Designs and Patents Act (1988) 25
copyright industries 79
  'core' xiii
  defined xii–xiii
  employment in 86–7
  growth xvi
  'total' xiii
Cornish, W. R. 34–5, 44
Costello, Elvis 62
Costner, Kevin 177
Coward, Noel 12
Craft, Robert 132
crafts 97–8, 123, 149
  defined 97
'create to', defined 8
creation myths 16
creative capital 206, 218–20
creative economy
  conventional economy and xvi–xvii
  the creative equation xiv
  defined xiv, 85
  dominant economic form xiv–xvii
  fragmented and elusive data 84
  growth xvi, 86–9, 123–4
  and the 'property contract' 29
  size of 123
  summed up 220
  worth 123–4
creative equation xiv
creative industries 84–124
  defined xiii–xiv
  employment xv, 87
Creative Industries Task Force xiii, 75
creative product
  characteristics x
  the creative equation xiv
  defined x
  difficult to quantify and value 84–5
creativity 1–18
  analysis 16–17
  and the arts x, xi, xiii, xiv
  attributes for development 11–12
  a basic element of life xvii–xviii, 10
  and business xvii
  characteristics 10–15
  collaborative 186, 191–2, 195–8

and competition 13
and consciousness 5
defined ix, xi, 4–10, 84, 167, 182
and economics 127–32, 159
as fun 12–13
generating product 4, 17–18
God and 7–8
Jung describes 5
lack of intrinsic moral quality 14–15
managing *see* managing creativity
meaningful 6, 9–10
and the nature of ideas 129–30
original 6, 7–9
personal 6, 7–9
personality traits 13–14
present at all levels of business xi
private and personal 4
relationship with economics viii–x, 17
and the sciences xi, xiii, 4
self-sufficiency 10–11
sense of competition 13
as a spiritual exercise 6
as surprising 14
in a team 7
and technology 183–6
tests of 16
two stages 4
a universal talent 11
unprotected 57
Crippen, Dr 15
cultural imperialism 77
Curl, Robert 2
Curry, Andrew xv
Curse of the Golden Flower 105

Daimler/Chrysler 113
Dali, Salvador 14
Damiasio, Antonio 5
Darwin, Charles 183
Davies, Donald 192
deal-making 155–6, 179
debt 152–3
DeButts, John 145
deckchair.com 125, 127
DeCSS (decryption code) 65
Defoe, Daniel 56
Dell Computers vii, 40
Denison, E. F. 208
Department of Trade and Industry [UK] 75, 113, 187
design xiii, 85, 99–100, 123, 149
and copyright xii
defined xii
exploitation 22
a form of intellectual property xi
intangible property right x
international conventions 26
owners 21
patents 86
registration xii, 70
rights xii, 70
Design Acts [UK] 99
Deütsche Telekom 170
developing countries 88–9
communal ownership traditional 80
and intellectual property law 30–31
Devlin, Dean 177
Diamond v. Chakrabarty 48
Diamond v. Diehr 39, 40
digital coding 183, 185–6
digital copying 22, 42
digital detective agencies 67
'digital flip', the 58
digital information, and copyright 58–61
Digital Millennium Copyright Act (1998) 25
digital technologies xiv, xvi, 72, 81, 199–200
Diller, Barry 175
diminishing returns 129–30
discovery, and invention 47
Disney Company, The Walt 20, 154, 169, 171, 172, 176, 178, 213
Buena Vista 167
Disney, Walt 166
DNA 45, 48, 49
Dolly the sheep viii, 32, 48
domain names 210
Donne, John 8
Doom (video game) 198
Dot.com (a piglet) 48

DragNet system 67
Drahos, Peter 77
dramatic works, and copyright 54, 107
drawings, and copyright 57
dreamlike state 5, 6, 14
dreams 11, 16–17, 164, 168
droite de suite (resale tax) 95
Drucker, Peter 129–30, 139
drugs, Indian 30
Du Pont 175
du Pont, Ben 51
Dutch government 49
DV (Digital Video) 188
DVD 64, 102, 103, 104, 110
  video games 120
Dylan, Bob 10
Dyson, Esther 60–61
Dyson, James 13

e-poetry 199
eBooks 200
economic clusters 147–9, 173, 174–5
economic growth 207–8
'economic rights' 22, 29, 32
economics
  creativity and 127, 129, 159
  defined ix
  economic theory xvii
  irrationality in 129
  relationship with creativity viii–x
The Economist 76, 108
economy
  defined ix
  of ideas 131
education 212, 220
Edvinsson, Leif 211–12, 214, 215
Edward IV, King 34
Einstein, Albert 3, 131, 155, 182, 183
electric market 198–202
Electronic Arts 122
Electronic Frontier Foundation 59
electronic publishing 110
electronic watermarks 67, 74
electronics, manufacturers 170
Eli, Lily 78
Eliot, T. S. 14
Elliott, Tony 138
Emerson, Ralph Waldo 134
EMI 61, 62, 105
Emmerich, Roland 177
employment
  copyright industries xvi
  freelance 139, 141
  full 139, 140, 141
  new opportunities xv
  part-time 139, 140, 141
  the post-employment job 139–42
  self-employment 87, 139, 140–41, 161
  young people xv
encryption 60
The English Patient 176
engravings, and copyright 57
Ensemble software 198
entertainment conglomerates 170
Entertainment Software Alliance 122
entrepreneurs 135–8, 162–3
entropy 10–11
  negative 11
equity 152, 153
Eternet networking 183
Ethics 3, 14–15, 44–50, 77–8
Europe
  compared with America 158
  number of patents xvi
  public/private broadcasters 169–71
European Commission 27, 43–4, 149, 152, 158, 220
European Court of Human Rights 182
European Court of Justice 49
European Patent Convention 27, 44, 47
European Patent Office 26, 27, 35, 37, 43–4, 46, 113, 116
European Union 27, 29, 87
  Directive on computer programs (1991) 38
  Directive on copyright (2000) 66
  Directive on Biotechnology (no.98/44) 49–50
Everyman's Dictionary of Economics 129

Evslin, Tom 189
excitement 16, 17, 164
Exxon 85
Eye Image, New York 146

Fairtlough, Gerard 146
fakes 71
fame 163–4
fashion 101–102, 123
Faulkner, William 21
Federal Communication Commission 190
Festen (Celebration) 188
Feynman, Richard 12–13
file-sharing systems 23, 63–5
film 81, 102–105, 123
  copyright xii, 31, 54, 61
  cost of processing 187
  costs and box office receipts 103
  distribution 176
  non-Hollywood film-makers 179–82
  rules for film-making 167
  theft statistics 73
  video rights 27
  see also Hollywood
'first to file' system 36
'first to invent' system 36
Fitzgerald, F. Scott 13
Flickr 88
Flint, Michael 69
Florence City Council 34
Ford, Gerald 74
Ford, Henry 155
Ford Motor Company 113, 163
Fortune 500 companies 213
Fortune vii
Foster, Norman 93, 145, 182
Four Weddings and a Funeral 104, 177
Fox, Twentieth-Century 102, 104, 167, 169, 171, 176, 177, 178
Fox, William 171
France
  art market 97
  attitude towards foreign nationals' works 26
  film production 102
  natural law approach to authors/inventors 29
  size of economy 87
  starting businesses 158
France Télécom 170
France Télévision 169
free-riding 128
Fremantle Media 119
Free Software Foundation (FSF) 193
FreeNet 63, 64, 193
freeware 80, 195
Fry committee 35
The Full Monty 104, 176

games *see* toys and games (excluding video games); video games
Gandhi, Mahatma 77
Gap 200
Gates, Bill 211, 212–13
Gehry, Frank 93
Geis, George 106
Geldof, Bob 125–7
Gemstar TV International 200
General Agreement for Trade and Tariffs (GATT) 75–6
General Motors 113, 209
General Public Licence (GPL) 193–4
genetics 32, 38, 45, 47–50, 78
gentian 77–8
Germany
  advertising market 91
  art market 97
  expenditure on R & D 84
  film production 103
  size of economy 87
  starting businesses 158
Getty Images 20
Geus, Arie de 146
Gillette 60
Giuliani, Mayor Rudi 149
Glaxo Welcome 154
Gleik, James 41, 42
Global Anti-Counterfeiting Group 73
Global Business Network xvii, 158
globalization 74–8
GNU 193, 194
GNU/Linux 192, 193

Gnutella 63, 64, 193
God, and creativity 7–8
Goethe, Johann Wolfgang von 14
Goffmann, Erving 13
Goldman, William 170
Goldstein, Paul 28–9
goods 130
  defined x
government
  bias towards manufacturing 85
  and intellectual property 22, 24–5
  tax systems 141
Granada Media 169
Grateful Dead 59, 181
Gravity, Law of 131
Gray, Thomas 8
GrayZone Inc. 67
Greece 87
gross domestic product (GDP) 87, 87–8, 208
Groupe Serveur 95
growth, economic 86–9, 207–8
Grubman, Jack 175
Guardian 78
Guggenheim Museum, Bilbao 93
Gutenberg, Johannes 109

H-Creativity (historical creativity) 8
Hadid, Zaha 93
Hall, Ernest 125
Hampden-Turner, Charles 163
Handy, Charles 9, 163
HarperCollins 178
Hartmann, Peri 40, 41
Harvard University 46
Hauser, Hermann 137, 144
Hayward, Peter and Christine Greenhalgh 29
health-care viii, 212
Henley Centre, London xv
Hewlett-Packard 114
'hierarchy of desires' xiv, 87
Hieron, King 15
Hinduism, and intellectual property 23, 30, 55
Hirschberg, Jerry 209
Hirst, Damien 32
Hitachi 121
Hitler, Adolf 15
hits 156–7, 179
Hobbes, Thomas 28, 57
Hollywood 102, 168–80
  the dream factory 168–70
  Hollywood lessons 170–79
  marketing budgets 176
Holstein, Johan Staël von 150
Houston, Whitney 177
Howard, George 145
Howe, Michael 11–12
Howells, Kim 21–2
Hoyle, Fred 3
Hubbard, Tim 198
Huddersfield 149
Huizinga, Johan 12
human capital 208–9
human genome 45, 46, 49
Human Genome Mapping Project (HGMP) 46, 47, 48, 198
humanism 7, 8, 55–6
Hundt, Rex 190

IBM 42, 114, 195
Icon Medialab 150
ideas
  in business 10
  and competition 129–30
  and copyright laws 9
  and deal making 155, 156
  the economy of 131
  and hits 157
  ideas business 84–5
  non-rivalrous 128, 129
  prioritising 162–163
  and a products economic value x
  rivalrous 128
  scavenging for 163
idiot savants 11
Idris, Kamil 10
increasing returns 131
incubation 16, 164
Independence Day 177
India 89
  dogbane 77

drugs 30
film production 102, 103
music market 107
Industrial Design Society of America (IDSA) 99
industrial process, and patent law 31
Industrial Revolution 34–5, 139
industry earnings and market size
defined 89
advertising 90–92
architecture 93–4, 123
art 95–7, 123
crafts 97–8, 123
design 99–100, 123
fashion 101, 123
film 102–3, 123
music 105–7, 123
performing arts 107–8, 123
publishing 111–12, 123
R & D 112–16, 123
software 116–17, 123
toys and games (excluding video games) 117–18, 123
TV and radio 119–20, 123
video games 121–22
inflation xvii
information feudalism 77
Innovation Potential Indicator 16
intangible industries xiv
Intel 186
intellectual capital 211–16, 218
defined 212
Intellectual Capital Management Group 211–12
intellectual investment 208
intellectual property x–xii, 3, 19–81
banks' attitudes 154
copyright *see* copyright
defined xi
designs *see* designs
economic trade value 78
government and 24–5
individual reward/social value balance 19
intangibility 24, 71
international conventions 26–7
justifications
disclosure 27, 28, 33
human rights 27, 28
incentive 27–8, 33
reward 27, 28, 33
the marketplace of 22
opting out 31
ownership/control v. use/access 28
patents *see* patents
powerful influences of ix
privatization of 32, 43
as property 23
property contract 28–31, 67
reforms, agenda for 80–81
seven principles
similarity with landlord-tenant relationship 60
trademarks *see* trademarks
see also copyright; designs; patents; trademarks
Intellectual Property and Communications Omnibus Reform Act (1999) 25
InterDigital 51
International Federation of Periodical Publishers (FIPP) 110
International Federation of the Phonographic Industry (IFPI) 63
International Intellectual Property Alliance (IIPA) xiii, 73, 86
Internet 120
advertising 91
effect on companies xi
the essence of 59
freeware and open source software 80
naturally avoids obstructions 65, 74
protocols (IP) 31, 190
and record companies 61, 106
revenue from downloaded music 106
seen as democratic and copyright-free 59–60, 60
technical principles 185–6
volume of traffic 185
Internet Patent News Service 52
Internet Underground Music Archive (IUMA) 62

invention
  authorship 197
  and discovery 47
Investor, Doug 178–9
IP (Internet protocols) 31, 190, 191
IP Warehouse Inc 67
IPNetwork 51
Iron Maiden 154
Isenberg, David 189–91
Islam, and intellectual property 23, 30, 55
Italy
  art market 97
  government 49
  RAI 216–18
  size of economy 87
ITV 104, 107

Jackson, Judge Penfield 196
James, William 5
Japan
  advertising market 91
  art market 97
  expenditure on R & D 87
  film production 102, 103
  first patent law (1885) 35
  patent system 33
  size of economy 87
  'utilitarian' approach to authors/inventors 29
Japanese Patent Office 35, 50, 114, 115–116
Java 191
Jefferson, Thomas 24, 32, 59
Jevons, Stanley 218
Johansen, Jon 65
John of Speyer 34, 38
Johnson, Dr Samuel 8, 12
Johnson, Philip 145
Johnson and Johnson 113
Johnstone, Keith 150–51
Jones, Jim 15
Jonscher, Charles 6–7
Jordan, Michael vii
Joyce, James 21
judicial courts 25
Jung, C. G. 5, 17
just-in-time person 142–3, 167

Kant, Immanuel 29
Kao, John 150
Kasparov, Gary 137
Katzenberg, Jeffrey 176
Kaye, Tobias 98
Keats, John 1
Keen, Ben 61
Kelly, Kevin 187
Kendrick, J. W. 208
Keynes, John Maynard 207–8
The Killing Fields 166
Kiln & Co. 213
King, Stephen
  'The Plant' 200
  'Riding the Bullet' 200
Kinko's copy-shops 64
knowledge management 215
'knowledge parasites' 210–11
Knox, Henry 32
Kodak 71
KPF Inc. 93
Kroto, Harry 1–4, 7, 112
Kuhn, Thomas S. 47
Kurokawa, Kisho 93

Laddie, Hugh 23
Laemmle, Carl 171
Lang, Johannes 43
Laughton, Charles 14
Lavoisier, Antoine Laurent 47
law of diminishing returns 129, 186
Lawlor, Laurie 177
'learning curve' 208
Lehman, Bruce 21
leisure activities xv
leisure budgets xv–xvi, 74
Lenin, Vladimir Ilyich 203
Lessig, Lawrence 42, 196
letters patent 34
Life is Beautiful 154
Lincoln Center, New York 107
Linux 192–3
The Lion King 192–5, 198
literary works, copyright in xii, 54
Little Women 177–8

Litton industries 71
Live Aid 125, 126, 127
Lloyd-Weber, Lord 108
Lloyd's
 headquarters 182
 insurance market 213
Locke, John 28, 57
Loew, Marcus 171
logos 1, 68, 85, 90, 99
London Business School 99, 158
 Business Strategy Review 212
London Stock Exchange 213
L'Oréal 78
Lotus 39
Louvre, Paris 93, 97
Luther, Martin 55
LVMH 101

Macaulay, Thomas Babington 57
McCabe, Ed 82
McCartney, Paul 211
McDonald's 178
machines, and creativity 6
Machlup, Fritz 208
magazine publishing 110, 111
management information systems 215
managing creativity 125–65, 166–80, 220
 creative management principles 131–57
 the creative entrepreneur 135–8, 173
 creative people 132, 170–71
 deals and hits 155–7, 179
 the economic cluster 147–9, 173, 174–5
 finance 151–55, 176–9
 how to grow 151, 152–4
 how to start 151–52
 the job of the thinker 133–5, 171–3
 the just-in-time person 142–3, 173
 the network office 145–7, 149–51, 178
 the post-employment job 139–41, 163
 setting up a company 151, 152–4
 teamwork 150–51
 the temporary company 143–4, 171, 174
 what to do if it goes wrong 151, 154–5
 the economics of the imagination 127–31
 ten rules for success 162–5
 'Tom's Beautiful Career' 160–62
 zest for wealth 157–9
manufacturing industry 207
 automation xv
 in Britain 75
 government bias 85
Margenau, Henry 10–11
Margolis, Esther 177–8
market size *see* industry earnings and market size
Marshall, Alfred 147, 207
Martin, Peter 195
Marx, Karl 207
Marxism 207
Maslow, Abraham xiv, 87
Massachusetts Bay Colony, General Court of 57
Matsuhita 175
Maugham, W. Somerset 17
'maximalists' 28–9, 79
Mayer, Louis B. 171
'mechanical' rights 31
Mediaset 169
Mendes, Sam 6, 7
Merrill Lynch 39
Metcalfe, Robert 183–4
Metcalfe's value 184
MGM 171
Microsoft 20, 31, 39, 113, 169, 181, 212
 Document Rights Management System 67
 'Halloween Report' 195
 Microsoft NT 194–5
Midnight Express 166
Mill, John Stuart 207
Millennium Dome, Greenwich 182
Milton, John 56
'minimalists' 28–9, 79

Miramax 176
Les Misérables 108
MIT Media Lab 150
Mitchell, John 11
Miyamoto, Shigeru 121
monopolies
  benefits 128
  entrepreneurs and 136
  the nature of 81
  rights 80
Monopoly board game 118
Moore, Gordon and Laws 186–7, 208
Moore, John, and his spleen 46
'moral rights' 22, 25, 29–30, 32
Morgan Stanley Dean Witter 140
Morita, Akio 205
motor racing 148–9
Motorola 114, 185
The Mousetrap 108
MP3 (Motion Picture Experts Group, Layer 3) 62, 63, 65, 72
MP3.com 42
MP4 72
Mr Bean 104
multiple works 197
Murdoch, Rupert 175, 176
Museo Nazionale delle Arti del XXI Secolo, MAXXI 93
music 62, 63, 65, 72, 81, 89, 105–7, 123, 124, 198
  clips 61
  copyright 31, 54, 61–5, 105, 107
  musicians' websites 202
  performance rights 31, 105
  performances 57
  publishing 105, 109, 199
  recording rights 31, 105
  software applications 188
  theft statistics 73
Musical Instrument Digital Interface (MIDI) 188
MySpace 88, 117

N2K 150
Napoleonic Code 29
Napster 23, 63, 64, 65, 81, 193, 200, 201, 202
National Endowment for Science, Technology and the Arts (NESTA) xiii–xiv, 158, 168
National Endowment for the Arts 96, 107
National Gallery, London 97
National Lottery 96, 104, 109
Natural History Museum 97
natural rights 28, 200–201
Nature 2
Navratilova, Martina 164
Needham, Simon 138
Negroponte, Nicholas 150
Nestlé India 78
Netscape 195
network office 145–7, 149–51, 178
networks
  becoming more obedient 189
  hard-wired 184, 189
  intelligent 189
  law of 183–4
  soft 184
  stupid 186, 189–91
new economy 187, 203
New York
  Broadway vii, 108, 149
  and economic clusters 149
New York Times 41
Newmarket Communications 177–8
News Corp 169
newspapers 111–12, 112
Newton, Sir Isaac 80, 131
Nice Girls 188
Nike 68, 99, 214
Nintendo 121
Nissan 209
Nissan Design International 209
Nobel Foundation 1
Nobel Prize 2, 3, 13
Notting Hill 104
Noyce, Robert 186
Nunn, Trevor 7, 17

OECD xv, xvi, 25, 113, 141, 185
Office of National Statistics 140
Ogilvy, David 90
Ogilvy & Mather 90

Ohga, Norio 214
Olivier, Laurence 14
Oncomouse 46
OPEC (Organization of Petroleum Exporting Countries) 74
Open Market 41–2
open source 80, 193, 195, 196
opting out 31
O'Reilly, Tim 80

P & T 94
P-creativity (psychological creativity) 8
Paine, Thomas 57
paintings and copyright 57, 70
Palm Pilot 183
Paramount Pictures 169, 176
Paris convention on patents, trademarks and designs (1893) 26, 76
Paris Review 15
Parker, Alan 164
passing off 69–70
Patent Cooperation Treaty (1970) (PCT) 26–7, 37
patent industries 21, 79
  defined xiii
'patent mining' 51
patent offices 28, 32, 33, 35–6, 38, 41, 43, 47, 50–54, 81, 113
  as central banks 50–52
  need for reform 53–4
patent rights, and competition 27
patents xii, 32–54, 75, 85
  biological material and 44–50
  borrowing against 154
  business methods patents 40–44
  computer software 38, 40–44
  and copyright 36
  exclusions 37
  fees 33, 36–7
  the first recorded patent 34
  'first to file' system 36
  'first to invent' system 36
  genes and 44–50
  growth in numbers xvi, 86, 113–16
  as intangible property rights x
  and international competitiveness 33
  international conventions 26
  as monopolies 32
  penalties for infringement 71
  'person skilled in the art' 36, 41
  principles 33
  prior art 36, 37–52
  R & D 110, 112–15
  registration xii, 26, 35–8, 81
  rules of ownership 54
  'stacking' 80
  technical effect and 42–3
  technological invention 33, 80–1
  term of xii, 24–5, 33
  tests 9, 33, 35, 37–8, 39, 81
Patents Act (1977) 25, 37
Patterson, Fiona 16
Patterson, Jeff 62
Paul Smith Ltd 102
Pearsall Smith, Logan 7
Pei, I. M. 93
Pentium-4 chips 183
performance rights 31
performances, copyright in 57
performing arts 107–9, 123, 149
Perl 192
Perry, Rupert 61
'personal rights' 29
personal secrets xii
Pfizer 79, 154
The Phantom Menace 203
Phantom of the Opera 108
pharmaceuticals 30, 33, 154, 210
Philips 42
photographs, copyright in 57
Piano, Renzo 181
Picasso, Pablo 6, 20, 183
picture libraries 20
plagiarism 72
Plant Patent Act (1930) [US] 44
Plant Varieties and Seeds Act (1964) [UK] 44
plants
  gentians 77–8
  patents for 44–5, 87
  propagation viii
  varieties 78
poetry 199

Polaroid 71
Polly the sheep 48
Polygram 61, 104, 175
pornography, Internet self-censorship 74
portfolio working 143
Powdermaker, Hortense 168, 173
Powell, Anthony 61
'power curve' 187
PPL Therapeutics 48
Priceline.com 41
PricewaterhouseCoopers 213
Priestly, Joseph 47
Prigogine, Ilya 14
Prince's trust 138
print-on-demand 199–200
printing 34, 56, 109
  digital 199–200
'prior art' 36, 37–8, 52
privacy xii
private copying 64–5, 66, 81
privatization 32, 43, 76, 79
prodigies 11
Production hybrids 203
program kernel 192
property, intellectual *see* intellectual property
property contract 28–31, 46, 66, 78, 79–81, 220
  definition 28
  need for reform 80
  and prosperity 220
property rights 197
  intangible x
  'maximalists' 28–9
  'minimalists' 28–9
Proust, Marcel 147
publishing 19–20, 81, 109–112, 123, 149
  educational 111
  electronic 110
  music 105, 110, 199
  professional 111
Puttnam, Lord (David) 164–5, 166–8

QED 51
Quad 75, 76, 78

radio 118–20, 130
Radio-Television Italiana (RAI) 216–18
Raffan, Richard 98
raising money 159
Raleigh, Thomas 23
Randolph, Edmund 32
Raymond, Eric: 'The Cathedral and the Bazaar' 195
Read, Sir Herbert 98
reality checks 16, 17, 164
RealJukebox 63
record companies 61, 105, 106
Recording Industry Association of America (RIAA) 62, 63
recording rights 31
Red Hat 193
Reeve, Christopher 171
Reichstag, Berlin 93
Relativity, Theory of 3, 131
Release 1.0 60
Renaissance 7, 55–6
research and development (R & D) 112–16, 123
  creativity in xi
  expenditure on 87
  in patent industries xiii
Resurgence 204
review 16, 164
Ricardo, David 130, 131, 136, 186
RiceTec Inc. 78
RIDER process 16–17, 134, 164
Rifkin, Jeremy 60
rights management systems 66–7
Rio Convention on Bio-Diversity (1991) 78
Rivarol, Antoine de 204
Rivette, Kevin 51, 52
RMB 94
Robin Hood: Prince of Thieves 177
Rocket eBook 200
Roddick, Anita 204–6
Rogers, Everett M. 147, 148
Rogers, Richard 93, 132, 181–3
Ronan, Colin xi
Roslin Institute 48–9
Royal Academy of Arts 97

Royal Albert Hall 107
Royal Court Theatre 150
Royal Institute of British Architects (RIBA) 93
Running Time 202
Russia
  advertising market 92
  and copyright theft 73, 74

Saatchi, Charles 164
Sachs, Jeffrey 76–7
Saffo, Paul xv
St Luke's advertising agency 146
Saint-Onge, Hubert 217
Salomon Brothers 175
Samara, Noah 133, 134
Samit, Jay 62
Samsung Electronics 113, 114
satellite systems
  broadcasting digital radio signals 133
  direct-to-cinema 171
Say, Jean-Baptiste 136, 139
Schiller, Herb 77
Schrage, Michael 183, 184
Schumpeter, Joseph 136, 138, 139, 158
Schwartz, Peter xvii
Science Museum 97
sciences
  and arts xiii–xiv
  collaboration on international projects 149
  creativity in xi, xiii, 4
  freely available 80
scientific instruments, theft of 73
Scott, Ridley 164–5
sculpture 57
search engines 201
Second Life 117
Sega 121
self-awareness 5
self-employment 87, 139, 140–41, 161
SendMail 192
server market 194–5
service industries xv, 208
service marks 69
services, defined x
Seth, Vikram 133, 134
Shakespeare in Love 176
Shakespeare, William 10, 20
Shanghai and Hong Kong Bank 145
Shaw, George Bernard 218
Sherrington, Charles 5
Shonfield, Andrew 136
Siemens 113
Sightsound.com 42
silicon chips 183
Silicon Valley 186
Sitte, Camillo 182
Skandia 211
sleep 4–5
Smalley, Richard 2
Smith, Adam 129, 136, 143, 207
Snow, C. P. xvii
Snyder, Allan 11
social needs xv
Socrates 10
Softbook 200
Softlock 67
software *see* computer software
Somerville, James 138
Sony 42, 61, 105, 121, 169, 170, 175, 188, 205, 214
Sony BMG 105
sound recordings, copyright in xii
South Korea 89
Spark Team 146
Spielberg, Steven 15, 16, 191
Stalin, Joseph 15, 155
State Street bank & Trust Co. v. Signature Financial Group Inc. 40, 43
'Statement of Patent Practice' [UK] 80
stationer's guild 56
Statute of Monopolies (1624) 34
Steinbeck, John 155
Stewart, Rod 154
Stewart, Thomas A. 215, 216
Stiglitz, Joseph 131
Sting 161
Storr, Anthony 13, 14
Story, Supreme Court Justice 21, 71, 81

Stravinsky, Igor 132
streaming 191
structural capital 209, 210–11
Subcharoen, Dr Pennapa 78
Sulston, John 46–7
Sun 195
Sunhawk.com 199
Swicord, Robin 177
Swiss Tourist Board vii
Sydney Opera House 107
Szent-Györgyi, Albert 190

Tabulating Machine Company 42
Takahashi, Korekiyo 35
Task Force on National Information Policy 74–5
Tate Britain 96
Tate Modern 96
Taylor, Frederick Winslow 163
TBWA Chiat/Day 90
'technical' copying 66
technology/technologies
  communication xv
  creativity and 183–6
  digital xvi, 67, 72, 81
  volatile xi
Telecom (Geneva 1999) vii
telecommunications 170
temporary companies 143–4, 173, 174
textile designs, copyright in 57
texts' downloaded 199–200, 202
TF-1 169
Thailand 89
Thaler, Richard 129
theatre vii, 107–8, 108, 149
thermodynamics, second law of 11
Thomas, David 188
3-D imaging xvi
3 Com 183
Time Code 2000 188
Time Out 138
Titanic 102, 170
Tobin, James 214–15
Toffler, Alvin 155
Tolkien, J.R.R. 17
Tolstoy, Count Leo 151
Tomato advertising collective 150
Torvalds, Linus 193, 194
Toy Story 170, 203
Toyota 113
toys and games (excluding video games) 117–18, 123
Toys 'R' Us 178
trade associations 73
Trade Marks Act (1994) 25, 69
trade secrets xii, 70
trade statistics 85
trade unions 142–3
Trade-Related Intellectual Property Rights (TRIPS) 27, 76
trademark companies xiii, 20
trademarks 68–70, 79, 85, 210
  defined xii
  exploitation 22
  a form of intellectual property xi
  as intangible property rights x
  international conventions 26
  law 31
  ownership 20, 21, 31
  passing off 69–70
  registration xii, 86, 99
Trilateral Working Group 113
Troggs 177
Tunstall, Jeremy 77
Turkey, and copyright theft 73
TV 102, 103, 117, 123, 149, 171
  TV programmes and copyright 54, 61
Twain, Mark 21
Twentieth Century Fox *see* Fox

UIP 167
unemployment 139, 140
Unesco (United Nations Educational, Scientific and Cultural Organization) 75
United Kingdom
  advertising market 91
  architecture market 94
  art market 96
  common law 25, 29
  copyright laws 27
  and copyright theft 73

crafts market 97–8
creditor-friendly 159
design market 100
employment in creative industries 87–8
fashion market 101–102
film market 102–103, 104
Labour Government xiii, 75, 158–9
manufacturing industry 75
ministry of Agriculture 48–9
music market vii, 107
national research councils 213
patent law 25
performing arts market 108–9
publishing market 111–12
R & D market 114–15
size of economy 87–8
software market 117
spending on copyright work 87–8
starting businesses 158
toys and games market 118
TV market 120
video games market 122
West End theatres vii, 108–9, 109, 149
United Nations 80
United States of America
advertising market 91–2, 91
architecture market 93–4
art market 96
attitude towards foreign nationals' works 26
Broadway theatres vii, 108, 149
common law 25, 29
copyright the number one export vii
and copyright theft 73
Court of Appeals 40
crafts market 98
debtor-friendly 159
Department of Commerce 185
Green Paper on *The Internet and Copyright* 59
design market 99–100
fashion market 101
film market 102–103
'first to invent' system 36
intellectual property in its Constitution 35
low inflation xvii
music market 106–7
number of patents xvi
Park Service 78
performing arts market 106
publishing market 111
R & D market 113–14
rules on copyright and patent protection 76
Senate Committee on Foreign Relations 74
size of creative economy in 86
size of domestic market 158
software market 117
springboard to globalization 74
starting businesses 158
Supreme Court 39–40, 45, 48, 50–51
Thirteenth Amendment to the Constitution 46
toys and games market 116
TV market 120
'utilitarian' approach to authors or inventors 29
video games market 122
zest for wealth 157–9
Unix language 193
US National Academies 61
The Digital Dilemma 59
US Patent and Trademark Office 32–3, 35, 40, 41, 220
and bio-organisms 45–6
Business Methods 42, 43, 53
computer programs 39–40
examiners 52
favours patenting genes 50
on 'invention' 47
mission of 50
number of patents (1999) vii–viii, 86, 113–14
revenues 50
widening the scope of what can be patented 23
US Patents Act (1970) 25
user-generated material 88, 117

VA Linux 193
Vacchs, Andrew 177
Van Gogh, Vincent 9
Van Gogh Museum, Amsterdam 93
Variety 102, 177
Vega Science Trust 1, 4
Versaware technologies 199
Viacom 122, 169
Victoria and Albert Museum, London 97
Vidal, John 78
video 103
video games 117, 120–121, 123, 135, 198
video rights 27
Vinterberg, Thomas 188
Virgin Interactive 122
Virtual Studio Technology (VST) 188
Visa 201
Vivendi Universal 105, 169, 171, 175
see also Polygram
Vroom Valley 148–9
VW Beetle 99

Wal-Mart 39
Walker, Jay 41
Walker Digital 41
Walkman 214
Wall Street Journal 175
Walpole, Horace 8
Walton, David 2
Ward, Victoria 146
Warhol, Andy 164
Warner, Jim 166
Warwick University: Employment Unit 140
Washington, George viii
Webster, Noah 57
Wehr, Tom 165
Wellcome Trust 46
West End theatres, London vii, 108–9, 109, 149
Wet Wet Wet 177
Whitford Committee's Report on Copyright (1977) 56
Who Wants to be a Millionaire? 119
Wilmut, Ian 48
Wilson, Edward O. xi
Wodehouse, P.G. 20
Wolff Olins 213
Woodmansee, Martha 55, 197
Wordsworth, Dorothy 148
Wordsworth, William 148
World Bank 30, 80, 87, 131
World Financial Centre, Shanghai 93
World Intellectual Property Organization (WIPO) 10, 26, 27, 75
conference (Geneva, 1996) 66
World Learning Network 167
World Trade Organization (WTO) 27, 29, 30, 31, 76, 78, 79
World Wide Web 184, 192
WorldSpace Corporation 133, 134
Wylie, Andrew 19–21, 31

The X Files 178
Xerox 31
Xian Dai 94

Yahoo! 169, 201, 202
Yates, Paula 126
Yellowstone National Park 78
YouTube 88, 117

Zander, Benjamin 150
Zenith Media 92
Zukor, Adolph 171